The Genius of John Paul II

The Genius of John Paul II

The Great Pope's Moral Wisdom

RICHARD A. SPINELLO

SHEED & WARD

Lanham, Chicago, New York, Toronto, and Plymouth, UK

The author gratefully acknowledges permission from Libreria Editrice Vaticana to quote from the encyclicals and other papal documents of Pope John Paul II.

Published by Sheed & Ward
An imprint of Rowman & Littlefield Publishers, Inc.
A wholly owned subsidary of The Rowman & Littlefield Publishing Group, Inc.
4501 Forbes Boulevard, Suite 200
Lanham, MD 20706

Estover Road
Plymouth PL6 7PY
United Kingdom

Distributed by National Book Network

British Library Cataloguing in Publication Information Available

Library of Congress Cataloging-in-Publication Data

Spinello, Richard A.
  The genius of John Paul II : the great pope's moral wisdom /
Richard A. Spinello.
    p. cm.
  Includes bibliographical references and index.
  ISBN-13: 978-1-58051-206-0 (cloth : alk. paper)
  ISBN-10: 1-58051-206-2 (cloth : alk. paper)
  1. John Paul II, Pope, 1920–2005. 2. Christian ethics—Catholic authors.
  3. Catholic Church—Doctrines—History—20th century. I. Title.
  BJ1249.S637 2006
  241'.042092—dc22   2006017192

Printed in the United States of America

⊚™ The paper used in this publication meets the minimum requirements of American National Standard for Information Sciences—Permanence of Paper for Printed Library Materials, ANSI/NISO Z39.48-1992.

Dedicated to the Most Reverend Lawrence J. Riley, S.T.D.

1914–2001

Contents

Acknowledgments

I AM ESPECIALLY indebted to my wife, Susan T. Brinton, for her work in typing and editing major portions of this book. Her moral support and encouragement during the writing of this book have also been invaluable. I also wish to thank Boston College for its ongoing support for my scholarship. Special thanks to Joyce O'Connor and Sandra Howe of the Carroll School of Management for helping me to handle the logistics of manuscript preparation.

Thanks are due to my editor at Sheed & Ward, John Loudon, for his enthusiastic support for this project. Special thanks also to Sarah Johnson and Sheila-Katherine Zwiebel for their cooperation and assistance.

Like all scholars, I have stood on the "shoulders of giants" in order to research and write this book. In this case, the "giants" have been moral theologians and philosophers who helped me to appreciate the subtleties of natural law philosophy. I have relied heavily on the work of Germain Grisez, John Finnis, Patrick Lee, and William May. I also want to single out the magnificent philosophical works of Father Norris Clarke, S.J., which are cited throughout this book. Father Clarke, a true pioneer in the work of Saint Thomas Aquinas, taught me Thomistic philosophy at Fordham University many years ago, and I can still remember his infectious enthusiasm for the thought of this great saint.

I wish to thank in a special way the Sisters of the Precious Blood at the Monastery of the Precious Blood in Manchester, New Hampshire, along with the nuns of Our Lady of the Angels Monastery in Hanceville, Alabama. I am quite sure that their prayerful support has led to the successful completion and publication of this book.

Finally, the book is dedicated to the memory of Bishop Lawrence J. Riley, S.T.D., a former auxiliary bishop for the Archdiocese of Boston. Bishop Riley was a close friend and an exemplary spiritual leader of this archdiocese. In his quiet and unassuming way he bore witness to the demanding life of the Gospel throughout his distinguished career as priest, scholar, and teacher. He inspired many of the faithful in this city with his deep faith, his holiness, his keen intelligence, and his unrivaled rhetorical skill. Bishop Riley was a noted moral theologian in his own right and wrote a book called *The History, Nature and Use of* Epikea *in Moral Theology*, published in 1948 by Catholic University of America Press. It is fitting, therefore, that this modest work on Pope John Paul II's moral theology will in some small way honor his memory.

Bishop Riley was one of many holy priests who have dutifully served the Catholic Church at my parish, Most Precious Blood, in Hyde Park, Massachusetts. The devoted work of these humble men, including the present pastor, Father Peter Nolan, C.S.Sp., has been an inspiration to me. Without their prayerful example, which has helped nurture and sustain my Catholic faith over many years, this book would not have seen the light of day.

Richard A. Spinello
February 11, 2006
Feast of Our Lady of Lourdes

Preface

This is not a Pope from Poland; this is a Pope from Galilee.
ANDRÉ FROSSARD, French journalist

AT THE WEARY age of eighty-four and after a long sojourn, Pope John Paul II was called home to his Heavenly Father. Despite the illnesses that plagued this holy man toward the end of his pontificate, his prolific vitality never diminished. He wrote at length on a wide range of theological and philosophical topics. But one area that received his focused attention was moral theology. To be sure, part of the reason for this keen interest in moral theology stemmed from the fact that Karol Wojtyla was an avid student of ethics long before he became Pope John Paul II. He had written his second doctoral thesis on the German philosopher Max Scheler, a well-known ethicist. As a young priest he had also taught ethics at the University of Lublin in Poland, where his courses included "Goodness and Value," a series of lectures on the need to find objective standards of morality. He once observed that "perhaps of all philosophical disciplines, ethics is the most intriguing to people in general."[1] Thus, he came into the papacy well prepared to teach and write about moral issues.

However, John Paul II was also deeply troubled about the erosion of traditional moral values such as those embodied in the Decalogue. Some philosophers and theologians have de-emphasized both the salience and absoluteness of these values as a way of accommodating cultural demands, while others have insisted that the entire fabric of Western morality must be rewoven. As a result, John Paul II clearly saw the need to correct some unsound moral teachings propagated by certain Catholic theologians and to intervene in society's debate about moral issues, especially those bearing on the sanctity of life. He sought to articulate a moral vision that was consonant with Sacred Scripture and the "living Apostolic tradition" (VS, 5).

This short book is a systematic presentation and defense of John Paul II's essential teaching on morality. That the pope's teaching would need to be defended may come as a surprise to some, but, as we shall demonstrate, John Paul II's moral writings have been subjected to strident and sometimes unfair criticism.

Before the reader plunges into this material, a few caveats should be mentioned. This book is merely a broad overview, and so it certainly does not purport to be a comprehensive treatment of the intricacies of John Paul II's moral theology. Such an effort would require several volumes of more precise and in-depth analysis. Nor does it seek to present John Paul II's extensive social teachings as articulated in encyclicals such as *Centesimus Annus* and *Sollicitudo Rei Socialis*. We will address some of these teachings when we deal with the issue of human rights, but this is a vast topic that would divert us from our main axis of discussion. Also, we will not consider in any depth the works written before John Paul II became pope, such as his philosophical treatise *The Acting Person*. We will refer to those works, however, when they provide corroboration for the arguments advanced in the encyclicals or other material composed during John Paul II's papacy. At times, for example, the positions enunciated in John Paul II's encyclicals presuppose certain philosophical underpinnings that are developed in earlier works such as *Person and Community*, where we see more clearly how Thomism infuses his moral outlook.

Our goal is to present a precise rendition of John Paul II's prophetic moral vision and to explain how he answers the primal ethical question asked by everyone: "What should I do?" In laying out that vision, special attention will be given to his magnum opus on ethics, *Veritatis Splendor*. John Paul II offers us a distinctive perspective on morality inspired by Scripture and firmly grounded in the natural law philosophy of St. Thomas Aquinas, though he gives that philosophy a personalist slant. The late Holy Father particularly sought to enlighten those who have fallen victim to the relativistic secular humanism that has insinuated itself into so much contemporary ethical reasoning.

Such thinking still persists, of course, and it was even evident in the mainstream media's crude assessment of John Paul II's tenure as pope. Often his moral teachings were gravely misrepresented. One unbalanced critique after another attacked John Paul II's "rigidity" and his "myopic" stand on key moral issues with no understanding of the philosophical depth or intellectual substance that girds his reasoning. The *Economist*, for example, boldly called upon Pope John Paul II's successor to repudiate his moral principles and to embrace the more flexible framework of proportionalism. According to the *Economist*, the Church's principled morality has intractable implications for public policy. The magazine's editors suggested that by adopting a more pliant moral system that permits abortion in hard cases, contraception, and euthanasia, the Church will have found a "new way to affirm the sanctity of life."[2]

Of course, society's acquiescence to this type of utilitarian reasoning was precisely behind the Holy Father's intention to devote so much energy to the theme of ethics. How is it possible to authentically affirm the sanctity of life by opening the door to life's destruction, even in difficult circumstances when doing so *appears* to be compassionate and sensible? The assumption that we should destroy or impede the basic good of human life in order to "save" it represents one of the many contradictions of the postmodern world. In response to the relativists and the proportionalists, John Paul II sought to demonstrate the critical importance of affirming moral objectivity. Moral truth transcends culture, politics, and even historical epochs, and it cannot be customized to satisfy the whims of "secular common sense."[3]

But is John Paul II's moral vision an antiquated one, as some suggest, or is it really adequate for this new millennium? Can it provide a moral compass in a hyperfast world of nanotechnology, genetic engineering, and transhuman cyborgs? In the course of explaining John Paul II's *moral theology*, we will also disengage his *moral philosophy*, a theory of morality that is based purely on reason. We will see how this philosophy, a synthesis of natural law and personalism, can be applied to our most daunting moral challenges. Contrary to what the critics say, John Paul II's moral teachings are not rigid or myopic; instead, they are supple, rich, and progressive. He offers the world a more authentic version of humanism that calls upon all human beings to respect the dignity that is proper to their own human nature.

When John Paul II died in April 2005, the world lost a gifted spiritual leader and a profound moral thinker. He stood for true freedom that is never severed from the truth. And he called upon the world to resist technology's hubris and civil society's slide into the culture of death. We invite readers to explore this critical aspect of the late Holy Father's comprehensive thought and to thereby better appreciate his genius and optimistic spirit. We can learn much from his fidelity to the quest for moral truth. That truth is always "splendid" and never concealed from those who prayerfully seek it out.

Notes

1. Karol Wojtyla, "Human Nature as the Basis of Ethical Formation," in *Person and Community: Selected Essays*, trans. Theresa Sandok (New York: Peter Lang, 1993), 95.

2. "The Future of the Church," *Economist*, April 9, 2005, 9.

3. "The Future of the Church," 9.

Abbreviations

Encyclicals of John Paul II

CA	*Centesimus Annus*, 1991
DM	*Dives in Misericordia*, 1980
DV	*Dominum et Vivificantem*, 1986
EE	*Ecclesia de Eucharista*, 2003
EV	*Evangelium Vitae*, 1995
FR	*Fides et Ratio*, 1998
LE	*Laborem Exercens*, 1981
RH	*Redemptor Hominis*, 1979
RMat	*Redemptoris Mater*, 1987
RMis	*Redemptoris Missio*, 1990
SA	*Slavorum Apostoli*, 1985
SRS	*Sollicitudo Rei Socialis*, 1987
UUS	*Ut Unum Sint*, 1995
VS	*Veritatis Splendor*, 1993

In all cases the editions used have been published by Pauline Books and Media and use the official Vatican English translation.

Other Writings of John Paul II

CTH	*Crossing the Threshold of Hope* (New York: Alfred A. Knopf, 1994)
FC	Apostolic Exhortation, *Familiaris Consortio*, 1981
LFam	Apostolic Letter, *Letter to Families*, 1994
MD	Apostolic Letter, *Mulieris Dignitatum*,1988

MI   *Memory and Identity* (New York: Rizzoli International Publishers, 2005)

RHV   *Reflections on Humanae Vitae: Conjugal Morality and Spirituality* (Boston: Daughters of St. Paul, [1984] 1993)

RP   Aposotolic Exhortation, *Reconciliatio et paenitentia*, 1984 (*Acta Apostolicae Sedis* 77, 1985)

SCdn   *Sign of Contradiction* (New York: Seabury/Crossroad, 1979)

SD   Apostolic Letter, *Salvifici Doloris*, 1984

TB   *The Theology of the Body: Human Love in the Divine Plan* (Boston: Pauline Books and Media, 1997)

*References in the text are to page numbers in these books. In all other cases the references are to paragraph numbers.

Works of St. Thomas Aquinas

The text refers to a number of works of St. Thomas Aquinas. These are the editions and translations that have been used unless otherwise noted in the references.

Commentarium et Reportatio super Epistolam Primam ad Corinthios (Commentary on St. Paul's First Letter to the Corinthians), ed. Raphael Cai, O.P. (Turin: Marietti, 1951).

De Unitate Intellectus contra Averroistas (Aquinas against the Averroists on There Being One Intellect), English edition used trans. Ralph McInerny (West Lafayette, Ind.: Purdue University Press, 1993).

Opera Omnia Sancti Thomae Aquinatis Doctoris Angelici. Abbreviated as *Opera.* Leonine edition edited by Commission of Dominican Scholars, 50 volumes, 1882–.

Quaestiones Disputatae De Anima (Disputed Questions on the Soul). Referred to as *De Anima. Opera* 24/1.

Quaestiones Disputatae de Malo (Disputed Questions on Evil). Referred to as *De Malo.* English edition used: *On Evil*, trans. Richard Regan (Oxford: Oxford University Press, 2003). References are to question (q.) and article (a.).

Quaestiones Disputatae de Potentia (Disputed Quesitons on the Power of God). References are to question (q.) and article (a.). Latin ed: *Sancti Thomae Aquinatis Doctoris Angelici, Opera Omnia* vol. 13, eds. S. E. Frette and P. Mare (Paris: L. Vives, 1889–1890).

Quaestiones de Quodlibet (Disputed Questions), in *Opera* 25. References are to question (q.) and article (a.).

Scriptum super Libros Sententiarum Petri Lombard (Commentary on the Sentences of Peter Lombard). Abbreviated as *Sent.* References are by book (I, II, III, IV), distinction (d.), question (q.), and article (a). Latin ed: *Sancti Thomae Aquinatis Doctoris Angelici, Opera Omnia,* vols. 7–11, eds. S. E. Frette and P. Mare (Paris: L. Vives, 1889–1890).

Summa Contra Gentiles (A Summary against the Pagans), English edition used trans. Anton Pegis (Notre Dame, Ind.: Notre Dame University Press, 1977). References are to book (I–IV) and chapter.

Summa Theologiae (Summary of Theology), 3 volumes, trans. Fathers of the English Dominican Province (New York: Benziger Bros., 1947–1948). References are to the four parts (I, I-II, II-II, and III), question (q.), and article (a.).

CHAPTER 1

Faith, Reason, and Morals

THIS BOOK IS a reflection upon John Paul II's presentation of the transcendent moral truth that reveals the path of righteousness. The late Holy Father diligently unfolded that truth throughout his greatest encyclicals, such as *Evangelium Vitae* and *Veritatis Splendor*. But is that truth discoverable by faith alone, or do we need the help of reason? Before we examine John Paul II's writings on morality, we must understand something about his methodology and his approach to these issues. In articulating his bracingly clear moral vision, is John Paul II writing primarily as a moral theologian, an ethicist, or a Christian moral philosopher? Is that message, which affirms the moral substance of the faith, an authoritative Church teaching exclusively for Catholics? Or does John Paul II make a decisive contribution to moral philosophy as well? Are his moral teachings relevant for the skeptical secular mind as well as for Catholics? We need to provide some type of framework in this chapter for answering these questions.

The Relationship between Faith and Reason

In the opening lines of the famous encyclical *Fides et Ratio*, Pope John Paul II poetically described faith and reason as "two wings on which the human spirit rises to know the truth about itself" (FR, introduction). This statement evokes the principal theme of the entire encyclical: the human search for truth, especially those truths that penetrate to the heart of our being, such as the meaning of life or the nature of the good. John Paul II is so convinced that the quest for truth is a vital part of what it means to be human that he defines the human person "as one who seeks the truth" (FR, 28). But how do we find this truth, especially moral truth, which seems to be so elusive?

Through our own natural reason we can discover certain truths about ourselves and about the world. Scientists, for example, use various methods to understand the laws of nature or the biological structure of animals. But we know the truths of the faith through revelation, which is a communication of God to humanity. As Scripture tells us: "In times past, God spoke in fragmentary and varied ways to our fathers through our prophets; in this, the final age, he has spoken to us through his Son" (Heb. 1:1–2). Thanks to revelation, even certain truths inaccessible to reason, such as the mystery of the Holy Trinity, can be believed with assurance.

Although faith and reason are two distinct sources of knowledge, each one supports and confirms the other. According to John Paul II, each "influences the other, as they offer to each other a purifying critique and a stimulus to pursue the search for deeper understanding" (FR, 100). For example, in Aquinas's view, there are certain truths of the faith that natural reason can in principle discover on its own, such as the existence of God and the fact that there is only one God.[1] In addition, reason provides a deeper explanation for many precepts of the faith, especially those with an "ontological content" (FR, 82). Thus, reason is capable of affirming and even illuminating key doctrines of the Church. At the same time, faith is a touchstone for the validity of reason's work, especially philosophical endeavors that explore questions about the nature of the human self or the source of moral obligation. If a philosophical system deviates far from the fundamental truths of the faith, if it contradicts the Word of God, one can infer that it has surely lost its way. Also, while reason, even in its fallen state, can attain objective truth, it needs the guidance of faith to pursue pathways to truth that might otherwise be ignored (FR, 76). The philosopher needs a reference point, "a friendly star" as Pope Leo XIII called it, in his or her pursuit of the truth, and that star can only be the faith itself.[2] Thus, there can be no real conflict between faith and reason. According to John Paul II, "The truth revealed in Christ does not oppose the truth discovered by philosophy" (FR, 34).

This mutually supportive relationship between faith and reason has been forcefully reaffirmed in John Paul II's encyclical *Fides et Ratio*. Why did the Holy Father write an entire encyclical on this topic? The reason is that the intimate connection between faith and reason, once assumed by most philosophers and theologians, has been questioned and even ridiculed in the modern, secular era. Science has emerged as the only reliable source of authentic knowledge. As a result, the bond between faith and reason has been ruptured, and they are now seen as antinomies. Autonomous reason disdains and excludes the faith that once nurtured it. For example, modern philosophers like Martin Heidegger believed that faith and reason were naturally separated by a great chasm: "The absoluteness of faith and the doubtfulness of thought represent two different domains divided by an abyss."[3] At the same time, some contemporary Protestant theologians like Paul Tillich have argued that God and His mysteries are knowable only by faith and religious experience. For Tillich, reason will not help our efforts to understand the supernatural.

The Catholic Church has consistently looked unfavorably on this sort of "fideism" or reliance on "faith alone," because it denies the role of reason in understanding the faith (FR, 55). Faith should not be suspicious of reason, since without the help of reason, faith "runs the grave risk of withering into myth or superstition" (FR, 48). Faith without reason often leads to an overemphasis on emotion and experience, thereby making it difficult for the doctrines of the faith to be properly assimilated and asserted as "universal propositions" (FR, 48). Unlike Heidegger, John Paul II sees a unity between faith and reason, not a division, and that unity comes from the one truth that is sought, whether through revelation or through the light of reason.

This interdependence of faith and reason has been firmly entrenched in the Catholic tradition since the time of Justin Martyr, St. Augustine, and St. Anselm, when *credo quia absurdum* ("I believe because it is absurd") began to give way to *fides quaerens intellectum* ("faith seeking understanding"). There was a need in the early Church to thematize or understand the faith, and so some theologians and Church Fathers turned to philosophy, the pursuit of wisdom as first practiced by the Greeks such as Plato and Aristotle. Philosophy provided conceptually reliable categories to explain some of the mysterious truths of the faith. Platonic metaphysics and epistemology, for example, provided the conceptual underpinnings for certain theological doctrines. One might say that the faith was clarifying and disclosing itself by the intellectual understanding that came from Greek philosophy. But, as John Paul II explains, these Church Fathers "confronted the relationship between philosophy and faith critically: with the help of the faith they deepened secular philosophy, disclosing what remained 'implicit and preliminary'" (FR, 41).

In *Fides et Ratio* John Paul II provides a clear account of this interdependence of faith and reason. He reminds us of the call not only to be hearers of the Word (*auditus fidei*) but also to be comprehenders of that Word (*intellectus fidei*) (FR, 65). And the tools of reason, especially philosophy, help us to comprehend the Word, to lay bare the assertions of revelation, which often possess an unmistakable "philosophical density" (FR, 61). Rational reflection also helps integrate the truths of the faith into our systems of knowledge and experience.

The dialectic of faith and reason continued through the late Middle Ages and arguably received its most profound expression in the work of St. Thomas Aquinas. With the help of Aristotle's philosophy, Aquinas developed a systematic theology that "illuminated the mysteries of faith by reason working in the light of faith."[4] The Scholastic philosophers like Aquinas took great comfort in the certitude that the faith offers. They also had confidence in the reliability of the natural light of reason to discover some of the truths articulated by the faith, while recognizing that there were certain mysteries of the faith such as the Trinity "that exceed every capacity of human reason."[5] Thus, for Aquinas, part of the faith's content is beyond the power of human reason to grasp, and so faith must play a permanent role in religious life. Reason can never displace the role of faith.

Aquinas's writings are a model of how faith and reason interact, and in his moral treatises one detects an especially close affinity between secular philosophy and theology. Aquinas skillfully integrated key insights of Aristotle into his natural law ethic, while going beyond Aristotle's understanding of the moral good and human fulfillment. Aquinas creatively appropriated the secular philosophy of Aristotle in order to better explain Catholic moral teaching. In his earlier writings, Karol Wojtyla had expressed the view that "the assimilation of Aristotelian ethics by St. Thomas Aquinas [was] an excellent example of a Christian striving toward truth."[6] Aquinas also used Aristotelian texts such as the *De Anima* (On the Soul) to help him work out a philosophical anthropology clearly implicit in the teachings of the Church.

Pope John Paul II constantly praised Aquinas's achievement, especially in his *Fides et Ratio* encyclical, where he refers to Aquinas as "the authentic model for all who seek the truth" (FR, 78). He cites Aquinas's fidelity to the truth and to the voice of the Church, characterized as his "sincere and total adhesion . . . to the solemn and infallible Magisterium of the councils and Supreme Pontiffs."[7] John Paul II is careful to state, however, that the Magisterium has no intention of imposing a philosophical system on the faithful: "The Church has no philosophy of her own nor does she canonize any one philosophy in preference to others" (FR, 49). At the same time, it is the Magisterium's duty to respond when philosophical errors contradict "the right understanding of revealed truth" (FR, 49).

Given the important interplay between faith and reason, it is no surprise that John Paul II repeatedly encouraged in his writings a retrieval of authentic Christian philosophy where faith and reason could easily coexist and support each other. In this broad conception of philosophy, "faith purifies reason and it liberates reason from presumption" (FR, 76). But what exactly is "Christian philosophy"? Etienne Gilson's definition is still the most suggestive and controversial: "I call Christian every philosophy which, although keeping the two orders [of faith and reason] formally distinct, nevertheless considers Christian revelation as an *indispensable auxiliary* to reason."[8] Christian philosophy, therefore, involves truths accessible to reason, but also included in or implied by divine revelation. Gilson's definition also implies that without the true light of faith, the human search for wisdom is bound to be incomplete, since philosophers must utilize all sources of truth available to human beings, including the truths of divine revelation, especially if they seek to develop and defend a metaphysical vision of reality.

John Paul II, however, would not necessarily agree completely with Gilson if he meant to suggest that the development of philosophy independently of theology was a futile endeavor. John Paul II did accept that there can be valid philosophical systems outside of faith—through sheer reason and logic it is possible to attain the truth. The work of Aristotle and other great pagan philosophers seems evidence of that proposition, for "to argue according to rigorous rational criteria is to guarantee that the results attained are universally valid" (FR, 75). Thus, John Paul II supports "philosophy's valid aspiration to be an autonomous enterprise" (FR, 75).

But according to Avery Dulles, John Paul II was also "keenly aware that an autonomous philosophy cannot be self-sufficient; the journey of philosophy . . . cannot be completed without faith."[9] If philosophy turns its back on the truth, it is prevented from deepening its understanding of reality. As John Paul II observed,

Revelation clearly proposes certain truths which might never have
been discovered by reason unaided, although they are not of themselves inaccessible to reason. Among these truths is the notion of a
free and personal God who is the Creator of the world, a truth
which has been so crucial for the development of philosophical
thinking, especially the philosophy of being. (FR, 76)

Reason's limitations and obvious lack of self-sufficiency leave it open to
receive the truths of divine revelation to complement what it can discover on its own.

What are the specific implications for this interconnection between
faith and reason for the study of ethics? First, we can look to both revelation and reason to tell us how we ought to live. We can choose to follow
two different paths, but they will lead us to the *same moral truth*. Second,
reason is capable of discovering sound, fundamental moral norms or principles on its own. In an essay written before he became pope, Karol Wojtyla
wrote that "the content of revealed [moral] precepts can also be known and
is in fact known without revelation, in a natural way."[10] Many other contemporary theologians would concur. As Germain Grisez points out,
Christian faith does not "add any principles to those naturally knowable."[11]
But revelation can confirm how these norms are consistent with the
proclamation of God's Word, and it can demonstrate how those norms fit
into a distinctively Christian morality. Finally, for the faithful who turn first
to revelation for moral truth, reason can deepen their understanding by
exposing the metaphysical underpinnings of that truth and by clarifying
the meaning of related moral concepts such as freedom and responsibility.

John Paul II as Moral Theologian

Despite the fact that John Paul II was frequently called the "philosopher
pope," he clearly gives priority to theology and revelation in his presentation of moral issues. Thus, in encyclicals such as *Veritatis Splendor*, he is
primarily engaged in the task of moral theology, not moral philosophy.
Theology is a reflection upon Scripture and other sources that bear witness to the faith of the Church. John Paul II defines theology as "a reflective and scientific elaboration of the understanding of God's word in the
light of faith" (FR, 64). In a speech given at Rome's Gregorian University
early in his papacy, the Holy Father described theology as an "ecclesial

science" that "grows in the church and works on the church." Unlike other academic disciplines, theology does not exist for its own sake but for the good of the Church and "the formation of Christians."[12]

Moral theology is the study of Christian moral principles, and hence it has a normative orientation. According to Wojtyla, most moral theology is positive theology, "an *exegesis* of the doctrine of Christian morality contained in revelation (scripture and tradition), in keeping with the magisterium of the Church."[13] As we have implied, moral theology is not reducible to philosophical ethics. Nor should it be reduced to a set of propositions, a practice that typified the manualist tradition prior to Vatican II. Rather, moral theology should be centered on Christ and constantly nourished by Sacred Scripture. The Second Vatican Council called for a renewal of moral theology so that it could manifest "livelier contact with the mystery of Christ and the history of salvation."[14]

In encyclicals such as *Veritatis Splendor* and *Evangelium Vitae*, John Paul II was undoubtedly attempting to fulfill the Council's call for renewal. His moral theology is thoroughly Christocentric, and it relies heavily on Sacred Scripture. It also seeks to demonstrate the supernatural calling of Christian life and to highlight "the obligation to bring forth fruit in charity for the life of the world."[15] But, according to Wojtyla, the real purpose of moral theology is to "'get to the bottom' of the reality of morality in light of the teachings on morality contained in the sources of revelation."[16]

Given this ambitious objective, it stands to reason that John Paul II would make liberal use of philosophical sources throughout his career, since philosophy provides an avenue for getting to the "bottom" of things. Thus, John Paul II, the moral theologian, relies in various ways on the work of certain philosophers to organize and thematize his reflections on the nature of the human person, freedom, and the source of moral obligation. This approach is obviously in keeping with his belief that reason and faith should support each other. John Paul II's work is a prime example of "theology calling upon philosophy . . . as a partner in dialogue" to confirm and elaborate the moral requirements that are revealed in Scripture (FR, 77). The moral truth of the faith has complete primacy, and philosophical insights are incorporated into that truth in order to provide a richer and sharper moral vision.

Thus, encyclicals such as *Veritatis Splendor* are not only an articulation of Catholic moral teaching; they also stand as a contribution to the ongoing philosophical debate about ethics. By drawing philosophy into the discussion so directly and by developing certain arguments on the nature of the moral life without appeal to divine revelation, John Paul II expands his moral vision so that it has something to offer the nonbeliever. Even if someone does not accept the moral norms that are articulated in Scripture, he or she may find the philosophical arguments used to explain and support those norms to be convincing. By adopting and defending the natural law framework along with the insights of personalism, John Paul II's work can engage those who do not have a Catholic or even a Christian worldview.

Of course, one might also say that John Paul II is writing as a Catholic philosopher, engaged in philosophy in the broadest sense as the pursuit of wisdom drawing upon all sources of truth, including divine revelation. But the difference is immaterial, given the close association between philosophy and theology in his moral writings. The distinction between a Catholic philosopher who feels free to rely on divine revelation in the quest for truth or a theologian using philosophy begins to blur since the tasks are so similar.

With all this in mind, we will attempt to distill John Paul II's moral teachings and philosophical observations into a moral framework that would be intelligible for both Christians and non-Christians. Thus, while our primary focus is on John Paul II's *moral theology*, we also want to make the case that one can derive from his writings a *moral theory*, a creative synthesis of natural law and personalism. This ethical framework deserves our attention, since it is a valid contribution to current moral discourse.

Nonetheless, since our primary task is to uncover and elaborate upon John Paul II's moral theology, it will be beneficial in this first chapter to review his methodology as a theologian. In the process of this exposition we will also consider the issues involved in working out a coherent theological framework that properly unites the "two wings" of faith and reason. The tight relationship between philosophy and theology in the development of Christian moral doctrine will become apparent as the argument of this book unfolds.

Theological Method

As we have noted, moral theology is the study of Christian moral principles and norms. But what is the relationship between faith and morality? Does the Gospel still have moral relevance in our secular culture? Can it respond to the great moral challenges of the twenty-first century? Or has morality become a purely profane affair? John Paul II expresses concern about dangerous trends that separate faith from morality, but he insists that the faith has *specific* moral content, and that content is presented to each believer through various forms of revelation (VS, 88). Sacred Scripture reveals what is truly human and shows forth "the personal dignity and inviolability of man on whose face is reflected the splendor of God" (VS, 90). Since the categorical principles articulated in the Decalogue or in other Scriptural passages protect that dignity, they have surely not lost their power to offer us something by which we can find our moral bearings.

All moral theologians, therefore, should recognize the critical importance of Scripture. The Gospel itself is normative for Christian life and for our conduct as Christians. As St. Paul exhorts us, "let your manner of life be worthy of the gospel of Christ" (Phil. 1:27). Jesus reveals in the Gospel how all men and women should live in response to His merciful love. According to Vatican II, the Gospel proclaimed by Jesus is "the source of all saving truth and moral teaching."[17]

In keeping with the tradition of the Second Vatican Council, John Paul II's ultimate reference point for moral theology is Sacred Scripture, where we find God communicating to us specific moral requirements through His Word. This approach is consistent with John Paul II's general theological method, since he regards the Word of God accepted in faith as the primary basis for all areas of sacred theology (FR, 73).

In *Veritatis Splendor* John Paul II alludes to the central role that Scripture must play in moral theology as he discusses the purpose of the encyclical: "To set forth with regard to the problems being discussed, the principles of a moral teaching based upon Sacred Scripture and the living Apostolic Tradition" (VS, 5). John Paul II was deeply inspired by Scripture for the formulation of his moral vision. For this pope, the moral relevance of Scripture was beyond dispute, and his writings bear this out.

In three of the major works devoted to moral issues, *The Theology of the Body, Evangelium Vitae,* and *Veritatis Splendor,* the Holy Father relies on a biblical narrative as the context and backdrop of his discussion. It should be remarked that *The Theology of the Body* is not an encyclical, but a collection of Wednesday addresses on matters of sexual morality. Nonetheless, when these talks are assembled, we end up with a work that manifests the same thematic unity as the Holy Father's other writings.

In *The Theology of the Body* he uses the creation story as the basis for developing his insights on anthropology and sexual ethics. For example, the Holy Father demonstrates that the words of Genesis have a profound ethical dimension, as confirmed in Christ's statements about the indissolubility of marriage (Matt. 19:3–10, or Mark 10:7–12). Recall Christ's specific words when asked by the Pharisees about the lawfulness of divorce (Matt. 19:3–6): "Have you not read that the Creator from the beginning made them male and female?" (Gen. 1:27). Jesus goes on, "For this reason man must leave father and mother, and be joined to his wife and the two shall become 'one flesh' (Gen. 2:24). So, they are no longer two but one body. What therefore God has joined together, let no man put asunder." Thus, Jesus Himself retrieves the text of Genesis to illustrate the primordial meaning of the marriage relationship. According to John Paul II, Christ affirms "the principle of the unity and indissolubility of marriage as the very content of the Word of God, expressed in the most ancient revelation" (TB, 79).

In *Veritatis Splendor* (6–27) he uses the narrative of the rich young man in Matthew (19:16–21) in order to illustrate how the Scripture contains a profound answer to our deepest questions about the nature of the moral life. The young man asks Jesus, "what good must I do to inherit eternal life?" This is an "essential and unavoidable question for the life of every man" (VS, 8). Jesus tells the young man, "If you wish to enter into life, keep the commandments." When the young man answers that he has already done so, "the Good Teacher invites him to enter upon the path of perfection, 'If you wish to be perfect, go, sell your possessions and give them to the poor, and you will have treasure in heaven; then come follow me' (Matt. 19:21)" (VS, 16). John Paul II uses this text to express the essence of the moral life: "the moral life of the commandments represent the absolutely essential ground in which the desire for perfection can take root and mature," yet moral perfection "demands that maturity in self-giving to which human freedom is called" (VS, 17).

Finally, in *Evangelium Vitae* (7–21) John Paul II once again uses the book of Genesis, particularly the story of Cain and Abel (Gen. 4:2–16), to illustrate how God has mandated reverence for life as an unconditional moral standard. Recall God's question to Cain: "What have you done? The voice of your brother's blood is crying to me from the ground"

(Gen. 4:10). That question still haunts us today. According to John Paul II, "The Lord's question, 'What have you done?' which Cain cannot escape, is addressed also to the people of today, to make them realize the extent and gravity of the attacks against life which continue to mark human history" (EV, 10). His opening reflection on this passage of Genesis sets the stage for the central theme of the encyclical: the epic conflict between the ethic of life and the culture of death, a culture that has now become entrenched in certain segments of modern society.

Why does John Paul II first turn to Scripture to present a defense of the basic good of human life? Beyond any doubt, the Holy Father is implicitly exhorting us to consult Scripture for moral guidance, because the Word of God confers graces that open our hearts to truth. He is hopeful that the moral truth we confront in the Word will begin to overcome the baleful effects of darkened consciences, which have permitted the value of life to be trivialized in contemporary society.

Thus, Scripture for John Paul II is the first key for unlocking the meaning of the moral life, since it directly answers the question "What should I do?" It would be an exaggeration to claim, however, that the propositions of Scripture exhaust moral truth. While the Gospels prescribe specific moral norms proper to Christian life, they do not give us a complete code of conduct. There are other sources that amplify and help elucidate the basic truths of Scripture. Accordingly, John Paul II uses Scripture as a point of departure for reflections on moral issues that will encompass philosophical discourse and draw from the teachings of the Magisterium. In the three works cited above, John Paul II moves from reflections on Scripture to a deeper philosophical analysis of moral actions based on the natural law framework. For example, in *Veritatis Splendor* he demonstrates why there are intrinsically evil acts, and in *Evangelium Vitae* he offers a sophisticated explanation of why actions such as abortion or the destruction of embryos for research fall into that category. But, for John Paul II, the Holy Scripture is always his most reliable reference point and the place to begin his exploration of the most profound and consequential moral truths.[18]

Some theologians have critiqued John Paul II's work for his "uncritical" appropriation of Scripture and for using it to support his presuppositions about certain moral issues. Underlying this invalid criticism seems to be skepticism about finding valid moral norms in Scripture that are intelligible for everyone and do not involve some prejudicial reading of the Scriptural text. Several dissenting theologians, for example, have called into question the validity of the Gospel teaching on the indissolubility of marriage (Matt. 19:3–10, or Mark 10:7–12), which the Holy Father accepts and repeats in many of his writings. Recall Jesus's admonition that "whoever divorces his wife and marries another, commits adultery against her" (Mark 10:11). As we observed, John Paul II relies upon these passages for reinforcing this theme of the permanence of marriage in *The Theology of the Body* (TB, 25–72). According to Josef Fuchs, S.J., while this teaching may represent a "valid moral affirmation," it is not necessarily "an absolute in the sense of a universal norm."[19] This means that Jesus's teaching on divorce should be regarded merely as an exhortation, a word of encouragement about the ideal of permanence in married life. It should not be taken as an absolute moral norm that proscribes divorce. In the view of most revisionists, Jesus's teachings on this and other moral matters are not prescriptive, but parenetic.

But why not understand this text the way it has *always* been understood throughout the long Catholic tradition? Why should anyone now come along to suddenly reinterpret this text and "soften" Jesus's teaching? In contrast to these dissenters, Rudolf Schnackenburg and many other Scripture scholars have regarded the forbidding of divorce precisely as a universal moral norm given to us by Jesus Himself. As Schnackenburg says, "We must let the words of Jesus stand in their severity and ruggedness," rather than reinterpret them to mitigate their meaning so that the message conforms to the current cultural context.[20] If Jesus's social and moral teaching, including his instruction to feed the hungry and clothe the naked (Matt. 25:31–40), does not impose moral demands upon us, the Gospel loses much of its prophetic power. If God's Word is merely suggestive and hortatory, how can it inspire us in the ways envisioned by the Psalmist: "the voice of the Lord breaks down cedars" and "flashes forth flames of fire" (Ps. 29)?

In addition to Scripture, John Paul II relies heavily upon the "living tradition" of the Catholic faith (VS, 27). As support for his positions and for his theological approach, he cites a long list of the Church's major teachers and doctors such as the early Church Fathers along with St. Augustine and St. Thomas Aquinas. He also frequently cites the extensive teachings of the papal Magisterium and the documents of Vatican II, especially *Gaudium et Spes*. He has enunciated that the primary task for the Church in this stage of its history is "the implementation of the doctrine of the great Council" (DM, 1), and so one could interpret his moral teachings as making more explicit the moral doctrine incorporated in the Vatican II documents. The encyclicals of his predecessors are also a key source for John Paul II, particularly the controversial *Humanae Vitae* and social encyclicals such as *Rerum Novarum*.

It should also be remarked that Pope John Paul II fully accepted the teaching authority of the Magisterium. He believed that the apostles and their successors enjoyed an unerring charism of truth. The Magisterium, the pope and the bishops, have the authority to decide what belongs to revelation. John Paul II took great comfort in the Holy Spirit's promise to guide the Vicar of Christ when he conveys and interprets the truth of revelation. The pope, of course, has the authority to speak infallibly either as head of the episcopal college or ex cathedra as successor of Peter. While John Paul II did not make any ex cathedra pronouncements on dogma, he did use his authority to reinforce infallible teachings on several moral issues such as abortion, confirming the faithful in matters that have become the common moral doctrine of the Church (EV, 62).

There has been some confusion on whether or not infallibility applies to the area of morality. But consider Vatican II's straightforward statement on this matter:

> Although the bishops individually do not enjoy the prerogative of infallibility, they nevertheless proclaim the teaching of Christ infallibly, even when they are dispersed throughout the world, provided that they remain in communion with each other and with the successor of Peter and that in authoritatively teaching on a matter of *faith and morals* they agree in one judgment that is to be held definitively.[21]

Thus, it is evident that the Magisterium can teach infallibly on moral questions when the bishops in communion with the pope enunciate the same position to the faithful throughout the world.

John Paul II also recognized the Holy Spirit's presence in the whole People of God and their "sense of faith" (*sensus fidei*). But *sensus fidei* should not be interpreted to mean that the faithful have an independent spiritual insight into moral truth such that if there were a divergence between Church teaching and the sentiments of the faithful the latter should prevail. While John Paul II appreciated Vatican II's teaching that the faithful have a "supernatural sense of faith," he admonished those who sought to base Church dogma or moral teachings purely on the consensus of the majority:

> The "supernatural sense of faith," however, does not consist solely or necessarily in the consensus of the faithful. Following Christ, the Church seeks the truth, which is not always the same as the majority opinion. She listens to conscience and not to power, and in this way she defends the poor and the downtrodden. The Church values sociological and statistical research, when it proves helpful in understanding the historical context in which pastoral action has to be developed and when it leads to a better understanding of the truth. Such research alone, however, is not to be considered in itself an expression of the sense of faith. (FC, 74)

Once again there has been criticism, especially from dissenting moral theologians, for taking such a "hierarchical approach." Some argue that the Magisterium does not and should not have the same role to play in moral matters that it plays in dogmatic ones. This is plainly false, however. As we have seen, Vatican II has certainly asserted the Church's competence in both faith and morals. Until recent years, most theologians accepted and defended the infallibility of the Magisterium in moral matters. Moreover, it is the Church's solemn task to guide people to salvation, and this demands firm moral teaching regarding specific issues, not just exhortations. Moral issues are complex and controversial, and people who want to follow Jesus in good faith must be given the right moral orientation so that they can live according to the light of the moral truth. It is simply false to say that the Church can only give general advice in moral matters, as some dissenters would have us believe. The Church has been the source of specific moral guidelines, that is, exceptionless moral norms, for centuries, as evidenced by this pronouncement at the Council of Trent against polygamy: "If anyone says Christians are permitted to have several wives simultaneously, and that such a practice is not forbidden by any divine law (cf. Matt. 19:4–9): let him be anathema."[22] That same Council also staunchly defended the Church's teaching on the indissolubility of marriage.

Beyond any doubt, John Paul II was on firm ground in following this tradition whereby the Magisterium asserts moral norms that must be definitively held by all Catholics. John Paul II makes this quite clear in a statement about the definitiveness of the norm excluding contraception:

> The Church teaches this norm, although it is not formally (that is, literally) expressed in Sacred Scripture, and it does this in the conviction that the interpretation of the precepts of natural law belongs to the competence of the magisterium.
>
> However, we can say more. Even if the moral law, formulated in this way in the Encyclical *Humanae Vitae* [HV], is not found literally in Sacred Scripture, nonetheless, from the fact that it is contained in Tradition and—as Pope Paul VI writes—has been "very often expounded by the Magisterium" (HV, 12) to the faithful, it follows that this norm *is in accordance with the sum total of revealed doctrine contained in biblical sources*. . . .
>
> Precisely against the background of this full context it becomes evident that the above-mentioned moral norm belongs not only to the natural moral order, but also to the moral order revealed by God: also from this point of view, it could not be different.[23]

John Paul II is asserting that even though this norm is not explicitly presented in Sacred Scripture, it has been consistently taught by the Magisterium and so it has become a permanent moral truth in the Church's tradition. Therefore, this norm is part of God's revelation and *it could not be otherwise.*

Finally, John Paul II's moral theology should be seen in the context of his overall theology, his orthodox views on Christology, eschatology, and ecclesiology. For example, in terms of Christology, John Paul II puts great emphasis on Christ as Redeemer and as the Source of Truth. On more than one occasion he described how Christ reveals the "truth about man . . . in his fullness and depth" (DV, 1). According to John Paul II, "in Christ and through Christ man has acquired full awareness of his dignity, of the heights to which he is raised, of the surpassing worth of his own humanity, and of the meaning of his existence" (RH, 11). If we want to know what it means to be authentically human and morally good, we need look no further than the life of Christ. The redemptive act of Christ, who suffered and died for our sins, reveals how much God loves us and how precious we are in the eyes of the Creator, who gave his only Son that we might have eternal life. In the mystery of redemption "man must find again the greatness, dignity, and value that belong to his humanity" (RH, 10). The moral life of each person involves living out this mystery, recognizing one's own dignity *and* the dignity of others. Human love, which recognizes the other's dignity, should be modeled on the love that Christ has shown us in His Incarnation and Redemption. In this way, each person's moral life represents cooperation with Jesus's redemptive action.

Much more could be said about John Paul II's Christology and its relationship to his moral theology. More could also be said about the remaining portions of John Paul II's theology, such as his ecclesiology and eschatology, and their relationship to his moral theology. However, a thorough treatment of John Paul II's theological presuppositions is well beyond the scope of this book. Interested readers should consult the book *The Splendor of Faith* by Avery Cardinal Dulles, which is a masterful and lucid summary of the late Holy Father's whole theological enterprise.[24]

Moral Theology and Philosophy

Now that we have clarified John Paul II's methodology as a moral theologian, we must return to a treatment of the role philosophy plays in his writings. Like many of his predecessors, John Paul II borrows liberally from philosophy to shape and support his moral theology.

As we have been at pains to insist in this chapter, moral theology must be carefully differentiated from ethics or moral philosophy. Most ethicists, like Aristotle, Immanuel Kant, or Max Scheler, do not rely on revelation, but develop an ethical system through reason and logic. Therefore, the arguments of philosophical ethics are accessible to anyone. But what is the conventional definition of philosophical ethics? Ethics refers to the domain of philosophical inquiry focusing on issues of right and wrong, good and evil, virtue and vice. Descriptive ethics merely "describes" moral beliefs or convictions without passing judgment. Normative ethics, on the other hand, seeks to present and defend objective norms of behavior.

It is worth noting that Karol Wojtyla had criticized ethical systems that "sacrificed normativeness" for descriptiveness or systems that were preoccupied with the "logic of norms."[25] In contrast to such approaches he defines ethics as "a science that deals with morality in its normative, not just descriptive, aspect and that aims at 'objectifying' norms, and thus above all at ultimately justifying them, not just presenting them."[26]

Normative ethics, clearly favored by the Holy Father, is also distinct from the discipline of metaethics, which is merely the study of moral discourse, the meaning of ethical terminology, and the provability of ethical judgments. Metaethics deliberately eschews the old Socratic questions that are also asked by Aristotle and Aquinas: "How should life be lived?" or "What is the good life?" Normative ethical inquiry, on the other hand, is a quest for the practical truth of how one's choices and actions will be good and worthwhile. The goal of normative ethics is not an appreciation of the structure of moral language, but an identification of the real and true human goods and the realization in our actions of those goods. Ethics seeks the truth, but it's the truth about the good and about the rightness of one's choices and actions.

In John Paul II's view, philosophical ethics has the power to discover fundamental moral norms and to help clarify normative questions of right and wrong. As a result, it can lend its support to moral theology and revelation. The value of a purely philosophical ethic is its reach beyond the community of believers. If the moral requirements made manifest in Scripture are also demanded by practical reason, those requirements can be accepted and appreciated by *all* reasonable men and women. As a philosopher, John Paul II presents convincing arguments in encyclicals such as *Veritatis Splendor* that the moral law revealed to us by God is the same as the moral law understood and imposed by right reason. According to John Paul II, "the divine law of the Decalogue is also binding, as natural law, for those who do not accept Revelation: do not kill, do not commit adultery, do not steal, do not bear false witness. . . . Each of these commands from the Sinai code seeks to defend a fundamental good of human and social life" (MI, 133).

In addition to affirming the moral norms revealed by faith, philosophy can also help us comprehend metaphysical concepts such as freedom, the will, and the nature of the human person. Moreover, it provides us with an understanding of the inextricable linkage between the natural goodness of God's creation and moral goodness, which, for John Paul II, is of crucial importance for understanding the nature of moral obligation. According to Wojtyla, philosophy (or speculative theology that makes use of philosophy) "throws light on the data of revelation and insightfully arranges them by means of metaphysical categories."[27]

In a revealing passage of *Fides et Ratio*, John Paul II makes several observations about why philosophy provides such invaluable support for moral theology:

> In order to fulfil its mission, moral theology must turn to a philosophical ethics which looks to the truth of the good, to an ethics which is neither subjectivist nor utilitarian. *Such an ethics implies and presupposes a philosophical anthropology and a metaphysics of the good.* Drawing on this organic vision, linked necessarily to Christian holiness and to the practice of the human and supernatural virtues, moral theology will be able to tackle the various problems in its competence, such as peace, social justice, the family, the defense of life and the natural environment, in a more appropriate and effective way. (FR, 98; my emphasis)

John Paul II clearly underscores in this statement the vital dependence of theology on philosophical ethics. He insists that a plausible philosophical ethics must be grounded in both a proper anthropology and a "metaphysics of the good." But what precisely does he mean by this?

Philosophy must provide an analysis of the nature of the human person because such an analysis is essential for coming to terms with related concepts such as freedom and moral accountability. As the Holy Father has reiterated many times, unless we understand the "truth about man" we will not get ethics right (DV, 1). Some biologists and scientists, for example, postulate such a reductive view of the person that concepts such as moral responsibility and personal freedom lose their coherence. For example, the famous scientist, Carl Sagan, once boasted, "I, Carl Sagan, am nothing but a collection of atoms bearing the name 'Carl Sagan.'" However, how does a "collection of atoms" know or make choices unless it is unified into a whole person? Also, how else can we explain the immaterial activity of knowing unless there is a spiritual intellect that transcends our material properties? A human being must be much more than a mere collection of atoms.

In addition, we cannot fully appreciate moral goodness unless we understand metaphysical or ontological goodness, the intrinsic value of God's creation. As chapter 4 will show, moral reasoning must begin with the assumption that being and goodness are convertible terms: all things created by God are good. Once we accept this premise about the natural goodness of things, we can discern the objective human goods (such as human life) and enter into the domain of moral reasoning.

The link between ethics, metaphysics, and anthropology that is expressed in *Fides et Ratio* has been a major theme of John Paul II's work on ethics. It was first developed by the Holy Father and his colleagues at the University of Lublin, and it appears in his book *Love and Responsibility*. As Christopher West points out, the "Lublin School" was a "bold philosophical initiative" that sought to unite these three disciplines.[28] Thus, John Paul II's claim that ethics is inadequate without a grounding in anthropology and metaphysics should be no surprise to those familiar with his early writings.

But the discipline of philosophy is in a state of grave crisis. The antimetaphysical bias, so evident in postmodern philosophy, is particularly troubling. As we will see in the next chapter, many postmodern thinkers proclaim this to be an epoch of "postmetaphysical thought." Gianni Vattimo describes with approbation how philosophy has become "weak thought," or "a thinking that is more aware of its own limits, that abandons its claim to global and metaphysical visions."[29] Theologians who rely heavily on those philosophers will surely end up with an incomplete moral theology. According to John Paul II, "a philosophy which shuns metaphysics would be radically unsuited to the task of mediation in the understanding of revelation" (FR, 83).

Many philosophers follow the legacy of Nietzsche and question the ability of reason itself to know any universal truth. They regard the quest for absolute truth as nothing more than a manifestation of the will-to-power. As a result, the hegemony of moral relativism continues unabated. Other philosophers opt for positivism, which contends that all moral norms are constructs of society. Pope John Paul II sees this situation as an urgent one, since the Church has "always considered philosophy as a way to come to know the truths about human life" (FR, 5).

Still other contemporary philosophers, who shun the naive position of pure relativism, have advocated reductive models of practical reasoning such as utilitarianism. The utilitarian deliberates about moral issues by trying to find the alternative that will yield the overall net good. A number of revisionist moral theologians have embraced variations of this moral theory, which permits evil acts to be done for the sake of a good end. This framework, known as proportionalism, will be analyzed more fully in later chapters. The problem with proportionalism is its denial that there are intrinsically evil acts. This position flatly contradicts the moral truth of Scripture along with the tradition of Catholic theology.

Consequently, philosophy is in dire need of systematic reform for two reasons: (i) the secular world urgently needs a more satisfactory form of philosophical ethics than utilitarianism, which is insensitive to the universality of basic human rights; and (ii) without a proper philosophical grounding, moral theology will be hard pressed to realize its promise or to achieve the organic vision that John Paul II has in mind.

Philosophers need to address more directly and honestly the sapiential questions about human life and the good, rather than devote their energies to formal questions about language and interpretation. If the great insights of metaphysics cannot be retrieved, and moral philosophy cannot be liberated from the skeptics and the nihilists, theology will suffer. When philosophical reasoning is impaired, the human intellectual spirit becomes disabled and so finds it more difficult to discern the truth about itself. Thus, it is not surprising that we find an exhortation in *Fides et Ratio* for the renewal of Christian philosophy that takes Christian anthropology and metaphysics seriously, since that philosophy is so necessary in order to do theology properly.

As one might expect, John Paul II's own moral theology is strongly influenced by the Christian philosophy of St. Thomas Aquinas. In this regard, John Paul II follows the teaching of the Second Vatican Council, which called St. Thomas Aquinas an "exemplary" philosopher for understanding "how faith and reason meet in the one Truth."[30] In his writings the late Holy Father adheres carefully to the natural law tradition presented so capably in the philosophy of Aquinas. According to that philosophy, our own God-given human nature determines the shape of moral responsibility. The natural law tells us that some actions are intrinsically evil no matter what the consequences because they go against our human nature. In addition, Aquinas's ethical system is deeply grounded in his philosophical anthropology and his metaphysics of the good.

Like Aquinas, John Paul II carefully links his moral theology to a philosophical anthropology. That anthropology is based on the work of Aquinas, but it includes more attention to the subjective interior life overlooked by Aquinas. John Paul II's moral theology also depends upon Aquinas's philosophy of being or his metaphysics. According to the late

Holy Father, "Saint Thomas celebrates all the richness and complexity of each created being, and especially of the human being" (CTH, 31). Unless we reawaken our convictions about the innate goodness of creation we will not be able to properly comprehend the meaning of moral goodness.

But John Paul II does not rely exclusively on Thomistic philosophy. In keeping with his background as a phenomenologist, the pope adds a personalist perspective to natural law morality that has distinctive Kantian overtones. John Paul II's thought manifests respect for Aquinas and the Scholastic tradition, but it also represents a creative reappropriation of Aquinas's philosophy. In so doing John Paul II hopes to amplify the Catholic wisdom (*sapientia*) of Aquinas. What we find in John Paul II, therefore, is a personalist approach to natural law that emphasizes the unique dignity of the person rather than specific precepts. The person, not the moral law, is at the center of morality.

John Paul II has been influenced by the work of contemporary personalists such as Roman Ingarden and Max Scheler. These philosophers helped John Paul II to understand the notion of self-giving love expressed in community (solidarity), and the role "assigned to intentionality in the grasp of ethical values."[31] Wojtyla described that he was attracted to Scheler because he "investigated the ethical experience of the human person as a lived experience."[32] Duty, for example, must be understood as the lived experience of "I ought," "an inner coercion that constitutes a distinctive modification of the experience 'I want.'"[33]

In addition, the eighteenth-century philosopher Immanuel Kant becomes a "partner" for dialogue. While Kant's formal moral philosophy has many problems, his emphasis on the person and on human dignity is particularly notable. The late pope's biographer, George Weigel, reports that Karol Wojtyla's "wrestling with Kant's second categorical imperative was 'particularly important' for his later thinking."[34] For Kant, there is one simple moral law, the categorical imperative, which in its second formulation states, "Act in such a way that you treat human beings always as an end and never simply as a means."[35] According to this imperative, we must strive always to respect the dignity of all persons. No person should be exploited or be manipulated through coercion or deceit. Rather, since each person is a free, rational being, he or she deserves to be always treated with respect. Karol Wojtyla had devoted many days as a scholar to an investigation of personhood. This effort culminated in his book *The*

Acting Person. In a letter to Henri de Lubac he explained why that focus was so important: "The evil of our times consists in the first place in a kind of degradation, indeed in a pulverization, of the fundamental uniqueness of each human person. This evil is even more of the metaphysical order than of the moral order. To this disintegration . . . we must oppose, rather than sterile polemics, a kind of 'recapitulation' of the inviolable mystery of the person."[36] For Wojtyla, Kant's imperative concisely captured the moral dimension of this "recapitulation."

The problem with Kant's moral philosophy lies in his flawed anthropology, which reduces the human person to a rational intellect. As we will see, John Paul II insists upon an anthropology that conceives of the human being as an embodied spirit, a unity of body and soul. With John Paul II's anthropology, personhood becomes an all-inclusive category— *no* human being is excluded, even those in the earliest stages of life or those with a terminal illness who are approaching death. Nonetheless, Kant's emphasis on an unconditioned moral principle of human dignity and the moral law protecting that dignity will become the bedrock foundation of John Paul II's moral vision.

In summary, the theologian must turn to philosophy in order to unfold the full moral truth and its presuppositions, to explore the philosophical depths of the Christian faith. As John Paul II explains in *Fides et Ratio*, moral theology "requires a sound philosophical vision of human nature and society, as well as of the general principles of decision-making" (FR, 68). As we noted, John Paul II is not proclaiming that every theologian must become a Thomist, but he is saying that they must choose philosophies for dialogue that will be worthy of attention and respect. If superficial philosophies are assimilated into moral theology, the inevitable result is a theology that is only superficially reflective. Thus, as Cardinal Dulles points out, "The bonds between philosophy and theology must be forged anew."[37]

A Distinctive Approach to Moral Theology

Beyond any doubt, one of John Paul II's great contributions to moral theology consists in working out a new methodology that is especially evident in both *Veritatis Splendor* and *Evangelium Vitae*. In contrast to classical moral theology, which often veered toward voluntarism, John Paul II puts far more emphasis on Christian fidelity and discipleship. Moral reflection begins and ends in the person of Christ. As Lois Malcolm observes, for John Paul II "Christian morality finds its center and criterion in the person of Jesus."[38]

As a result, his writings on morality are a careful blend of Scriptural exegesis, prophetic criticism of lax moral standards in contemporary society, and an exhortation or "instruction" on how to live up to the moral demands of the faith. As we noted earlier, the discussion on life in *Evangelium Vitae* is framed by the biblical narrative of Cain and Abel in the book of Genesis because "the fullness of the Gospel message about life was prepared for in the Old Testament" (EV, 31). The encyclical also contains strong moral rhetoric on the "culture of death," where "the right to life is being denied or trampled upon especially at the more significant moments of existence: the moment of birth and the moment of death" (EV, 18). The exhortation consists in teaching Catholics how to promote and support the new culture of life. Thus, teachers, catechists, and theologians are strongly encouraged to assume "the task of emphasizing the anthropological reasons upon which respect for every human life is based" (EV, 82).[39]

The moral standards manifest in Scripture such as "life is always a good" (EV, 34) are probed more deeply through theological and philosophical analysis that hews broadly to the natural law tradition. The arguments advanced against abortion (EV, 55–62) seek to demonstrate the absoluteness of the right to life and the intrinsic evil of abortion. Although John Paul II does not make substantial use of natural law in his encyclicals, it is always lurking in the background of his normative arguments. In *Evangelium Vitae*, for example, he appeals to the natural law, which forbids the taking of innocent life, in his elaborate discussion on the morality of abortion and euthanasia (EV, 62).

Thus, John Paul II presents the Word of God on a moral issue, illustrates how society or the Church falls short of living up to the Word, and exhorts his followers to renew their commitment to the Gospel's call to live a morally superior life. In support of this instruction and exegesis are various philosophical arguments usually drawn from the natural law tradition, but with a strong personalist slant. Christian morality is properly re-centered on the person of Jesus, but its moorings in philosophical ethics are not untethered.

Summary

We have covered some difficult ground in this chapter, so a brief summary of the main points is in order:

- John Paul II emphasizes the interdependence of faith and reason, which work together to explore the philosophical depths of Christian experience and to reveal the moral truth in its fullness. The truth revealed in Sacred Scripture and tradition does not oppose the truth discovered by philosophy. Faith turns to reason in order "to understand God's Word better" (FR, 73), but faith also supports reason because it "sharpens the inner eye" (FR, 16) and "perfects wisdom" (FR, 43).
- Accordingly, John Paul II believed that the basic content of the moral law is capable of being known by everyone. Some arrive at moral truth through philosophical reasoning, while others learn the truth through Revelation. As a result, "the divine law of the Decalogue is also binding as the moral law for those who do not accept Revelation" (MI, 133).
- In writing about moral issues, Pope John Paul II follows the path of revelation and thus speaks to us primarily as a moral theologian. John Paul II's moral theology is Christocentric, relying heavily upon Sacred Scripture; it also relies on the Catholic theological tradition and the teachings of the Magisterium in order to illuminate the moral requirements of the faith.
- John Paul II's moral theology depends on the insights of philosophy. Moral theology can profit immensely from philosophical ethics, but it must be an ethic that "presupposes a philosophical anthropology and a metaphysics of the good" (FR, 98).
- Catholic moral theology must be circumspect in borrowing from modern and contemporary philosophy, which often deny key assumptions of Catholicism. Moral theology needs philosophy as a "partner in dialogue," but it cannot afford to choose the wrong partners, who contradict the moral principles of the faith. Without the right philosophical support, moral theology runs the risk of compromising the faith to suit a fashionable ideology or superficial ideas. Theology must look instead to "exemplary" philosophers such as St. Thomas Aquinas.

- Thanks to John Paul II's generous use of philosophy, we can disengage from his theological writings an innovative approach to philosophical ethics, a synthesis of natural law morality and the "personalist norm" derived from the philosophy of Immanuel Kant.
- In John Paul II's major encyclicals we can discern a new method of moral theology that integrates Scriptural exegesis, prophetic critique of the culture's moral laxity, and an exhortation on how to live up to the demands of the Gospel. All of this is accompanied by deeper philosophical reflection on the relevant moral issues.

According to the philosopher Alasdair MacIntyre, in *Veritatis Splendor* John Paul II presents a "theology of moral philosophy."[40] I take this to mean that John Paul II, the moral theologian, is using philosophical reasoning to interrogate the meaning of ethical issues such as freedom and the good in order to elaborate upon the biblical teachings with moral import. In so doing, Pope John Paul II draws attention to the "philosophical commitments" of the Catholic faith.[41] Those commitments are primarily to Christian philosophies such as Thomism that take seriously the realities of being, truth, and goodness.

It should be remarked, however, that anyone looking for a systematic philosophical ethics will not find one in John Paul II's teachings. Although John Paul II relies on natural law, he does not expound on this theory or attempt to elucidate the nuances of Aquinas's natural law system. For a fully developed natural law ethic, readers must look to philosophers such as John Finnis or Germain Grisez or to theologians like Martin Rhonheimer (see the bibliography for works by these authors). Nonetheless, because of his appeal to natural law theory complemented by personalist philosophy, John Paul II provides an ethic that is intelligible to the secular world. Beyond any doubt, the secular world, battered by postmodern despair and the ideologies of evil, certainly needs a more credible moral framework, as evidenced by the burgeoning of the culture of death. Thus, as MacIntyre points out, "*Veritatis Splendor* is and will remain a striking Christian intervention in moral debate."[42]

John Paul II was not afraid to confront the reality of evil. He was particularly determined to combat perverted notions of the human person and to expose the moral obtuseness that justified the taking of innocent human life through acts like abortion. He was also anxious to demonstrate how far the dissenters in his own church had wavered from revealed moral truth. The next chapter will present a better sense of the need for John Paul II's intervention. We will survey the confused state of contemporary philosophy along with the misguided views that persist among some moral theologians.

Notes

1. St. Thomas Aquinas, *Summa Contra Gentiles*, I, 3.

2. Pope Leo XIII, "Aeterni Patris: Encyclical Letter on the Restoration of Christian Philosophy," in *One Hundred Years of Thomism: Aeterni Patris and Afterwards—A Symposium*, ed. U. C. Brezik (Houston: University of St. Thomas, 1981), 107.

3. Martin Heidegger, *Was Heißt Denken* (Tübingen: Niemeyer, 1954), 110.

4. Germain Grisez, *Living a Christian Life* (Quincy, Ill.: Franciscan Herald Press, 1983), 28.

5. St. Thomas Aquinas, *Summa Contra Gentiles*, I, 3.

6. Jaroslaw Kupczak, O.P., *Destined for Liberty* (Washington, D.C.: Catholic University of America Press, 2000), 55.

7. John Paul II, "In Pontificia Universitate S. Thomae Aquinatis, Saeculo Expleto a Datis Encyclicis 'Aeterni Patris,'" *Acta Apostolicae Sedis* 71 (Aug.–Dec. 1979): 1472–1483.

8. Etienne Gilson, *The Spirit of Medieval Philosophy* (New York: Charles Scribner & Sons, 1932), 37 (my emphasis).

9. Avery Dulles, S.J., "Can Philosophy Be Christian?" *First Things* (April 2000): 24–29.

10. Karol Wojtyla, "Ethics and Moral Theology," in *Person and Community: Selected Essays*, trans. Theresa Sandok (New York: Peter Lang, 1993), 105.

11. Germain Grisez, "Presidential Address: Practical Reason and Faith," *Proceedings of the American Catholic Philosophical Association* 58 (1984): 2.

12. John Paul II, "Address to the Pontifical Gregorian University," *L'Osservatore Romano*, January 21, 1980, 3–5.

13. Wojtyla, "Ethics and Moral Theology," 101.

14. *Optatam Totius*, in *Vatican Council II: The Conciliar and Post Conciliar Documents*, ed. Austin Flannery, O.P. (Northport, N.Y.: Costello, 1975), 16. All references to the Vatican II documents in this volume are to paragraph numbers.

15. *Optatam Totius*, 16.

16. Wojtyla, "Ethics and Moral Theology," 102.

17. *Dei Verbum*, in *Vatican Council II: The Conciliar and Post Conciliar Documents*, 7.

18. See John Conley, "Introduction," in *Prophecy and Diplomacy: The Moral Doctrine of John Paul II*, ed. John Conley and Joseph Koterski (New York: Fordham University Press, 1999), xv–xvi.

19. Josef Fuchs, S.J., "The Absoluteness of Moral Terms," in *Readings in Moral Theology No. 1: Moral Norms and Catholic Tradition*, ed. Charles Curran and Richard McCormick, S.J. (New York: Paulist Press, 1979), 97–98.

20. Rudolf Schnackenburg, *The Moral Teaching of the New Testament* (New York: Herder and Herder, 1965), 88.

21. *Lumen Gentium*, in *Vatican Council II: The Conciliar and Post Conciliar Documents*, 25 (my emphasis).

22. Henricus Denzinger, *Enchiridion Symbolorum Definitionum et Declarationum de Rebus Fidei et Morum*, 34th ed. (Frieburg im Breisgau: Herder, 1967), 1802.

23. John Paul II, "General Audience of July 18, 1984," *L'Osservatore Romano*, July 23, 1984, 1.

24. Avery Cardinal Dulles, S.J., *The Splendor of Faith* (New York: Herder and Herder, 2003).

25. Wojtyla, "Ethics and Moral Theology," 101.

26. Wojtyla, "Ethics and Moral Theology," 101.

27. Wojtyla, "Ethics and Moral Theology," 103.

28. Christopher West, *Theology of the Body Explained* (Boston: Pauline Books, 2003), 36.

29. Gianni Vattimo, *Belief*, trans. Lucas DeSanto and David Webb (Stanford, Calif.: Stanford University Press, 1999), 35.

30. *Gravissimum Educationis*, in *Vatican Council II: The Conciliar and Post Conciliar Documents*, 10.

31. Gerald A. McCool, S.J., "The Theology of John Paul II," in *The Thought of Pope John Paul II*, ed. John McDermott, S.J. (Roma: Editrice Pontificia Università Gregoriana, 1993), 39.

32. Karol Wojtyla, "The Separation of Experience from Act in Ethics," in *Person and Community: Selected Essays*, 33.

33. Karol Wojtyla, "The Problem of the Theory of Morality," in *Person and Community: Selected Essays*, 152.

34. George Weigel, *Witness to Hope* (New York: HarperCollins, 1999), 29.

35. Immanuel Kant, *Foundations of the Metaphysics of Morals*, trans. Lewis Beck (Indianapolis: Bobbs-Merrill, 1959), 16.

36. See Henri de Lubac, *At the Service of the Church* (San Francisco: Ignatius Press, 1993), 171–172.

37. Dulles, *The Splendor of Faith*, 89.

38. Lois Malcolm, "Freedom and Truth in *Veritas Splendor* and the Meaning of Theonomy," in *Ecumenical Ventures in Ethics: Protestants Engage Pope John Paul II's Moral Encyclicals*, ed. Reinhard Hütter and Alan Mitchell (Grand Rapids, Mich.: Wm. B. Eerdmans, 1997), 164.

39. For a similar view see John Berkman, "Has the Message of Evangelium Vitae Been Missed? An Analysis and a Future Direction for Catholic Biomedical Ethics," *The Thomist* 63 (October 1999): 461–480.

40. Alasdair MacIntyre, "How Can We Learn What *Veritatis Splendor* Has to Teach?" *The Thomist* 58 (April 1994): 171–195.

41. MacIntyre, "How Can We Learn," 188.

42. MacIntyre, "How Can We Learn," 195.

CHAPTER 2

Competing Moral Visions

THERE IS AN old story about the German poet Goethe that occasionally surfaces at convention smokers or in philosophy seminars. Goethe is supposed to have said that reading Immanuel Kant's *Critique of Pure Reason* for the first time was like walking into a brilliantly lighted room: everything suddenly became clear! Those who are familiar with Kant's dense and impenetrable work on epistemology may be startled and amused by Goethe's unusual claim. Nonetheless, the broader point is that there are certain philosophical or intellectual works that are distinctively enlightening and transformative. It seems safe to assert that John Paul II's radical treatise *Veritatis Splendor* will be regarded as just such a work, since, in the words of Cardinal Ratzinger, it "opens new horizons to moral theology."[1] *Veritatis Splendor*, which seeks to recover the true essence of Christian morality, offers all readers a luminous message of grace and truth. It crystallizes essential elements of Catholic moral theology so carefully elaborated by the Magisterium but in danger of being relativized by some dissenters.

In contrast, many of the moral theories in vogue today are riddled with philosophical ambiguity and have little to offer searchers of moral truth. These theories are superficial and are often typified by a narrow rationality. Their proponents typically support cultural relativism or positivism and scoff at the ideas of objective moral truth or ontological goodness. But John Paul II's major encyclicals on morality expose the deficiencies and inconsistencies of competing ethical visions. The pope relied on both philosophical reasoning and the authority of revelation to convince us that there really is an objective and transcendent moral truth.

Veritatis Splendor was the first papal encyclical ever written devoted exclusively to the theme of moral theology. The encyclical's subtitle, *De Fundamentis Doctrinae Moralis Ecclesiae* (On the Fundamentals of the Church's Moral Teaching), sends a clear signal that the encyclical will deal directly with the "fundamental truths of Catholic doctrine which, in the present circumstances, risk being distorted or denied" (VS, 4). The fact that such an encyclical was necessary is an indication of the serious difficulties that have befallen moral theology and the philosophies from which it elicits support.

John Paul II was deeply concerned about the drift of moral reasoning both within the Church and in secular society. He regarded the current situation as a "genuine crisis" in need of immediate attention (VS, 5). In *Evangelium Vitae* he described a "profound crisis of culture, which generates skepticism in relation to the very foundations of knowledge and ethics" (EV, 11). Pope John Paul II knew that the Church urgently needed to address this state of affairs. Thus, encyclicals such as *Veritatis Splendor* and *Evangelium Vitae* represented an earnest and prayerful attempt to reaffirm the moral substance of Christian belief.

John Paul II's moral writings represent a strong protest against an impoverishment of moral reasoning taking a heavy toll on Western culture. Specifically, there are three fundamental problems that have been frequently cited by the late Holy Father:

(i) The pervasive problem of ethical relativism, "which reigns unopposed" with a "sinister result" (EV, 20). This viewpoint is expressed most stridently in postmodern philosophy, which has dissolved any claims of moral objectivity. Relativists object not only to fixed ethical norms but also to the metaphysical presuppositions of traditional morality; they insist on the ambiguity of the moral life. According to John Paul II, however, "life cannot be grounded upon doubt and uncertainty" (FR, 28).

(ii) The reliance on questionable moral frameworks such as utilitarianism or proportionalism; these moral systems are "excessively concerned with efficiency" (EV, 12). In John Paul II's last book, *Memory and Identity*, we find a harsh assessment of utilitarian reasoning: "Utilitarian anthropology and the ethic derived from it set out from the conviction that man tends essentially toward his own interest or the group to which he belongs" (MI, 35).

(iii) The overemphasis on personal freedom and autonomy of the self, including ethical autonomy; freedom is an important value, but the Holy Father frequently wrote about the need to recover "the necessary link between freedom and truth . . . [because] when freedom is detached from objective truth it becomes impossible to establish personal rights on a firm rational basis" (EV, 96).[2]

As one might surmise, John Paul II is not alone in singling out such problems. Philosophers like Charles Taylor have voiced similar concerns. Taylor, for example, has talked about modern "malaises" in his book *The Ethics of Authenticity*. One "malaise" that he describes is the primacy of "instrumental reason," that is, utilitarian thinking that determines rightful conduct by measuring efficiency, by weighing costs and benefits and choosing the alternative with the greatest net benefits. The problem with this form of reasoning is that "the independent ends that ought to be guiding our lives will be eclipsed by the demand to maximize output."[3] Similarly, Oliver O'Donovan warns against the "lure of effectiveness" because it can corrupt our vision of moral truth.[4]

Charles Taylor describes the second malaise afflicting modern society as rampant individualism that accompanies excessive freedom, freedom that is disconnected from truth and moral goodness. As Taylor observes, "modern freedom was won by breaking loose from older moral horizons," but the price of that freedom is a loss of purpose, a "centering on the self, which both flattens and narrows our lives, makes them poorer in meaning, and less concerned with others in society."[5] Some ethicists have sought to accommodate individualism by giving preeminence to the moral principle of autonomy. Taylor, like John Paul II, recognizes the perils of inflating the value of autonomy or promoting freedom for its own sake.

It is important for us to appreciate the superficiality of contemporary philosophical ethics and the problems that arise when instrumental reason dominates ethical analysis. We must also address the ill effects these modes of thinking have had on moral theology. If we are proposing the cogency of John Paul II's moral vision as an antidote to problematic ethical paradigms, it is essential that we understand precisely the specious philosophies and the erroneous assumptions that contradict Church teaching. We cannot begin to grasp how *Veritatis Splendor* enlightens unless we first survey the surrounding darkness. With this in mind, let us explore in more depth each of the three major problems cited repeatedly by John Paul II. All of these problems have helped to foster a definite "split between the Gospel and culture."[6]

Ethical Relativism and the Postmodern Paradigm

The ongoing diffusion of moral relativism threatens to undermine sensible reasoning about ethical issues. This matter was of great concern to John Paul II. In *Evangelium Vitae* he elaborated upon the "the ethical relativism which characterizes much of present-day culture" (EV, 70). The Holy Father was especially worried about "those who consider such relativism an essential condition of democracy, inasmuch as it alone is held to guarantee tolerance, mutual respect between people and acceptance of the decisions of the majority, whereas moral norms considered to be objective and binding are held to lead to authoritarianism and intolerance" (EV, 70). The issue remains a source of worry for his successor, Pope Benedict XVI, who warned about a "dictatorship of relativism" at his opening homily for the conclave that elected him.

The theory of ethical relativism presumes that the good is not the same for all persons. Each of us has different beliefs about the moral good. After all, the relativist opines, who are we to question another person's perception about what is good? The ancient Sophist philosopher Protagoras put it quite simply: "man is the measure of all things." Accordingly, each moral agent is the "measure" of his or her own moral code.

Relativists argue, therefore, that morality is purely a matter of individual, subjective opinion, and what is right for one person may be wrong for someone else. They typically claim support for this viewpoint by pointing to the ample evidence of moral diversity in society—if people cannot agree even on fundamental moral issues like abortion and human cloning, how could there possibly be any single moral truth? The frequency of ethical disagreement and the incidence of obduracy about moral issues seem to undermine the possibility of objective moral truth to which *all* can give their assent. John Paul II saw that these successful efforts to relativize and privatize morality were beginning to encroach on the moral authority of Scripture and revelation. Therefore they could not go unchallenged.

The encroachment of relativism on virtually all academic disciplines is beyond dispute. The most popular form of relativism is known as cultural ethical relativism, which argues that moral values are relative to a given culture. Ethicists who subscribe to this philosophy regard moral imperatives on the same level as custom and social convention. Like customs, moral norms are "prescriptive"—they prescribe certain behaviors and tell us what to do. Hence, relativists reason, their authority is equivalent to the authority of local customs. Ethical norms, therefore, have only local validity. Just as the customs of Japan are not followed in the United States, the same could be said for the ethical standards of Japan, which have validity only within Japan. Thus, moral norms are not fixed or reliable standards, since they are relative to a specific social or cultural context. According to this view, morality has little stability: just as customs change and evolve, so too do moral standards.

Many traditional philosophers, of course, who have written in depth about ethics would steadfastly reject any claim that would regard ethical principles merely as an extension of our customs and manners. But thanks in part to the widespread influence of political correctness and an exaggerated emphasis on tolerance, this type of relativism has become quite persistent and destructive.

Some relativists also cite the "historicity" of truth as justification for their position. According to John Paul II, "the great concern of our contemporaries for historicity and for culture has led some to call into question the immutability of the natural law itself, and thus the existence of 'objective norms of morality'" (VS, 53). The assumption is that truth has a historical character, which means that it changes and evolves through history. If this is so, moral truth too must be contingent, always evolving, and always conditioned by the current cultural climate. Some dissenting moral theologians appear to subscribe to a version of this philosophy, arguing that neither the Old Testament nor the New Testament includes statements that are "independent of culture and thus universal and valid for all time."[7] Apparently, for these theologians, the meaning of God's Word is completely contingent upon the historical and cultural context. But, as John Paul II observes, "the word of God is not addressed to any one people or to any one period of history. . . . [T]ruth can never be confined to time and culture; in history it is known, but it also reaches beyond history" (FR, 95).

Moreover, if the meaning of specific revelations such as the Ten Commandments is so culturally conditioned, one wonders why they still resonate today, several millennia later, with most reasonable and conscientious people? Also, what do the assertions of these dissenters imply about the rest of Divine Revelation? Do not the teachings and actions of Jesus last through history as sacraments and as the foundation of His Church? Jesus says of His own words that they "will not pass away" (Matt. 24:30). Is this just empty rhetoric? Jesus also tell his disciples "Go therefore and make disciples of all nations . . . teaching them to observe all that I have commanded you" (Matt. 28:19–20). But the fulfillment of this command presupposes that the truthful teaching proclaimed by Jesus is accessible to all nations and cultures through the course of history. According to John Paul II, "With the richness of the salvation wrought by Christ, the walls separating the different cultures collapsed. God's promise in Christ now became a universal offer: no longer limited to one particular people, its language and its customs, but extended to all as a heritage from which each might freely draw" (FR, 70). *There is no room for relativism or radical historicism if we take seriously what Jesus commands: the universal proclamation of the Gospel that is not bound by place, time, or culture.*

Nevertheless, the upshot of this historicist philosophy for ethics is significant: the impossibility of deriving absolute moral norms from Scripture or from anywhere else for that matter. Moral norms can have only provisional validity. They can never have transcultural, ahistorical, and universal validity. According to Father Josef Fuchs, S.J., "we can never exclude the possibility that future experience, hitherto unimagined, might put a moral problem into a new frame of reference which would call for a revision of a norm that, when formulated, could not have taken such new experience into account."[8] Father Fuchs does not advocate a philosophy of pure relativism since he does admit that there are some formal universal norms such as "fidelity to God's Word." But his theology precludes universal specific moral norms, and so it is a form of soft relativism because it gives people a great deal of behavioral latitude.[9]

Much of the momentum for ethical relativism emanates from postmodern philosophy, which, on balance, has had a negative impact on the state of philosophical ethics. Some moral theologians, however, are attracted to this post-Christian way of thinking, because they find fresh categories for understanding the human phenomenon. But postmodernism, which became popular in the 1970s, amounts to a critique of objective rationality. Postmodernity at its worst represents the subversion of the rationalist ideals of unity, continuity and identity. It recommends a "de-centering" of perspective so as to discern not what things or individuals have in common, but "otherness" and "difference" in the world. Some theologians accept this way of thinking within limits because it complements classical theology's focus on the immutable and the universal and gives greater recognition to the particular and the diverse. One could see why some postmodern philosophers might have little use for St. Thomas Aquinas, whom John Paul II called the "master of philosophical and theological universalism" (CTH, 31).

But John Paul II has been quite critical of the extreme claims advanced by many postmodern philosophers:

> Our age has been termed by some thinkers as the age of "postmodernity." Often used in very different contexts, the term designates the emergence of a complex of new factors which, widespread and powerful as they are, have shown themselves able to produce important and lasting changes. The term was first used with reference to aesthetic, social and technological phenomena. It was then transposed to the philosophical field, but has remained somewhat ambiguous, both because judgement on what is called "postmodern" is sometimes positive and sometimes negative, and because there is as yet no consensus on the delicate question of the demarcation of the different historical periods. One thing is certain: the currents of thought which claim to be postmodern merit appropriate attention. According to some of them, the time of certainties is irrevocably past, and the human being must now learn to live in a horizon of total absence of meaning, where everything is provisional and ephemeral. In their destructive critique of every certitude, several authors have failed to make crucial distinctions and have called into question the certitudes of the faith. (FR, 91)

The clear implication is that one must be circumspect about flirting with a philosophical movement that is so antithetical to "the certitudes of the faith."

This post-Christian and secular philosophy will probably one day pass from the intellectual scene as a pernicious fad, but in the interim it has convinced many that there are no fundamental truths underlying reality, only a multiplicity of perspectives. More moderate versions of postmodernism are suspicious of universal theories and skeptical that an overarching moral theory could ever be discerned. As Zygmunt Bauman writes, "the foolproof—universal and unshakably founded—ethical code will never be found . . . and ethics that is universal and 'objectively founded' is a practical impossibility."[10]

There is actually a two-pronged attack on traditional morality that emerges in postmodern philosophy. First there is an attack on the metaphysical assumptions of moral philosophy such as the nature of human nature and the notion of a unitary self who is responsible for moral choices. John Paul II has said that we need to know the nature of man before engaging in ethics, but most postmodernists would say that there is no fixed human nature, and, even if there were, we couldn't know it anyway! Second, we uncover this suspicion and questioning about the possibility of a unifying moral system or a single set of overarching, valid moral principles. Without universal principles applicable to all human beings, however, there is no possibility for an objective moral truth.

Let us turn first to the latter concern. Postmodern philosophy comes in many different stripes, so it is hard to categorize it in simple terms. But one thing most postmodern thinkers have in common is their rejection of "grand narratives," that is, attempts to find a totalizing or systematic explanation of reality.[11] Hence a foundationalist ethic, a system that tries to explain right and wrong in terms of the natural law or some other unifying principle, is considered suspect and invalid. Why? One reason is that situations are unique and it is difficult to derive some universal system that can fit different circumstances. Also, as French philosopher Michel Foucault suggests, it may be that our notion of a universal good is influenced by our political and sexual interests. How do we know that those who espouse some universal theory of the good are not just proposing that theory because it suits their own vested interests?

Thus, according to most versions of postmodernism, it is impossible to develop and defend a singular rational account of moral obligation that will give us some sort of grand moral principle such as Kant's categorical imperative. The best we can hope for, postmodernists believe, is a plurality of ethical viewpoints that "learn somehow to respect one another."[12] We are destined therefore to a future of uncertainty and inconclusiveness that comes with ethical pluralism. According to Lucas Introna, "To live a moral life is to live in the continued shadow of doubt, without hope for certainty."[13] Because of this stance, most postmodernists refuse to give definite, objective measures of what is just or unjust, right or wrong.

In addition, in the works of the prominent European postmodernists we find a full-scale assault on the metaphysical assumptions of traditional ethical frameworks. As we discussed in chapter 1, John Paul II links ethics with anthropology and metaphysics. However, thanks to the work of philosophers such as Heidegger and Derrida, the metaphysics of presence elaborated by Aquinas has been a victim of deconstruction. As a result, many postmoderns are united in the conviction that "philosophical questions regarding Being and nothingness, language and reality, and God and his existence are pointless."[14] We have entered into a new postmetaphysical era where there is no room for a moral order based on the principles of metaphysical realism.

One key metaphysical assumption has always been that there must be an ethical subject, a stable self (or soul), who is responsible for his or her actions. Without such a substantial self, which maintains its identity through time and change, human experience seems to be unintelligible. But postmodernists find fault with this conventional notion of selfhood. Let us review the positions of several French postmodernists who call into question our assumptions about the ethical subject. According to Jacques Derrida's thought, there is only multiplicity or *différance*, that is, different elements of reality that cannot be organized into higher levels of being such as a person or a self. And this notion applies to human subjectivity as well: "the subject is constituted only in being divided from itself, in becoming space, in temporizing, in deferral."[15] There is no unified self-conscious subject beyond the multiple elements (emotions, thoughts, relations, etc.) that constitute the human experience.

French psychoanalyst Jacques Lacan, like his postmodern contemporaries, has also questioned the very possibility of an ethical subject who can make and carry out moral decisions and therefore assume responsibility. He too argues that any experience of a stable subject underlying our choices is purely "imaginary." According to Lacan, "our experience of human life" is that it is "something which goes, as we say in French, *à la dérive*. Life goes down the river, from time to time touching a bank, staying for a while here and there, without understanding anything. . . . The idea of a unifying unity of the human condition has always had on me the effect of a scandalous lie."[16]

Postmodernists, then, have done a thorough job of deconstructing the notion of selfhood and other key metaphysical suppositions that underlie traditional moral theories. For example, they also reject any metaphysical anthropology that postulates a common or "universal" human nature. It is no surprise, therefore, that they have no use for Aquinas's natural law ethic, which is predicated on those principles. As an alternative, they offer only pagan and tentative approaches to defining right and wrong.

What exactly do supporters of the postmodern paradigm propose as a substitute for the moral principles of the tradition? Let us briefly consider a few examples. A good place to begin is Jacques Lacan, who proposes "desire" as the ultimate norm of moral correctness. In his discussions on ethics and psychoanalysis Lacan appears to give total priority to human desire. Lacan calls for a "revision" of ethics and a new basis for moral deliberation that focuses on this question: "Have you acted in conformity with the desire that resides within you? . . . The only thing one can be guilty of is to have compromised one's desire."[17] This revision of traditional ethics is aimed at rebuking the philosophies of Aristotle and Aquinas with their teleological thrust and emphasis on the objective good that all human beings seek (such human flourishing). Lacan wants to substitute desire for such a good, so that the foundation of morality is *within the subject* and not external to human experience. But does Lacan's ethic imply that there should be no constraints on our behavior as long as that behavior is consistent with our desire? How can one possibly build an authentic way of life by indulging one's every impulse without self-discipline or without care for the bonds of human solidarity? Moreover, even if we admit his false claim that ethics is all about desire, where do we locate the capacity to endorse that desire and see it through, given Lacan's rejection of a stable self? There must be a desiring subject who either compromises desire or embraces that desire and brings it to fruition over time. Human experience, including moral accountability for the past or fidelity to the future, is simply unintelligible unless we posit a radically responsible and consistent self.[18]

We find another example of a revisionist ethic in the work of the American pragmatist and postmodernist Richard Rorty. Rorty, inspired by Nietzsche, essentially advocates the replacement of ethical values with aesthetic ones. The ethical life is reduced to "self-creation" and the choice of appropriate values to fit one's current lifestyle. For Rorty, there should be no constraints on the range of human possibilities, no matter how perverse, aside from minimal demands of social utility. But is Rorty right to claim that there are no other limits to these subjective and self-appropriated values? Can I choose a value structure laced with racism and hatred or a life devoted to pointless activities and solitary sex? Hatred leads inevitably to the destruction of human goods in the one who hates and possibly in those around him or her, and yet it is apparently legitimized in Rorty's framework. Also, doesn't it matter if the values I choose are trivial or inane? Is a life devoted to counting grains of sand as good and worthwhile as a life devoted to the pursuit of scientific research? Must there not be other issues of significance besides mere self-creation? Once we abandon universal human goods and just let people select or "create" their own values with no parameters or horizons of goodness for guidance, we must be prepared for self-destructive choices and trivialized modes of life that are unworthy of human aspiration.

Rorty credits Freud for rejecting a teleological vision of humanity and giving desire its rightful place in constructing the "good life." As we have seen, Jacques Lacan would certainly concur. So would philosopher Jonathan Lear. He too praises Freud because he achieved "a deep rejection . . . of the teleological understanding of human being."[19] Instead, according to Lear, there should be no limits set on the range of human possibilities, which should not be constrained by religion or philosophy. But, says Lear, "to live with human possibility, one has to tolerate a peculiar kind of theoretical anxiety: the willingness to live without principle."[20] Ethics without principle, then, seems to be what we are left with, simply because there is no way that human goods and desires can be hierarchically ordered, and there is no *telos* (or goal) toward which we all strive.

A final example comes from the work of the postmodern philosopher John Caputo, who tries to deal with the problem of constructing a viable ethic in light of the disruptive philosophies of Martin Heidegger and the postmodernists. What are the ethical implications of living in a world where there is only *différance*, that is, disunity, multiplicity, and chaos? In Caputo's view, we have little choice but to throw up our hands in the face of this new reality. He writes that "there is nothing to do but face the worst, the play of the epochs, the play of the temporary constellations within which we live out our historical lives, to wade into the flux and try not to drown."[21] In short, the best we can hope for in this chaotic world is to "cope with the flux."[22]

By now, the poverty of postmodern ethical relativism should be evident—a missing ethical subject and hence no possibility of genuine moral responsibility or accountability, desire as the basis for ethics, ethics

as pure self-creation with the vaguest of boundaries, ethics without principle, or ethical conduct measured by how well one "copes with the flux"
of the postmodern world. But ethics must go beyond merely coping
with the flux, and it must mean more than satisfying desire. It must identify an objective good that orients our moral lives and provides a secure
basis for moral deliberation. How can one live a decent human life or
build a decent society based on these radical and implausible ideas that
come from postmodern philosophers?

And what about theologians who are tempted to turn to these contemporary philosophies for intellectual "invigoration"? As we have seen,
some moral theologians applaud the salutary effects of postmodern
thought such as its emphasis on particularity, difference, historical relativity, and the primacy of ethical pluralism. Although distancing themselves
from the more extravagant claims of postmodernism, other theologians
have embraced several key postmodern premises. Sister Margaret Farley,
for example, appears to accept postmodernism's deconstruction of the
stable self. For Professor Farley, we must concede that the metaphysical
self has been expunged by postmodern thought and "there is only
process and relation without agency."[23] The key to love and moral relationships in a postmodern world is attentiveness to "concrete lives of
individuals" and a willingness to privilege difference and otherness.[24]

Thus, we see that postmodernism has begun to have an unsettling
influence on moral theology, as some theologians repudiate the metaphysical presuppositions essential for a valid moral philosophy. There is
no problem, of course, with paying attention to the "particular" or to
those individuals who are at the margins of society. John Paul II has said
that "universality does not ignore the individuality of human beings, nor
is it opposed to the absolute uniqueness of each person" (VS, 51). But
when we focus exclusively or predominantly on difference and particularity, we lose sight of the universal, specifically, our common humanity,
which is the securest foundation for a common morality and universal
human rights.

One thing should be certain about postmodern philosophy: it is
hardly a worthy partner for a fruitful dialogue with moral theology.
Theologians who fall under its seductive spell could easily be duped into
questioning core Catholic beliefs about universal moral law, freedom,
and the nature of the person. As John Paul II reminds us in his last work,
Memory and Identity, unless we begin with "realist presuppositions" about

being and humanity, presuppositions that have so far been ignored and scorned by postmodernists, "we end up in a vacuum" (MI, 12).

Proportionalism and Consequentialism

When we turn from contemporary philosophy to theology, we find that the state of affairs is somewhat better, since most revisionist moral theologians have not been persuaded by the extreme views of postmodernism. However, the discipline of moral theology has been in disarray for some time, at least from John Paul II's perspective. He has regarded the ascendancy of proportionalism as especially problematic: "such theories [as proportionalism] are not faithful to the Church's teaching when they believe they can justify, as morally good, deliberate choices of kinds of behavior contrary to the commandments of the divine and natural law" (VS, 76). Proportionalism draws its inspiration from the philosophy of consequentialism or utilitarianism, which seeks to solve moral dilemmas by means of cost-benefit analysis. Moral thinkers such as John Paul II, Charles Taylor, and Alasdair MacIntyre are extremely wary about the primacy of instrumental or utilitarian reasoning.

Classic utilitarianism was developed by two nineteenth-century British philosophers, Jeremy Bentham and John Stuart Mill. According to this theory, the right course of action is to promote the general good. The general good can be described in terms of "utility," or human welfare (happiness), and this principle of utility is the foundation of morality and the ultimate criterion of right and wrong. Utilitarianism is a form of consequentialism since it maintains that the right thing to do is to optimize the consequences for everyone involved in a given situation. This theory often finds expression in a cost-benefit analysis, which is undertaken in order to determine which option would optimize the consequences or produce the greatest net benefits for all parties with an interest in the decision. The right course of action is determined by this moral calculus, this weighing of costs and benefits in order to ascertain which action maximizes social welfare. According to John Paul II, "*consequentialism* . . . claims to draw the criteria of the rightness of a given way of acting solely from the calculation of foreseeable consequences deriving from a given choice" (VS, 75).

Despite its flaws, consequentialism remains in vogue, especially in the sphere of professional ethics. Consult any textbook on business and society, legal ethics, or medical ethics and the popularity of this framework becomes readily discernible. That popularity is due to the theory's flexibility and its pragmatic approach to intractable moral problems that appear to require compromise or openness to "creative" solutions. At the same time, alternative theories that support moral absolutes are criticized for their inflexibility and their impracticality in a complex, fast-paced world. We are often told that in the real world it is sometimes necessary to perpetrate evil acts for the sake of a good end. This sentiment is eloquently expressed in the words of a communist leader named Hoederer in Sartre's play *Dirty Hands*:

> How you cling to your purity, young man! How afraid you are to soil your hands! What good will it do? To do nothing, to remain motionless, arms at your sides, wearing kid gloves. Well, I have dirty hands. Right up to the elbows. I've plunged them in filth and blood. But what do you hope? Do you think you can govern innocently?[25]

Of course, in the last century this pragmatic moral philosophy, where the end justifies the means, has been used to legitimize the most inhumane forms of tyranny and fascism.

It is probably no surprise that utilitarian reasoning has insinuated itself into the recesses of Catholic moral theology. Some contemporary moral theologians still subscribe to a "proportionalist" method of moral judgment. What does this mean and what does it have to do with consequentialism? John Paul II provides us with a brief explanation: "*proportionalism* . . . focuses on the proportion acknowledged between the good and bad effects of [a] choice, with a view to the 'greater good' or 'lesser evil' actually possible in a particular situation" (VS, 75). Quite simply, according to proportionalism, when a moral agent is confronted with a choice, that person should carefully consider the alternatives. Each alternative should be examined to determine the benefits and harms that will come about if it is chosen. One should choose the alternative that gives the optimal proportion of benefits to harms. Moral judgment, therefore, always represents a *comparative assessment* of the alternatives facing the moral agent. It is important to note that for most proportionalists there are no acts that are intrinsically evil, evil in their very nature, prior to judging if there is a proportionate reason for doing them. For example, lying is typically an evil thing to do because it causes injury to others, but if telling a lie yields more benefits than harm, lying is morally acceptable.

But why is it permissible to sacrifice what is good (such as truth) for a "proportionate reason"? The answer to this question lies in proportionalism's notion of the good. Proportionalism implicitly presumes a distinction between moral goodness and other goods that fulfill or satisfy human persons. The latter are called "premoral" or "ontic" goods, and they might include life, health, freedom from pain, friendship, security, and so forth. There are also "premoral evils" (including death, pain, and sickness). These premoral human goods and evils exist only in concrete instances, that is, in the state of affairs that results from making a particular choice.

Thus, one must choose the option that maximizes the balance of these premoral or ontic goods over premoral evils. In summary, the proportionalist's response to the question "What should I do?" can be expressed as follows:

> We ought to do that action which maximizes the good and minimizes the evil. How do we discover the right thing to do? We discover it by balancing the various "goods" and "bads" that are part of the situation and by trying to achieve the greatest proportion of goods to bads. What constitutes the right action? It is that action which contains the proportionally greatest maximization of good and minimization of evil.[26]

Some proportionalists recommend this method for resolving any moral dilemma, while others have said that it should be restricted to "hard cases" or "conflict" situations. According to Father Richard McCormick, "When one is faced with two options both of which involve unavoidable (nonmoral) evil, one ought to choose the lesser evil."[27] He and other proportionalists argue that in those situations one may choose a nonmoral evil and sacrifice a premoral good (such as life) provided that one has a proportionate reason for doing so. Other dissenting theologians try to distance themselves from utilitarianism, but admit that they accept a form of moral reasoning that is modeled on utilitarian thinking. For example, Father Charles Curran maintains that "reforming Catholic theologians generally speaking do not embrace utilitarianism." Instead they accept what "can be described as mixed consequentialism."[28]

But even a hybrid theory like "mixed consequentialism" leads its proponents to reject many Church teachings such as the teaching that direct abortion is *always* morally wrong. For example, some dissenting moral theologians like Father Charles Curran claim that abortion is justified if it is the lesser evil: "Abortion could be justified to save the life of the mother or to avert very grave psychological or physical harm to the mother with the realization that this must be truly grave harm that will perdure over some time and not just a temporary depression."[29]

This is not the place for an elaborate refutation of proportionalism. But a few remarks are in order. One can certainly appreciate the perilousness and precariousness of following proportionalist reasoning. Once one heads down this path in resolving moral problems, it seems difficult to find a principled breaking point. Consider the difficulty posed by abortion. As we just read, proportionalists like Curran claim that abortion is morally permissible under some circumstances. But what are those circumstances? Richard McCormick, for example, argues that "abortion of a fetus in order to avoid a medical (delivery) bill . . . is *always wrong* . . . because when taken as a whole, the nonmoral evil outweighs the nonmoral good."[30] But how can he be so sure? What if an extremely poor person in a developing country is offered a free abortion? In addition, the only alternative available to her is to spend her meager savings on medical bills for the delivery of her child, but payment of those bills might thereby deprive her other children of food and their own medical care. Under these circumstances, a proportionalist might reasonably conclude that an abortion to avoid a medical bill is justifiable.[31]

Proportionalism introduces an arbitrariness into moral reasoning by claiming that the moral act (such as abortion or adultery) no longer has an independent moral quality of its own. For the proportionalist, actions receive their moral character from their end, that is, from the state of affairs they bring about. As John Paul II pointed out, according to this framework, "concrete kinds of behavior could be described as 'right'" even if they "contradict a universal negative norm" (VS, 75). Moral rightness becomes completely adjectival to the good of utility.

The biggest difficulty with proportionalism is that these premoral goods (and bads) are incomparable, and so the whole calculus is really doomed from the start. Utilitarianism and proportionalism want to compare goods by using a common measure for all of them such as pleasure or "advantage," but proponents have been unable to find such an appropriate measure. How do we compare fundamental goods such as human life or free speech with each other, or weigh them against purely instrumental and secondary goods like money or financial security? There is simply no common denominator or measure for the qualitatively different goods or harms involved in moral choice. And if these goods are really incommensurable, searching for the "greatest net good" is a futile exercise.

Also, what about the subjectivity of consequences as experienced by each individual? We do not all experience the impact of consequences in the same way. The consequences or impact of an abortion might be felt and assessed differently by a woman with many children than by a woman with no children. According to Bartholomew Kiely, we are faced with two possibilities: "either one allows consequences as subjectively experienced to constitute potentially proportionate reasons, or else (as the only alternative) one calls for an objectification of consequences and says that given consequences *should* be experienced in a certain way."[32] The latter alternative seems to make little sense, and so proportionalists are forced to concede that this form of moral reasoning is further vitiated by this subjective element of how consequences are experienced by the acting person.

Moreover, there is a host of practical problems. How do we know which consequences to consider, and can we really predict those consequences? Do we consider just the immediate consequences or also the more remote ones? If the latter are to be included, can we really foresee the distant consequences of our choices, which often take a long time to unfold? Whose interests should be considered? John Paul II carefully explains that the search for the proportionately greater good is futile:

> Everyone recognizes the difficulty, or rather the impossibility, of evaluating all the good and evil consequences and effects—defined as pre-moral—of one's own acts; an exhaustive rational calculation is not possible. How then can one go about establishing proportions which depend on a measuring, the criteria of which remain obscure? How could an absolute obligation be justified on such debatable calculations? (VS, 77)

None of these objections to proportionalism have been answered in a convincing manner, despite the fact that they were raised decades ago by theologians such as Germain Grisez.

Finally, according to John Paul II, proportionalism "cannot claim to be grounded in the Catholic moral tradition" (VS, 76). Proportionalists contend that the moral concept of "proportionate reason" has a long pedigree within Catholicism. Some believe that this form of moral reasoning is traceable back to the philosophy of St. Thomas Aquinas. Father Richard McCormick, for example, cites Aquinas's rationale for self-defense to illustrate Aquinas's implicit endorsement of proportionalism: "An act done with a good intention can still be rendered illegitimate if it is not proportioned to the end. And so if someone uses greater violence than necessary in defending his own life, it will be illicit."[33] But Aquinas is saying something quite different from what the proportionalists advocate. He is arguing that if one is acting out of self-defense, that person must use only enough force to protect himself or herself and no more. Thus, if a small man attacks me with his fists, I have the right to defend myself but not with disproportionate force; if I can defend myself with my own fists, I am not allowed to pull out a gun and shoot this person in the name of self-defense. There is no weighing or calculus of goods and evils involved in this analysis, so Aquinas's idea is far removed from the proportionalist methodology that has been propagated by revisionist moral theologians.

John Paul II is right to reject proportionalism and to assert that "the faithful are obliged to acknowledge and respect the specific moral precepts declared and taught by the Church in the name of God, the Creator and Lord," regardless of the consequences (VS, 76). Within the proportionalist framework, all goods, even traditionally moral goods such as marriage and life, are treated as ontic goods that must contend with other premoral goods in the moral decision-making process. If a marriage isn't working out so well, divorce might be the choice that yields the optimal balance of premoral good over evil. Morality becomes a matter of efficiency, as intimated by Hans Küng's remark that "the morally good is what 'works' for man, what permits human life in its individual and social dimensions to succeed and to work out happily in the long run."[34] But surely anyone can see that not everything that "works" for man is morally good. Should we tolerate the abortion or infanticide of newborn babies with Down's syndrome just because it "works," by making life less stressful for their parents and easing the financial burdens on the health-care system? Jesus never spoke about morality in such crude utilitarian terms of what works for man, but in terms of the love of God and love of one's neighbor, which is at stake in all moral decisions. Whenever he condemned immoral actions such as adultery, he did so bluntly, simply, and without qualification, precisely because that action violated the good of a human person and could *never* be a manifestation of authentic love. As Christopher Dawson tells us, the Gospel "is essentially hostile to the spirit of calculation, the spirit of worldly prudence."[35]

The Idol of Autonomy

We have examined two of the three critical problems that have corrupted our moral vision: the rampant ethical relativism of contemporary Western culture and the overreliance on utilitarian or consequentialist reasoning. We now turn our attention to the third major difficulty cited frequently by John Paul II, that is, a preoccupation with individual autonomy and freedom.

Modern man is enthralled by his freedom. He is excited at the prospect of assuming more responsibility and control for the process of his own development. Man should cherish his autonomy, but he must clearly appreciate its nature and limits. In *Redemptor Hominis* John Paul II warns us against "illusory freedom, every superficial unilateral freedom, every freedom that fails to enter into the whole truth about man and the world" (RH, 36).

In philosophical terms, autonomy should be conceived as the power of self-determination, the capacity to determine one's own activities. One's dignity derives in part from this power of self-determination or free choice. The moral imperative to respect the autonomy of others is beyond question: arbitrary restrictions on a person's freedom are an affront to his or her dignity. Thus, moral agents should not be coerced or deceived into acting against their will.

But there are perverse effects when autonomy is absolutized or disconnected from its essential relationship to truth. According to John Paul II, "Freedom negates and destroys itself and becomes a factor leading to the destruction of others, when it no longer requires and respects *its essential link with the truth*" (EV, 19). For John Paul II, freedom is not a value-neutral concept. Unless freedom is subordinate to the good and to truth, it loses its moorings and devolves into anarchy. And, as Plato reminds us in the *Gorgias*, the good life requires order and self-control: "[man] must not allow his desires to run riot, nor, by striving to fulfill the endless torment of satisfying them, live the life of a brigand."[36] Thus, a young man who is an avid consumer of pornographic material may think that he is acting freely as he peruses his favorite salacious websites every day, but isn't he the victim of psychological compulsion? When someone is compelled by his or her instincts or passions to act in certain ways, that person is not free. Freedom is neither caprice nor arbitrary impulse; also, it cannot be defined as the absence of external constraints so one can do whatever one wants. We have real freedom only when we transcend our instincts and compulsions and make good choices that perfect our human nature.

The primacy attributed to undisciplined freedom and subjective experience exacerbates the problem of relativity. In the current climate, many people believe that the gift of autonomy implies the right to create their own moral values. For example, some dissenting theologians argue for the autonomy of conscience in relation to the Church's teaching. John Paul II laments this attitude in *Evangelium Vitae*: "individuals claim for themselves in the moral sphere the most complete freedom of choice" (EV, 69). We will see in the chapters ahead how John Paul II's moral theology will expose the conspicuous defects in this position.

In the political sphere, there is strong support for an unequivocal value-neutral right to autonomy. Accordingly, many philosophers and legal scholars demand the state's neutrality about moral values. This position was forcefully articulated in the "Philosopher's Brief" to the U.S. Supreme Court on behalf of the right to "assisted suicide." In that brief, Ronald Dworkin, John Rawls, and others argued that since doctors are allowed to preserve life at the end of a person's existence, they must also be allowed to terminate that life.[37] The same neutrality rationale surfaces in arguments about abortion: if a mother can choose life for her unborn baby, she should also be able to choose death. The central claim in the "Philosopher's Brief" was that the state must be neutral about basic moral values, including values of life and death. Although the Supreme Court ultimately rejected any right to assisted suicide, it has embraced an expansive right to human autonomy that does not augur well for a balanced approach to similar cases:

> Matters involving the most intimate and personal choices a person may make in a lifetime, choices central to personal dignity and autonomy, are central to the liberty protected by the Fourteenth Amendment. At the heart of liberty is the right to define one's own

concept of existence, of meaning, of the universe, and of the mystery of life . . . beliefs [that] define the attributes of personhood.[38]

Lost in this perspective is any sense that this undisciplined autonomy must be encumbered by fundamental human goods and the principles of practical reason.[39]

Moral autonomy, conceived as a right of absolute self-sufficiency, has also wreaked a particular havoc on the field of bioethics. Moral theologian Janet Smith explains that among bioethicists, autonomy has been transformed from a *prima facie* (or conditional) moral principle into an absolute value that takes precedence over all other values. According to Smith, "The autonomous choice has supplanted the good moral choice as the primary concern of bioethics."[40] As evidence she cites the support among bioethicists for the moral (and legal) acceptability of assisted suicide. According to the authors of a popular book on medical ethics, "if a person desires death rather than life's more typical goods and projects, then causing that person's death at his or her autonomous request does not either harm or wrong the person. . . . To the contrary, not to help such persons in their dying will frustrate their plans and cause them a loss, thereby harming them."[41] It is evident that in this situation the patient's autonomous choice trumps virtually all other considerations.

Autonomy is a critical moral value that must be weighed carefully in bioethics cases. But it must be properly understood and kept in perspective. Individual autonomy cannot provide a satisfactory foundation for a coherent bioethics. The end result of such a skewed approach is apt to be an inflated individualism, an overreliance on patient wants and interests, that will ultimately lead to an atmosphere of uncertainty and mistrust in the medical profession.

In addition, contemporary philosophy has failed us once again by refusing to consider the nature of human freedom as well as its relation to the good. Autonomy or freedom is not an end in itself. Nor can autonomy be unhinged from its necessary orientation to the good, since indeterminate willing is not true freedom. Once freedom is detached from the good, freedom will soon be abused to bring harm to others and even to oneself. John Paul II was cognizant of this unhealthy trend to absolutize autonomy and in many writings voiced his thoughtful objections: "If the promotion of the self is understood in terms of absolute autonomy, people inevitably reach the point of rejecting one another" (EV, 20).

More important, if we become preoccupied with man's freedom and self-sufficiency, we misapprehend what it means to be human. We overlook the priority of truth, especially the truth about fundamental human goods that perfect our nature according to God's great plan. According to John Paul II,

> Different philosophical systems have lured people into believing that they are their own absolute master, able to decide their own destiny and future in complete autonomy, trusting only in themselves and their own powers. But this can never be the grandeur of the human being, who can find fulfillment only in choosing to enter the truth, to make a home under the shade of Wisdom and dwell there. Only within this horizon of truth will people understand their freedom in its fullness and their call to know and love God as the supreme realization of their true self. (FR, 107)

Summary

We have sketched out in this chapter three fundamental errors that characterize modern ethical thinking. As we have seen, the current impetus for ethical relativism and skepticism comes primarily from postmodern philosophy. Some relativists and postmodern thinkers offer us nothing more than self-refuting arguments to support their thesis that all values are relative. Others are more cautious, as they advance tentative proposals for ethical pluralism, always reminding us that ethics cannot escape from the shadows of doubt and uncertainty. Postmodern philosophers themselves concede that this "post-metaphysical" culture is one characterized by "weak thought," which shuns questions about reality, Being, or goodness.[42] But this metaethical skepticism has terrible practical implications, since it undermines the resolution of even the most uncomplicated moral problems.

The ethical principles proposed by these philosophers, however tentatively, fail to do justice to fundamental rights and the common good. The idea that ethics can be reduced to the principle of desire or to "coping with the flux" of the postmodern age should provoke a sense of unease even among those who believe that traditional morality has lost some of its vitality. At the same time, proportionalism is too pragmatic and too willing on some occasions to allow for unjust means in order to achieve a good end. Proportionalism is the theological counterpart of utilitarianism, a theory that can rationalize infringement on the rights of the weak and innocent for the sake of some proportionately greater good. Finally, preoccupation with individual freedom with no limits yields a narcissistic and self-centered society, which celebrates the absolute sovereignty of the individual.

The ideologies that spring forth from relativism, instrumentalism, and individualism are often hostile to theism. They have fostered a "climate of secularism" and helped promote the "culture of death" (EV, 87). The ideology of secular liberal pluralism, for example, which repudiates the truth about the moral common good, has been especially damaging. It is expressed in John Rawls's prescription for law and politics, which urges that "we try, so far as we can, neither to assert nor to deny any religious, philosophical or moral views, or their associated philosophical accounts of truth and the status of values."[43]

At the deepest source of those ideologies, we uncover either a denial of the transcendent or a recalcitrance to the Word of God and to the inspiration of the Holy Spirit. As John Paul II writes in *Dominum et Vivificantem*:

> Unfortunately, the resistance to the Holy Spirit which Saint Paul emphasizes in the *interior and subjective dimension* as tension, struggle, and rebellion taking place in the human heart finds in every period of history and especially in the modern era its *external dimension*, which takes concrete form as the content of culture and civilization, as a *philosophical system*, an ideology, a *programme* for action and for the shaping of human behavior. (DV, 56)

Some of the philosophical misconceptions exposed in this chapter have yielded nihilistic ideologies that culturally embody this "rebellion" in the human heart. The result is our secularized modern culture, which fails to recognize the sanctity of life and the absolute dignity of every human person in the name of relativism, pragmatism, pluralism, tolerance, and "weak thought."

John Paul II, however, would certainly not acquiesce to "weak thought" or to an "epistemic humility"[44] that might deprive us of moral truth. He remained confident that reason "could rise to the higher planes of thought, providing a solid foundation for the perception of being, of the transcendent, and of the absolute" (FR, 41). There is something quite mysterious about being that simultaneously reveals and conceals itself. Martin Heidegger often cited a famous fragment of Heraclitus, "being inclines to conceal itself," and Heidegger himself wrote that concealment "lies in the essence of Being."[45] John Paul II would undoubtedly agree with this insight since he too has often spoken of the mystery of being. But being also reveals itself in the light of truth as ordered, intelligible, and good. Anyone with a positive experience of being, anyone who has enjoyed life and friendship, the beauty of nature, the joy of play and creative work, can appreciate that intelligibility and goodness, and thereby begin to fathom the metaphysical transparency that is so vital for morality.[46] John Paul II urges the renewal of a philosophy of being, "a dynamic philosophy which views reality in its ontological, causal, and communicative structures" (FR, 97). Only with such a metaphysical vision are we equipped to engage in serious ethical inquiry and rediscover the transcendent source of values.

But when reason becomes too modest, when it remains enshrouded in darkness and suspicion, we end up in a postmetaphysical world with the flimsiest of moral standards. How much more sensible to accept what reason and revelation tell us—there are horizons of goodness, certain core goods that all human beings and cultures require. These intelligible human goods, essential for human flourishing and based on "universal truth about the good" (FR, 98), are the foundation for formal principles and specific moral norms (or natural laws) that one can never set aside.

Skeptics may scoff at this reasoning, but if we accept the highly plausible assumption of a common humanity, we can deduce even without the help of revelation that there must be *some* basic moral goods that we all share. According to the philosopher Philippa Foot,

> Granted that it is wrong to assume identity of aim between people of different cultures; nevertheless there is a great deal that all men have in common. All need affection, the cooperation of others, a place in the community, and help in trouble. It isn't true to suppose that human beings can flourish without these things—being isolated, despised or embattled, or without courage or hope. We are not therefore simply expressing values that we happen to

have if we think of some moral systems as good moral systems and others as bad.[47]

Moreover, isn't it logical to accept the premise that evil or unjust means cannot be done *even* for the sake of a good end? Some acts, such as enslavement of other human beings or the taking of innocent human life, cannot be justified by any end, and therefore they must *always* be wrong. Otherwise, discourse about equal human rights has a hollow ring.

John Paul II's writings, on the other hand, stand in stark contrast to the darkness that abounds in postmodern thought. His moral philosophy rejects skepticism along with proportionalist reasoning that leads one down the sinuous path of soft relativism that implicitly fosters an insensitivity to absolute and *universal* human rights. Instead, John Paul II looks to our common humanity and a common basic moral law as the source of specific moral principles that always apply. And, above all, John Paul II turns first and foremost to the Incarnate Word, who has taught us how to live and where to turn for lasting moral truth.

But if we are to explore John Paul II's reconstruction of ethics and understand his call to build a moral system on the *"bonum honestum"* (the "just good"), we must begin with a deeper understanding of the human person and its capacity for self-determination (MI, 34). The next chapter takes up this theme.

Notes

1. Joseph Cardinal Ratzinger, "Morality Should Be Inspired by Encounter with Jesus," Congress on the Encyclical *"Veritatis Splendor,"* November 26, 2003.

2. See Alasdair MacIntyre, "How Can We Learn What *Veritatis Splendor* Has to Teach?" *The Thomist* 58 (April 1994): 191–195.

3. Charles Taylor, *The Ethics of Authenticity* (Cambridge, Mass.: Harvard University Press, 1991), 5.

4. Oliver O'Donovan, *Resurrection and Moral Order*, 2nd ed. (Leicester: Apollos, 1994), 20.

5. Taylor, *Ethics of Authenticity*, 4.

6. Pope Paul VI, *Evangelii Nuntiandi, Acta Apostolicae Sedis* 68 (1976): 20.

7. Josef Fuchs, S.J. *Moral Demands and Personal Obligations*, trans. Brian McNeil (Washington, D.C.: Georgetown University Press, 1993), 100.

8. Josef Fuchs, S.J. *Personal Responsibility and Christian Morality* (Washington, D.C.: Georgetown University Press, 1984), 140.

9. Josef Fuchs, S.J., "The Absoluteness of Moral Terms," in *Readings in Moral Theology No. 1: Moral Norms and Catholic Tradition*, ed. Charles Curran and Richard McCormick, S.J. (New York: Paulist Press, 1979), 97–98.

10. Zygmunt Bauman, *Life in Fragments: Essays in Postmodern Morality* (Cambridge: Blackwell, 1995), 8.

11. See, for example, Jean-François Lyotard, *The Post-Modern Condition: A Report on Knowledge* (Minneapolis: University of Minnesota Press, 1984).

12. Ronald Green, "Business Ethics as a Postmodern Phenomenon," *Business Ethics Quarterly 3*, no. 3 (July 1993): 219–225.

13. Lucas Introna, "The 'Measure of Man' and the Ethics of Machines," in Proceedings of Computer Ethics Philosophical Enquiry (CEPE) Conference, ed. Richard Spinello and Herman Tavani, Boston College, June 2003, 122–131.

14. Santiago Zabala, "A Religion without Theists or Atheists," in *The Future of Religion*, ed. S. Zabala (New York: Columbia University Press, 2005), 4.

15. Jacques Derrida, *Positions*, trans. A. Bass (Chicago: University of Chicago Press, 1981), 26.

16. Jacques Lacan, "Of Structure as an Inmixing of an Otherness," in *The Structuralist Controversy: The Languages of Criticism and the Sciences of Man*, ed. R. Mackey and E. Donato (Baltimore: Johns Hopkins University Press, 1972), 190.

17. Jacques Lacan, "The Seminar of Jacques Lacan," Book VII, in *The Ethics of Psychoanalysis*, ed. J. A. Miller, trans. D. Porter (New York: W. W. Norton, 1992), 314.

18. See William J. Richardson's commentaries on Lacan, which appear in many of his articles, including "Lacan and the Subject of Psychoanalysis," in *Interpreting Lacan*, ed. J. Smith and W. Kerrigan (New Haven, Conn.: Yale University Press, 1983), 51–74.

19. Jonathan Lear, *Happiness, Death and the Remainder of Life* (Cambridge, Mass.: Harvard University Press, 2000), 160.

20. Lear, *Happiness*, 165.

21. John Caputo, *Radical Hermeneutics: Repetition, Deconstruction and the Hermeneutic Project* (Bloomington: Indiana University Press, 1987), 278.

22. See William J. Richardson, S.J., "Heidegger's Truth and Politics," in *Ethics and Danger*, ed. A. Dallery and C. Scott (Albany, N.Y.: SUNY Press, 1992), 22.

23. Margaret Farley, "How Shall We Love in a Postmodern World?" in *The Historical Development of Fundamental Moral Theology in the United States*, ed. Charles Curran and Richard McCormick, S.J. (New York: Paulist Press, 1999), 321.

24. Farley, "How Shall We Love," 321.

25. Jean-Paul Sartre, *Dirty Hands*, in *No Exit and Three Other Plays*, trans. L. Abel (New York: Vintage International, 1989), 218.

26. Timothy O'Connell, *Principles for a Catholic Morality* (New York: Seabury, 1978), 152–153.

27. Richard McCormick, S.J., *Notes on Moral Theology, 1965–1980* (Washington, D.C.: University Press of America, 1981), 718.

28. Charles Curran, "Utilitarianism and Contemporary Moral Theology: Situating the Debate," in *Readings in Moral Theology No. 1: Moral Norms and Catholic Tradition*, ed. Charles Curran and Richard McCormick, S.J. (New York: Paulist Press, 1979), 354.

29. Charles Curran, *New Perspectives in Moral Theology* (Notre Dame, Ind.: Fides, 1974).

30. McCormick, *Notes*, 710 (my emphasis).

31. See Germain Grisez, *Christian Moral Principles* (Quincy, Ill.: Franciscan Press, 1983), 165.

32. Bartholomew Kiely, S.J., "The Impracticality of Proportionalism," *Gregorianum* 66 (1985): 676–683.

33. St. Thomas Aquinas, *Summa Theologiae* II-II, q. 64, a. 7.

34. Hans Küng, *On Being a Christian*, trans. E. Quinn (New York: Doubleday, 1976), 534.

35. Christopher Dawson, *The Dynamics of World History* (La Salle, Ill.: Sherwood Sugden, 1978), 206.

36. Plato, *Gorgias*, trans. W. C. Helmbold (Indianapolis: Bobbs-Merrill, 1952), 507.

37. Ronald Dworkin et al., "Assisted Suicide: The Philosopher's Brief," *New York Review of Books*, March 27, 1997, 44.

38. *Planned Parenthood v. Casey*, 505 U.S. 833, 851 (1992).

39. For more about the "philosopher's brief" and the *Casey* case, see John Finnis, "On the Practical Meaning of Secularism," *Notre Dame Law Review* 73 (March 1998): 491–516.

40. Janet Smith, "The Preeminence of Autonomy in Bioethics," in *Human Lives: Critical Essays on Consequentialist Bioethics*, ed. D. Oderberg and J. Laing (London: McMillan, 1997), 195–210.

41. Quoted in Smith, "The Preeminence of Autonomy in Bioethics," 202.

42. Santiago Zabala, "Dialogue with Richard Rorty and Gianni Vattimo," in *The Future of Religion*, 55.

43. John Rawls, "The Idea of an Overlapping Consensus," *Oxford Journal of Legal Studies* 7, no. 1 (1987): 4.

44. Farley, "How Shall We Love," 311.

45. Martin Heidegger, *Einführung in die Metaphysik* (Tübingen: Niemeyer, 1953), 87 ("liegt im Wesen des Seins . . .").

46. See Norris Clarke, S.J., *The One and the Many* (Notre Dame, Ind.: Notre Dame University Press, 2001), especially chapter 1, "What Is Metaphysics and Why Do It?"

47. Phillipa Foot, "Moral Relativism," in *Moral Relativism: A Reader*, ed. T. Carson and P. Moser (New York: Oxford University Press, 2001), 195–196.

CHAPTER 3

The Nature of the Human Person

B EFORE WE PROBE more deeply into the moral theology of Pope John Paul II, it is essential that we review his understanding of the human person or, in more technical terms, his philosophical anthropology. In *Dives in Misericordia* John Paul II describes the urgent need to understand "the truth about man" (DM, 1). Unless we understand this truth, we can never reach the right conclusions about how man should behave. Questions such as "Why should man be moral?" inevitably lead to the question "What is man?" Only when we know the truth about man can we discern the foundations of moral truth.

More specifically, we need to know the nature of the person in two crucial aspects: as a being possessing a rational nature who is a bearer of rights and deserving of full moral worth, and as a subject capable of making free and responsible choices. The wrong anthropology could easily lead us astray, since a sound moral system must be grounded in an accurate understanding of human nature. This is the reason for John Paul II's concern about dualism. In his *Letter to Families*, he warned that the "human family is facing the challenge of a new Manichaeism, in which body and spirit are put in radical opposition," and he expressed apprehension that adherence to this sort of dualistic framework would corrupt moral reasoning (LFam, 19).

For example, to some extent, resolving the moral problem of abortion depends on our understanding of the nature of the human person. Some defenders of abortion reason that since a fetus lacks consciousness or rational awareness, it could not possibly deserve "human" rights. But John Paul II believes that the right to life is based on a human being's rational nature, the natural capacity for conceptual thinking and free choice, and not on accidental qualities such as conscious awareness. Since human beings are persons with a rational nature, they are different in kind from other animals. Nonetheless, human persons are also by nature physical organisms, and they come into existence when the physical organism comes into existence, which is at the moment of conception. Thus, abortion can never be morally justified because it takes the life of a human person who deserves special intrinsic worth.[1]

In this chapter, we will first present a cursory overview of misguided conceptions of human nature or human selfhood. As we saw in the previous chapter, in addition to the problem of dualism, we must also deal with postmodernism's assault on the person as substance or as the subject of his or her actions. That philosophy has dismantled any notion of the continuity of selfhood by reducing the human person to his or her accidental qualities or to his or her relations with others. It regards the self as a multiplicity of conflicting emotions, drives, and impulses, always divided and with no interior unity. It was Nietzsche who first saw the self as a *dividuum*, lacking unity and coherence, where one force temporarily dominates. According to Nietzsche, the self is "a plurality . . . a war and peace, a herd and a shepherd."[2]

Nietzsche was not completely wrong in this metaphorical description of the self. There is strife or tension within the self, as St. Paul has reminded us in Romans (7:13–20), since we can never fully integrate all of our conflicting drives and emotions. Yet the vast majority of people are able to achieve some level of integrity and thereby function as moral persons. They are not at the mercy of their conflicting impulses. The self, therefore, is not a plurality but a unity-in-plurality with an abiding center that unifies its many relations, attributes, and qualities.

Nonetheless, French postmodernists such as Jacques Lacan and Jacques Derrida followed Nietzsche's lead, rejecting the immediacy of the subject as the ultimate source of activity. They postulated that the self was fissured and divided, and could not be considered as the ultimate term in a sequence of actions. These ideas have undermined the concept of moral responsibility, for how can we ascribe responsibility to a self that doesn't exist or to an unstable plurality of different "selves" with no interior center of unity? On the contrary, there must be some principle of self-identity through change in each human person. Otherwise, common human experiences such as making and keeping a promise, carrying out a project over time, or even the giving of one's self in marriage or friendship will lose their intelligibility.

At the same time, the ghosts of the Platonic tradition have haunted the area of philosophical anthropology for centuries. That tradition demeaned the body in favor of the soul. For example, neo-Platonists like Plotinus juxtaposed the purity of the spiritual soul against the inferior quality of the human body: "the soul becomes ugly by mixture and dilution and inclination towards body and matter."[3]

That early Christian philosophers would be impressed with a Platonic view of the person is not surprising, given their appropriation of many elements in Plato's philosophical system. According to Father Robert O'Connell, S.J., St. Augustine followed Plato and Plotinus in adopting the principle that "'the soul is the man,' the authentic 'I,' which means that the body is something alien to our true identity."[4] This body-soul dualism was also reaffirmed in the writings of certain modern philosophers, such as Descartes. In his *Meditations*, Descartes defined the person in terms of two substances, *cogitatio* (the intellect) and *extensio* (matter), so heterogeneous that they could not possibly interact with or affect each other. Although this Cartesian or Platonic conception of the person as a strange amalgam of body and soul has been decisively refuted by many great philosophers, it still bedevils Western culture, and it still exerts some influence on Catholic moral theology.

One also finds novel forms of dualistic thinking expressed in the work of theologians like Karl Rahner, S.J. Father Rahner, under the influence of Immanuel Kant, regarded the human person as a transcendental ego or spiritual inner self, which is the source of our knowledge and freedom. Thus, he juxtaposed this "personal spirit . . . in freedom and radical self-possession" with the person's "concrete human nature."[5] Rahner separated the person's pure transcendental nature from his or her human nature and argued that what belongs to this changeable human nature cannot be definitively determined. This unusual way of thinking seems to deny that one's concrete bodily life is an intrinsic part of the human person. Rahner's anthropology has become dogma for many revisionist moral theologians, who set the concept of person (as spirit or consciousness) in opposition to concrete human nature (or the body).

On the contrary, John Paul II, inspired by Thomistic philosophy and by the Old Testament accounts of creation in *Genesis*, regarded the human person as a tight unity of body and intellectual soul. The Holy

Father's affinity for Aquinas's metaphysical anthropology is quite evident in his earlier works. It is also evident in the *Letter to Families* and in several encyclicals such as *Veritatis Splendor* and *Evangelium Vitae* where the conception of the person as embodied spirit is presupposed. Finally, this anthropology is discernible throughout the talks he gave at the Vatican that have been collected as *The Theology of the Body*. George Weigel calls this great work a "theological time bomb," which may "prove to be the decisive moment in exorcising the Manichean demon and its deprecation of human sexuality from Catholic moral theology."[6]

We cannot give this magnificent book its due in this context, but let it suffice to say that a rich and nuanced view of the "nuptial meaning of the body" and the body as intrinsic to selfhood unfolds in its pages. While John Paul II takes seriously the human subject as a thinking being with free will, he insists that it is always an embodied subject. We will consider the essentials of John Paul II's position, but we must first say a few more words about the persistent problem of dualism.

Dualism and the Culture of Death

As we have seen, dualism regards the individual's "spirit" or personhood as distinct from his or her bodily life. Some philosophers or theologians implicitly or explicitly embrace substance dualism, which posits that the human being is a spiritual substance inhabiting a body. John Paul II asserts that this viewpoint became entrenched in modern anthropology thanks to the rationalism of Descartes, which "makes a radical contrast in man between spirit and body" (LFam, 19). Post-Cartesian versions of dualism do not focus on the soul but on consciousness "as an independent subject of activity."[7] The person is identified with consciousness, while the body is regarded as a mere organism like all other bodies in the natural world. This form of dualism also conceives freedom, which accompanies consciousness, "in opposition to or in conflict with material or biological nature, over which it must progressively assert itself" (VS, 46).

Thus, according to John Paul II, "the body is no longer perceived as a properly personal reality, a sign and place of relations with others, with God, and with the world. It is reduced to pure materiality: it is simply a couple of organs, functions, and energies to be used according to the sole criteria of pleasure and efficiency" (EV, 23). Dualism reduces the body to a material appendage of the true self, self-conscious awareness, such that the body becomes something at our disposal for a pleasurable experience. According to this viewpoint, we "have" our bodies or we "use" our bodies as an instrument, but they are distinct from who we really are.

When the body is viewed so crudely, detached from the reality of some consciousness or transcendental self, sexual promiscuity becomes more easily acceptable. One uses the body for pleasure, but the true self remains transcendent to this experience and so it is unaffected. As a result, sexuality is easily "depersonalized and exploited" (EV, 23). Within this anthropological perspective, "man thus ceases to live as a person and a subject . . . [and] he becomes merely an object" (LFam, 19).

This dualistic framework has become ascendant among many proponents of abortion, euthanasia, physician-assisted suicide, and contraception. The well-known ethicist Joseph Fletcher, for example, justifies "the right of spiritual beings [i.e., humans] to use intelligent control over physical nature rather than submit beastlike to its blind workings."[8] According to this perspective, the physical body is alien to our spiritual nature, and it must be tamed or it will interfere with our plans and projects. As John Paul II writes, the body becomes a "raw datum devoid of any meaning and moral values until freedom has shaped it in accordance with its design" (VS, 48). Thus, actions such as genetic manipulation or contraception are often justified according to this line of reasoning. That justification presupposes a dualistic anthropology wherein our spiritual intelligence regards the body as a premoral phenomenon, as raw material to be reconfigured as necessary.

Or consider the moral rationales often put forth for euthanasia or physician-assisted suicide. Once a person's cognitive abilities have ceased to function or have become impaired, the individual is no longer considered to be a true or authentic person. These individuals exist as biological entities, perhaps in a persistent vegetative state like the late Terri Schiavo, and they have lost any semblance of personhood.[9] For example, when asked by ethicist Wesley Smith whether Terri was still a person, consider the answer given by Bill Allen, a prominent bioethicist in Florida: "No, I do not. I think having awareness is an essential criterion for personhood. Even minimal awareness would support some criterion of personhood, but I don't think complete absence of awareness does."[10]

According to the dualistic framework, without consciousness or minimal awareness, the person is no longer "there," and the termination of life is considered appropriate. There is a complete dichotomy between one's sentient bodily life and the conscious life of the person. One's bodily existence has no intrinsic worth apart from the presence of traits such as self-awareness. Accordingly, John Harris, another bioethicist teaching in England, defines the person "as a creature capable of valuing its own existence."[11] Without the capability to know and value one's existence, there is no person, and if there is no person, it is a small step to argue that euthanasia is morally acceptable. Of course, this is a preposterous claim. What if a mentally handicapped person cannot properly value his or her existence according to the criteria of bioethicists like Harris? Or what about young infants? Are we to conclude that these individuals are not persons just because they lack full cognitive ability? Personhood does not depend on the presence or absence of accidental qualities such as conscious awareness (EV, 60). Every human being is a person, a personal being possessing a rational nature, and hence every human being qualifies for full moral value.

Even some Catholic moral theologians have jumped on this bandwagon in recent years. According to Father Richard McCormick, S.J., for example, "life in a P.V.S. [persistent vegetative state] is not a benefit or value to the patient."[12] Implicit in this claim is that life has no intrinsic worth unless it is a self-conscious or rational life. These theologians, therefore, seem content to let these patients die, perhaps through the deprivation of food and water, since without a minimal consciousness that patient's existence is considered to be virtually worthless.

These comments, perhaps startling to those who are unaware of the recent trajectory of bioethics, graphically illustrate the late Holy Father's concern with distorted notions of selfhood, which conceive the person as a spiritual self-conscious subject who *has* a body. But this is a false perception of personhood that leads ineluctably to a curtailment and a weakening of human rights. John Paul II writes that this dualistic mentality "carries the concept of subjectivity to an extreme and even distorts it, and recognizes as a subject of rights only the person who enjoys full or at least incipient autonomy" (EV, 19). When personhood is conceived independently of the body, and it is defined in terms of traits such as cognitive awareness or rationality, "the criterion of personal dignity—which demands respect, generosity, and service—is replaced by the criterion of efficiency, functionality, and usefulness: others are considered not for what they are, but for what they 'have, do, and produce'" (EV, 23). This attitude can only yield disastrous moral consequences since it implies that the lives of many human beings will be regarded as expendable unless they are productive in some fashion.

On the contrary, John Paul II has argued from his earliest days as a philosopher that the human subject cannot be reduced to consciousness. In one of his early philosophical essays he explains that "if consciousness or self-consciousness characterize[s] the person, then they do so *only in the accidental order.*"[13] The whole person as a composite of body and soul is the subject who acts or who makes choices, not one's consciousness. In *The Acting Person*, Wojtyla points out that this nondualistic approach "runs counter to another trend of modern philosophy," which seeks to identify a person with his or her cognitive function.[14] But Wojtyla wants to reverse this attitude and explain the anthropological structure of a person by investigating human action (*actus humanis*). Later in *Veritatis Splendor* John Paul II reiterates the dangers of reducing the person to consciousness and insists that the person be seen in his or her nondualistic wholeness: "*body and soul are inseparable*: in the person, in the willing agent and in the deliberate act *they stand or fall together*" (VS, 49).

Fatal Problems with Dualism

As we have seen, the endorsement of a dualistic vision of the person has led bioethicists and others to devalue bodily life when cognitive abilities appear to be absent or even diminished. Yet this dualistic framework is deficient, and it has had many detractors. Even Friedrich Nietzsche, the father of postmodernity, was quite uneasy with a purely instrumentalist view of the body. In a section of *Also Sprach Zarathustra* known as "Despisers of the Body," he condemned those who have contempt for the body because they fail to see the ongoing corporeal involvement in the life of the human spirit. In *Also Sprach Zarathustra*, the body is heralded as a "great reason" and an "unknown sage" because of its indispensable but neglected role in the process of knowing.[15]

Nietzsche seemed to appreciate that a dualistic framework cannot explain human action, the complex unity of our experiences. A violinist, for example, achieves success in mastering a great violin concerto through a subtle combination of senses, intellect, and physical technique. As this example implies, a person's living body is intrinsic to his or her personal reality. Once we accept each human being's unity of action, the dualism fallacy is quickly undone. And if we embrace the idea that the corporeal life is an essential and irreducible component of the human person, we are less apt to reach false conclusions on moral issues such as abortion and euthanasia.

Also, when the self is seen in dualistic terms, human freedom is often misconceived. Philosophers who reduce the self to consciousness exhibit a tendency to inflate the value of freedom. We end up with a Sartrean view of the person wherein the person constitutes himself or herself by making choices and is always in a process of change or "becoming." For the philosopher Jean-Paul Sartre, there is no such thing as a fixed human nature. Human beings are always beyond themselves, projecting and choosing new goals. Thus, Sartre writes that "the existentialist will never consider man as an end because he is always in the making."[16] In Sartre's view, "for human reality, to be is to *choose* oneself."[17]

When the self is regarded as pure consciousness, it is free to create its own reality, to make its own way, to find its own truth. John Paul II seemed to have Sartre in mind when he summed up the prevailing attitude toward freedom: "what matters is to be free, released from all constraint or limitation, so as to operate according to private judgement, which in reality is pure caprice . . . [but] such liberalism can only be described as primitive" (MI, 34).

Of course, this is precisely the sense of freedom that John Paul II so categorically rejected in *Veritatis Splendor* because it is license, not authentic freedom. According to John Paul II, "the natural law thus understood [in terms of a person's nature as embodied spirit] does not allow for any division between freedom and nature" (VS, 50). Freedom and nature are not opposed, but instead they are "harmoniously bound together" (VS, 50).

Dualists, especially those who "absolutize consciousness," also tend to falsely equate *being* a person with *functioning* as a person by exhibiting the human traits of consciousness and reasoning.[18] As a result, they make the mistake of attributing moral worth to human beings based on accidental attributes such as their level of intelligence or degree of conscious awareness. But full moral worth depends upon *being* a person, a personal being with an intellectual nature, and not upon *acting* as one. According to Wojtyla, "the reality of the person demands a return to conscious *being*; this being is not constituted in and by consciousness."[19] John Paul II appreciated that human personhood is a mode of being a person in which the fullness of an actually flourishing personal life is not there all at once. Unlike angels, who are also persons, we are persons with a human nature. And that nature, though always present, unfolds and develops over time through its actions. As the medieval scholastics were wont to say, *"agere sequitur esse"* ("action follows being"): a being's actions are the unfolding of its nature. But if those actions are latent for some reason, one should not infer that the underlying nature of this being is absent. Thus, even if a particular human person, such as a fetus or someone in a coma, is not acting or functioning in a fully human (or rational) way, that person's intellectual nature still exists.

A related problem with dualism is its failure to consider the proper dynamism of human nature by virtually ignoring *human potentiality*. John Paul II, as Karol Wojtyla, relied heavily on this concept when he wrote his philosophical treatise *The Acting Person*, in which he described potentiality as a "mode of being which proceeds towards a fulfillment it does not yet possess."[20] A little girl is a woman in potency, and an acorn seed is an oak tree in potency.

It is particularly important to follow the precedent of Aquinas by differentiating between an active and a passive potentiality.[21] According to Aquinas, a receptive or passive potency is the potentiality to receive something or to undergo change from outside the self. A piece of wood has the potential to become a cross, but only if someone makes it so. But an active potency is the capacity to develop and act from within; for humans this includes the capacity to speak, to know, or to love. A newborn child, a fetus, even an embryo, has this active potency associated with being human, this radical capacity to know and to love. Every nature, including human nature, is defined by its properties or its built-in potentialities for activity. The active potency of a cat (which can never know or love) is not the active potency of a human being because its nature is completely different.

But what is the ethical significance of all this? According to Patrick Lee, if we recognize the intrinsic value of "higher mental functions," then we must also appreciate that the entities that have the potentiality for these functions are intrinsically valuable. According to Lee, "if the entity itself is intrinsically valuable then it must be intrinsically valuable from the moment it exists."[22] Hence the claim by abortion defenders that a fetus is not a personal human life is a gross fallacy. As John Paul II observes, "from the time that the ovum is fertilized, a life is begun which is neither that of the father nor the mother; it is rather the life of a new human being with his own growth. It would never be made human if it were not human already" (EV, 60).

What are the broader implications of accepting this doctrine of active potency, the notion of inner openness to a limited spectrum of possibilities? No human being is ever fully present or complete, nor is any human being a nonperson because he or she lacks certain traits. Rather, at every stage of our existence we are "potentially functioning actual persons," and we are "always functioning in ways appropriate to our level of development."[23] Should we not esteem a human person because he or she is *always* a personal being with an intellectual nature, regardless of the person's level of awareness or activity? We value the life of a two-day-old baby in part because of what this child will become in his or her life. If that life is cut short for some reason, we perceive the baby's death as a tragic event. We are saddened in part because we are cognizant of this child's unactualized potency. Similarly, someone in a persistent vegetative state is still a person who possesses a human nature, despite the absence of its proper functioning.

Thus, we value human beings not just for what they are here and now in the present and not just for their accidental qualities such as their level of intelligence or consciousness, but for their distinctive human nature and their inner dynamic potency. A dualistic anthropology with its typical focus on actual conscious awareness and rationality as the criteria of personhood completely obscures the critical element of active potency. It diverts our attention away from the person as an intellectual substance, qualitatively different from animals, to that person's accidental characteristics.

The final problem with anthropological dualism and its prejudice against the body is its incompatibility with the nondualistic view of the person found in Sacred Scripture. According to John Paul II, the doctrine of the bodily resurrection exposes the falsity of dualism, since it demonstrates that bodily life, not just spiritual life, is an intrinsic good. In his words, "the resurrection means the restoring to the real life of human corporeity, which was subjected to death in its temporal phase" (TB, 238). St. Paul affirms that the risen life of the person will be physical as well as spiritual (1 Cor. 15:42–50). According to St. Paul, the physical body is God's gift and should never be despised or deprecated in any way. He also explains that the physical body of the risen person will be different in that it will have total infusion of the spirit. Following St. Paul, John Paul II agrees that the resurrection in the eschatological future perfects the person, but he insists that any spiritualization of that new body does not signify a "disincarnation of the body, nor, consequently, a 'dehumanization' of man" (TB, 241).

The Human Person as Embodied Spirit

John Paul II's understanding of the human person is radically distinct from this rationalistic and dualistic anthropology. In the opening chapters of *The Theology of the Body*, John Paul II provides a wonderfully evocative description of human personhood: "Man is a subject because of his self-awareness and self-determination, but also on the basis of his own body. The structure of the body permits him to be the author of a truly human activity. In this activity the body expresses the person" (TB, 40–41). Later in that same work he describes how the body "reveals the living soul" (TB, 61). We may be spirit, but we are incarnate spirit, and our spiritual activities of willing and reasoning are achieved and made manifest with the help of our bodies.

John Paul II presents a similar argument in *Veritatis Splendor*: "The person, including the body, is completely entrusted to himself, and it is in the unity of the body and soul that the person is the subject of his own moral acts" (VS, 48). The person is a natural unity of body and soul. The human person, therefore, is a finite *embodied spirit*, a spirit intrinsically related to matter. According to John Paul II, "the body can never be reduced to mere matter: it is a *spiritualized body*, just as man's spirit is so closely united to the body that he can be described as an *embodied spirit*" (LFam, 19). The term "embodied spirit," perhaps better than any other, captures John Paul II's understanding of what it means to be a human person.

This unity of body and soul strongly implies the body's role as a subject of freedom rather than an inert object of freedom separate from one's consciousness. The person as a body-soul unity is a moral agent and exercises freedom. The body, therefore, is not some premoral organism to be manipulated, but an integral part of the human subject. The body is not only an integral part of the concrete human person, but also has a "nuptial meaning," that is, a "capacity of expressing love, that love in which the person becomes a gift and—by means of this gift—fulfills the meaning of his being and existence" (TB, 58).

In the ethical writings published before he became pope, Karol Wojtyla consistently articulated the same theme: the human body as an integral part of personhood. He repeatedly referred to the importance of Aquinas's metaphysical anthropology, which develops in great depth the notion of the human person as a unity of body and soul. He also discussed the critical importance of these concepts for working out a viable moral framework. According to Wojtyla, "the natural law is possible only if we accept a certain metaphysics of the person."[24] Furthermore, in *The Theology of the Body*, John Paul II offers some positive commentary on Aquinas's anthropology during his discussion of the resurrection of the body (TB, 235–240). Given John Paul II's obvious affinity for Aquinas's presentation of these issues, it would be instructive to briefly review the Thomistic conception of personhood and human nature that has been assimilated by John Paul II. Aquinas's philosophy can guide our efforts to grasp the full import and implications of John Paul II's own metaphysical anthropology.

Aquinas, of course, regarded the person with the utmost esteem. Indeed, he described the person as "that which is most perfect in all of nature."[25] Wojtyla fully concurs: "in the created world the person is the highest perfection: the person is *perfectissimum ens*."[26] But just what is a person? Father Norris Clarke expresses Aquinas's definition of the person as follows: "an actual existent [i.e., with its own act of existence], distinct from all others, possessing an intellectual nature, so that it can be the self-conscious, responsible source of its actions."[27] The concept of person, however, is an analogous one since there are angelic persons and the Divine Person, God Himself. Of course, we are not spiritual persons like God or the angels. So what is the nature of the human person? Human persons have a soul, but they also have a body, which, in their case, is for the good of the soul. A human person's soul or intellectual nature needs the body as a "natural complement and mediating instrument to fulfill his destiny as a traveler to God through the material cosmos."[28] Thus, Aquinas saw each human person as a single unitary being, not two beings (body and soul) contingently or loosely linked together. Similarly, John Paul II writes that "man is a person in the unity of his body and his spirit" (LFam, 19).

The evidence for the truth of this proposition is the same evidence used to refute the dualistic fallacy: the unity of each person's operations. Aquinas offers his theory of knowledge as substantiation. For Plato, knowledge is strictly a function of the soul. But for Aquinas, when some-one says "I know," that knowing is a result of the cooperation of the body, senses, and intellect. Although human understanding is a spiritual act that transcends matter, it is connected to the senses. We understand intelligible concepts with the help of the senses. Like Aquinas, John Paul II accepted the fact that "human knowledge is primarily a sensory knowledge . . . [because] '*nihil est in intellectu, quod prius non fuerit in sensu*' ('nothing is in the intellect that was not first in the senses')" (CTH, 33). Furthermore, as Aquinas reminds us, there is no such thing as pure imageless thought. Each time we think of concepts or ideas they must be linked to an image that is supplied by the brain's imagination. Hence Aquinas insists that this union is for the good of the soul, that is, the lower is for the sake of the higher. The body neither imprisons the soul nor fetters its activities. Rather, it allows the soul to extend itself into the physical world and come to know that world. Our fulfillment as embod-ied spirits is always through the body in the natural world. As Aquinas writes at one point, the soul must be "led by the hand by material things."[29] Unlike the angels, who are pure spirit and who have perfectly intuitive knowledge, a human person is a more complex entity. He or she is an "incarnate intellect" with a soul capable of existing on its own but incomplete without a body.

As John Paul II pointed out, Aquinas decisively overcame the dichotomy of body and soul as proposed by Plato, who saw the body as the soul's "earthly prison" (TB, 240). Aquinas also preserved the teaching on the soul's personal immortality in the face of opposition from medieval philosophers like Averroes. To be sure, the soul has preeminence because it is "the principle of unity of the human being" (VS, 48). At the same time each human being "exists as a whole—*corpore et anima unus*—as a person" (VS, 48).[30] But if the soul is so tightly connected to the body, how can we account for its incorruptibility and immortality, important truths of revelation? What happens to the soul when the body dies?

Aquinas solves this problem by demonstrating that the soul must possess its own spiritual act of existence. According to Aquinas, "The human soul exists through its own being; and matter shares in this being up to a point without completely enveloping it, because the dignity of such a form transcends the capacity of matter."[31]

The human intellectual soul has its own act of existence, its own being in itself, and the body shares in that being. The soul, therefore, as "a spiritual substance" is capable of existing without the body. As Aquinas argues, "The intellectual soul has being in itself, absolutely, not dependently on the body."[32] But, as we have seen, the soul is incomplete without the body, and the body needs the soul. Quite simply, the soul has a dual role to play: it has its own act of spiritual being (or *esse*) and so it is a substance, but it also informs and animates the body, so it is a form as well. In Aquinas's world each substance is composed of form and matter, where the form is the inner natural shape of a being, its intelligible structure that makes that being what it is. Consider a forest of oak trees: each tree has its own *matter* and so each tree is different; yet they are all similar—they are all trees and so they share in common the same *form* of being a tree. In human beings the soul represents the form, but the soul is more than an ordinary form since it is also a substance. The soul is a form "emerging above matter" (*forma emergens*), since the soul's activities as the body's form do not exhaust its full spiritual capabilities. Nonetheless, like all forms, the soul is correlated with matter, and it is incomplete without the body.

Aquinas summarizes this notion of man as incarnate spirit with unusual clarity in his commentary on St. Paul's Letter to the Corinthians: "Now since the soul is part of the human body, it is not the entire human being, and my soul is not I. So, even if the soul reached salvation in another life, neither I nor any human being would thereby do so."[33] Since the separated soul is incomplete without its body, it is not a complete human person. Hence the need for the resurrection of the body that will perfect and complement the disembodied soul.

As we have demonstrated through several key citations, John Paul II unequivocally affirms Aquinas's teaching on the unity of body and soul in both his earlier philosophical works and his encyclicals. In *Veritatis Splendor* he explains that "the rational soul is *per se et essentialiter* the form of his body" (VS, 48). Of course, he also accepts the soul's immortality, but reminds us that the body will share in the soul's immortal glory because of the promise of the resurrection (VS, 48). Thus, although John Paul II does not go into the same level of detail as Aquinas, one can safely assume that his metaphysical anthropology seems to be in general harmony with Aquinas's philosophy.

Now that we have untangled the Thomistic conception of human nature we can look more closely at personhood. What does it mean to be a divine, angelic, or human person? From an ontological perspective the person, like all beings, is a substance that is actively present, but a person is much more than that given our innate capabilities. Aquinas's most familiar definition of the person was *subsistens distinctum in natura rationali*, or a "distinct substance in a rational nature."[34] As we saw earlier, a person is distinguished from the rest of creation because the person possesses a rational nature. But it is not enough to say that the person has a rational (or intellectual) nature—in order to be an autonomous being, the person must also have his or her own act of existence (*esse*). According to Wojtyla, "A rational nature does not possess its own subsistence as a nature, but subsists in a person. The person is a subsistent [i.e., autonomous] subject of existence and action, which can in no way be said of a rational nature. That is why God must be a personal being."[35] The human person has something in common with angelic and Divine persons because the human person has an intellectual nature, though the intellect is linked in a natural unity with a material body.

John Paul II, like Aquinas, saw the person as more than just an ordinary being or another member of a species. In a work he composed before he became pope, *Love and Responsibility*, he wrote: "The term *persona* has been coined to signify that a man cannot be wholly contained within the concept 'individual member of the species' but that there is something more to him, a particular richness and perfection in the manner of his being, which can only be brought out by the use of the word 'person.'"[36]

Following other Thomist scholars like Clarke, John Paul II conceived of personhood in terms of "self-possession" (TB, 27, 48). A person, unlike a tree or an animal, is aware of himself as present and as the source of his actions. Only a person can say "I" and know what that means, so only a person is present to himself or "possesses" himself through self-awareness. Thus, this self-possession that characterizes the person finds expression through self-consciousness or self-awareness and through self-determination. According to John Paul II, the person is a subject precisely because of his or her "self-awareness and self-determination" (TB, 40).

In the earlier philosophical writings, the theme of self-possession emerged as an important aspect of Wojtyla's anthropology, and it became a key concept for understanding human action. Wojtyla put particular emphasis on self-determination, as evidenced by this passage in *The Acting Person*,

Because "I will" is an act of self-determination at a particular moment, it presupposes structural self-possession. For only the things that are man's actual possession can be determined by him; they can be determined only by the one who actually possesses them. Being in the possession of himself, man can determine himself.[37]

Moreover, John Paul II, following Aquinas, attributes the moral dignity of human beings, who are made in God's image, to our capacity to be *dominus sui*, or master of oneself.[38] Thus, one of the most distinctive elements of personhood for John Paul II is that each person is a free, self-governing individual. Self-possession also makes possible the gift of self called for in the Gospel: "only if one possesses oneself can one give oneself."[39] No one can give of his or her self to another unless he or she has a "self" to give and some conscious "possession" of that self as belonging to him or her.

But we must keep in mind that personhood is never fully "achieved." Rather, *to be a human person is always to be on the way from potential self-possession to actual self-possession*. A young child grows or awakens into self-possession. That child slowly becomes *self-aware* through outside stimuli and especially through contact with others; and the child also develops a sense of responsibility as he or she comes to see himself or herself as *self-determining*, that is, as master of his or her actions. But this capacity is latent in the child's being from the time of conception. Even as adults we are continually awakened to the exercise of our personhood by external stimulation and through the initiatives of others, who can help us attain new levels of self-awareness and self-donation as we mature in life.

Thanks to our intellectual nature, each human being comes into existence with the intrinsic power to achieve self-possession, and herein lies the innate dignity of the human being. Full concrete functioning may not always be there, but a person's intellectual nature, the natural capacities for free will and conceptual thought, are always present. Therefore, each person has full moral worth and is deserving of our respect from the moment of conception. As we have argued, from all this follows an important consequence for bioethics: it is morally unacceptable to depersonalize the embryo or the fetus, since it possesses this intellectual nature or intrinsic power to achieve actual self-possession and is already "on the way" from potency to act.

We should also note the cardinal importance of this Thomistic anthropology adopted by John Paul II for overcoming the false postmodern notions of selfhood that interfere with the traditional conception of moral responsibility. When we look at a human person's ontological structure, we find that the person is a substance, a being that "stands out as a distinct, autonomous, self-governing moral subject in the community of persons."[40] The person cannot be reduced to sheer multiplicity, that is, to his or her relations with others or his or her accidental qualities. Therefore, the human self is changed by its experiences yet retains its self-identity through these accidental modifications (age, etc.), and it is irreducible to its relations with others. Some theologians such as Sister Margaret Farley appear to concur with postmodern assumptions that there are "many selves" and "only process and relation without agency."[41] But without a perduring substantial self, how could there be a "relation" between two beings? I can't say that X is related to Y and then say that Y is nothing but its relations, because then X is relating to nothing, and a relation must relate to something.

The human person, like all real beings, must be a synthesis of permanence and mutability, or, in metaphysical terms, *substance* (or underlying substrate) and accidents. Of course, unlike other substances, a human person is also a *subject* because of our self-conscious awareness and freedom. John Paul II likes to use the language of subjectivity in order to underscore the distinct interiority of the person. As Kenneth Schmitz observes, in his discussions on the person, "John Paul has in mind, not only the metaphysical sense of subject as *suppositum entis* [substrate] but also a corrected modern sense of subject as 'subjectivity' in distinction from the modern sense of 'object' as 'thing lacking interiority.'"[42] Many contemporary philosophers, however, have neglected the *suppositum* or substantial dimension of personhood, while dwelling extensively on the relational and accidental dimensions. But there must be an irreducible substantial self to ground our experiences and relations with others in the unity of a single being.[43]

Without such a principle, much of human experience loses its intelligibility. For example, the notion of self-giving in marriage, friendship, or religious commitment becomes unintelligible. Unless one has a distinct self to give, it makes no sense to promise the gift of that self to another person, whether that other person is one's spouse or God Himself. Moreover, it becomes impossible to hold a person responsible for anything if the self is a plurality in a state of constant change. If someone robs a bank and is caught one year later, it seems senseless to hold that person accountable for that crime unless the person is the same self who committed the crime. But how could this be if the self is never the same, always in flux, and always different?

John Paul II's conception of selfhood, however, does not imply some sort of static entity. Substance should not be understood as an inert substratum, but as the principle of self-identity (*suppositum*) through change. Every substance or underlying subject is dynamic and is changed constantly by accidental modifications of greater or lesser importance. However, in these accidental changes the substance is changed accidentally, not substantially. Self-identity is not to be confused with unchangeability. As Wojtyla insists, in all the subject's actions "it does not remain indifferent."[44] Each person is a subject and substantial being, capable of free, self-conscious activities, who is changed by those activities even while maintaining identity throughout those changes. John Paul II has always insisted upon the human self as a substantial subject in process and in relation with others. The human self is not a sheer plurality, but a *unity-in-plurality*.

Beyond Thomistic Anthropology

We have illustrated that Pope John Paul II subscribed to the essentials of Thomistic anthropology, fully embracing the notion that the human person is an embodied spirit, an intellectual nature (or soul) joined in a natural unity with a physical body. As an incarnate will and intellect, the soul lives and operates through the life of the body. In one of his many homilies the Holy Father described human life as the "concrete reality of a being that lives, that acts, that grows and develops."[45] The human person, therefore, is a "concrete reality," not a spiritual one, and as a consequence our bodily life is an intrinsic good that cannot be casually dispensed with for convenience or for utilitarian reasons. Also, it is the nature of a human being to always be a person; personhood is not something to be acquired. If so, personal dignity becomes equated "with the capacity for verbal and explicit, or at least perceptible, communication" (EV, 19).

But John Paul II goes beyond Aquinas in at least two ways. First, he gives his anthropology a personalist touch by focusing more attention on subjectivity. In one of his earlier works he proffers the following assessment of Aquinas:

> We can see how very objectivistic St. Thomas' view of the person is. It almost seems as though there is no place in it for an analysis of consciousness and self-consciousness as totally unique manifestations of the person as subject. . . . Thus St. Thomas gives us an excellent view of the objective existence and activity of the person, but it would be difficult to speak in this view of the lived experiences of the person.[46]

In other words, Aquinas does a great job of unfolding the objective dimension of the person, but he falls short in describing the interior, self-creative dimension.

As we have seen, John Paul II prefers the Thomistic notion of self-possession as a way of speaking about human personhood. The human person is both self-aware and self-determining, and John Paul II gives particular emphasis to the latter capability. But, unlike Aquinas, and in keeping with the modern focus on subjectivity, he emphasizes that we are not simply determining our specific actions, but we are also determining our selves: "I am not only the efficient cause of my acts, but through them I am also in some sense the 'creator of myself.'"[47] The conscious, free actions of the acting person not only produce an external effect; they also produce an internal one since the person is creating himself or herself through these actions. Let's say that Jane chooses to be deceptive in a hurtful way. She not only brings about harm to the victim of that deception (the external effect), but she also constitutes her self as a harmful deceiver.

This viewpoint is elaborated in great depth in John Paul II's earlier writings, particularly *The Acting Person*. In an important passage of that book Wojtyla states: "In point of fact, in all dynamizations [i.e., actions], the subject does not remain indifferent: not only does it participate in them . . . but it is itself in one way or another formed or transformed by them."[48] This wonderful insight echoes Aristotle, who wrote in the *Nicomachean Ethics* that "the man . . . must be a perfect fool who is unaware that people's characters take their bias from the steady direction of their activities."[49] John Paul II carries over this theme to his encyclicals and his later writings. For example, in *Veritatis Splendor* he explains that our free choices "do not produce a change merely in the state of affairs outside of man but, to the extent they are deliberate choices, they give moral definition to the very person who performs them, determining his profound spiritual traits" (VS, 71). Once again we see the close connection between ethics and metaphysics. It stands to reason that if the permanent substance is dynamic and is really changed in every accidental change, then the human subject will be shaped by his or her choices.

Each of us, then, has this capacity for "soul-making," that is, determining the interior self through the choices we make. Wojtyla emphasized that each self-determining action leaves upon us a mark or a trace. Thus, every time someone makes a choice we are keenly aware of the objective value of that choice and its outward impact along with the abiding effects on the chooser. Although Aquinas provides ample explanation of the outward dimension of our free choice as a cause of many possible external effects, he gives scant attention to the internal or soul-making effect on the chooser. And yet both sets of effects accompany one another in the choices we make—they are two aspects of the same reality.[50]

Second, John Paul II puts greater emphasis than Aquinas on the social and communitarian nature of the human person with his focus on solidarity. This notion certainly has its roots in Thomistic metaphysics, which defines being as actively present and self-communicative. Aquinas, for example, tells us that "communication follows upon the very intelligibility of actuality."[51] Of course, wherever there is self-communication there must be a relation of some sort between the being that "communicates" or acts and the being that is acted upon. This implies that self-communication and the capability to relate to others are ontological dimensions of being a substance. There is a dynamic and relational side of all beings, but this is especially true of persons, who have an intrinsic dynamism toward self-communication and sharing with others. We find the highest level of self-communication in human beings, who alone are capable of love, the highest form of self-giving and receiving. Authentic personhood, therefore, requires us to be persons in communion with others.

Although Aquinas does not focus extensively on this issue, it is surely implicit in his philosophy. Contemporary Thomists, however, such as John Paul II, put considerably more emphasis on the relational dimension of human beings, who are perfected through this dynamism of giving and receiving. We find the clearest statement of John Paul II's thinking on this issue in a work written before he was elevated to the papacy: "The human being is not a person, on the one hand, and a member of society on the other. The human being as a person is simultaneously a member of society."[52] John Paul II also reiterates this theme in *The Theology of the Body*, where he uses the text of Genesis to illuminate the meaning of our mutual interdependence:

> When God-Yahweh said "It is not good that man should be alone, . . . I will make him a helper" (Gen. 2:18) . . . He affirmed that "alone" man does not completely realize his essence. He realizes it only by existing "with someone"—and even more deeply and completely— by existing "for someone."
>
> This norm of existence as a person is shown in Genesis as characteristic of creation, precisely by means of the meaning of these two words: "alone" and "helper." These words indicate as fundamental and constitutive for man both the relationship and communion of persons. The communion of persons means existing in a mutual "for," in a relationship of mutual gift. This relationship is precisely the fulfillment of man's original solitude. (TB, 61–62)

This conception of the person as having a communitarian nature, as one who achieves self-identity and self-possession in authentic communion with others, has unmistakable ethical implications. According to John Paul II, the "fundamental dimension of man's existence . . . is always a coexistence" (CTH, 36). As we shall see in the next chapter, the theme of *solidarity* as a virtue, which calls for us to work responsibly for the common good and to recognize the interdependence of all people, pervades John Paul II's encyclicals and serves as the basis for several of his key social and ethical doctrines.

Solidarity, however, is not to be confused with liberalism's notion of fraternity. While fraternity is based upon "common citizenship of a given polity," solidarity is predicated upon John Paul II's anthropological vision grounded in his inspired reading of Genesis.[53] Solidarity, therefore, is a bond of love that aims at the values of peace and justice for all people who are one in Christ.

A Definition of the Human Person

We are now in a position to summarize John Paul II's metaphysical anthropology: a human being is an individual person possessing his or her own act of existence with an intellectual nature, always on the way from potential self-possession (self-consciousness and self-determination) to actual; the intellectual nature is tied to a physical body that anchors it in the physical world. The person, as an embodied spirit, a unity of body and soul, freely transforms himself or herself through his or her actions, and achieves fulfillment in communal solidarity or coexistence with fellow human beings.

Anthropology as Theology

This discussion of John Paul II's conception of the person would be incomplete without further consideration of the link between his anthropology and the theology of the body. As Christopher West explains, the novelty of John Paul II's approach to these issues lies in his belief that "an adequate anthropology must be a theology *of the body*."[54]

As we observed earlier, each person is created as an embodied spirit. The body expresses the person. As John Paul II writes, "The body, in fact, and it alone, is capable of making visible what is invisible: the spiritual and divine" (TB, 76). Each person is created in God's image, and so each person is ontologically destined to live in relation to others in imitation of the Trinitarian communion of persons. Therefore, "to be a person means both 'being subject' and 'being in relationship'" (TB, 371). Man is the only being that God creates for his own sake, but he is not called to live in solitude. Rather, man finds himself by living in communion with others through the gift of self. Marriage epitomizes that communion. According to John Paul II, the nuptial meaning of the body is "the body's capacity of expressing love: that love precisely in which the man-person becomes a gift and— by means of this gift—fulfills the very meaning of his existence" (TB, 63).

Thus, man is created for his own sake and yet only discovers and fulfills himself through the sincere gift of that self. According to Christopher West, "God created the rest of creation for *our* sake. We are free to use (but not abuse) creation for our benefit. The human person, however, since he exists 'for his own sake,' must never be used as a means to an end. He is an end in himself. Nonetheless, having been created for his own sake, man is not meant to live for his own sake, but to live for others."[55] We see once again how deeply ethics is rooted in anthropology. A person is not something, but some*one*, a subject, who should never be reduced to the status of object. We are made in the image of the Divine Subject, God Himself, and we are called to love as God loves, which means the giving of ourselves to others.

This anthropology is Christocentric because "Christ the New Adam . . . reveals man to himself" (RH, 2). In order to amplify this claim, John Paul II turns to a key text of *Gaudium et Spes*, which is cited in many of his encyclicals:

> The truth is that only in the mystery of the Incarnate Word does the mystery of man take on light. For Adam, the first man, was a figure of Him who was to come, namely Christ the Lord. Christ, the final Adam, by the revelation of the mystery of the Father, and His Love, fully reveals man to man himself and makes his supreme calling clear. It is not surprising, then, that in Him all the aforementioned truths find their root and attain their crown.[56]

Quite simply, Christ is the exemplary person, a model of giving and self-sacrifice, and we must look to Him in order to learn how to love and find fulfillment in giving ourselves to others. Any authentic humanism must be theocentric (DM, 1).

Regrettably, John Paul II's anthropology is totally at odds with the conventional notions of personhood that prevail in secular society. As John Paul II has lamented, "The unreserved gift of self, mastery of one's instincts, the sense of responsibility—these are notions considered as belonging to another age."[57] While the anthropology of the secular world is dualistic, utilitarian, individualistic, and self-centered, John Paul II's anthropology stresses inalienable dignity, integrity (the wholeness of the person as body and soul), the gift of self, authentic community, and responsibility.

Common Humanity as the Ground of Morality

One last word on this topic. John Paul II's clear and distinct views on anthropology become a secure foundation for his philosophical argument that there is a universal morality. Like Aquinas and others in the natural law tradition, he looks to our common human nature as the ground of common moral principles. In *Veritatis Splendor*, he explains that "the natural law has universality" thanks to the "nature which we all have in common" (VS, 51).

Although each human person is unique and different from everyone else, that person is not radically different because he or she shares the same intellectual nature as other persons. As we have seen, each human person possesses this intellectual nature and acts as a unity of soul and body (or form and matter). Each one of us shares the same form of humanity, and so we are all individuals with the same essential features (such as intellect and will), similar to other humans on a fundamental level. Yet we are all individuated by matter, that is, by our bodies so that no single human being exhausts the human species. If each person's situation were unique, if we were all completely different from each other and not members of the same species, a situational ethic might be more fitting. However, given that we are all members of the same human species, this is not the case. Since we share in a common human nature, it is reasonable to derive a common, transcultural morality or a moral law that applies to all members of that species. At the same time, "universality does not ignore the individuality of human beings" (VS, 51). We are all free to become unique individuals, to express ourselves in many different ways, within the general parameters of the natural law.

But what about the historicity of human nature? Isn't human nature mutable and always evolving, and might that not ground an ethic that is more validly situational? To be sure, human nature certainly undergoes accidental modifications as habits, instincts, or other qualities change. However, neither the most important characteristics of human nature such as the capacity for reasoning nor the possibilities for human fulfillment have been substantially altered despite the profound existential changes that have occurred in the course of human history. It is simply not possible to find *any* culture that does not esteem the basic human goods that are the source of normativity and the natural law. The people of each culture value life and health, require basic forms of knowledge for their survival and thriving as a culture, esteem the beauty of the physical world, and appreciate the harmony of friendship and communal life.[58] John Paul II is right to insist that human nature transcends cultural differences: "This [human] nature is itself the measure of culture and the conditions ensuring that man does not become the prisoner of any of his cultures" (VS, 53). Without human nature as a benchmark, we cannot judge the moral adequacy of a culture. We know that the slave trade is wrong even if it is sanctioned by a particular culture because it is dehumanizing and violates the right to self-determination. If cultural norms are the only standard of morality, and moral rightness is whatever a particular society approves, moral dissent becomes unintelligible, since there is no higher moral standard to which the moral dissenter can appeal.

It is fashionable today to argue against the preeminence of the human species when viewed in comparison to other species. Peter Singer and other contemporary philosophers reject the privileged or central position of the human being and regard such claims as a form of "species-favoritism." According to this viewpoint, the notion that the human species transcends all other species is prejudicial. John Paul II has consistently argued that morality must have the person as its central focus: "only the human being as person is the true center of morality."[59] But Singer argues for a "decentering" of ethics, a movement away from this central focus on the human person. How is this decentering justified? Singer contends that "the capacity for suffering and enjoyment . . . is sufficient for us to say that a being has interests—at an absolute minimum, an interest in not suffering."[60] Animals certainly have an interest in the avoidance of suffering, and since rights are based on interests, animals must have some sort of rights just like human beings. Although Singer and so-called biocentrists do not claim that animals or other living beings have the same rights as humans, they deny "the existence of rights in the full sense of the term" because they do not accept that human beings are different in kind from other living things.[61] Other philosophers like Lucas Introna take this argument even further and claim that even machines such as computers have interests. Introna advocates that we must "move beyond any centre, whatever it may be—anthropological, biological, etc."[62] Thanks to this enterprise of radical decentering, human interests and human rights must now compete with animal interests (and perhaps even machine interests!) within a framework of crude utilitarian reasoning.

But this line of argumentation denies the obvious: the distinctive reality of personhood—as human persons, each of us has the intrinsic capabilities of spiritual intellect and will. Unlike the members of any other species, humans have the intellectual capacity to be able to judge their status in the universe. Human beings are qualitatively different or different in kind from all other beings. If animals and machines had spiritual intelligence, they might begin to ask questions about their place in the order of created being, but animals are not persons. They lack this gift and cannot even begin to raise such questions. There is not the slightest hint of self-possession among animals who cannot say "I" and know what that means. Nor are animals capable of determining themselves in any purposeful way. Human beings alone are persons with an intellectual nature that makes them deserving of special moral worth.

Also, John Paul II believes that this unwillingness to give a privileged place to human beings in the world is connected with the growing rejection of God the Creator:

> When the sense of God is lost, the sense of man is also threatened and poisoned. . . . Man is no longer able to see himself as "mysteriously different" from other earthly creatures; he regards himself merely as one more living being, as an organism which, at most, has reached a very high stage of perfection. Enclosed in the narrow horizon of his physical nature, he is somehow reduced to being "a thing" and no longer grasps the "transcendent" character of his existence as man. (EV, 22)

We must never lose sight of our distinctive nature as human beings, and never let anthropology become detached from its roots in theology and our understanding of God's creative power.

There is something uniquely valuable about the human species, and it seems beyond dispute that our common humanity supports a common morality that we share with all fellow humans. At the core of that morality is what makes us distinct from all other creatures—because of our God-given personhood we stand out in the universe and therefore have a certain dignity that commands respect. Each member of the human species deserves respect, deserves to be treated with special intrinsic worth, because the person is a rational nature, an embodied soul with spiritual capacities of will and intellect.

Finally, revelation confirms the insights of philosophy regarding the uniqueness of the human person. As John Paul reminds us in *Veritatis Splendor* and elsewhere, Scripture repeatedly tells us that each one of us is made in the image and likeness of God. Moreover, by virtue of our personhood we are similar to angels and God Himself, who are also persons. According to John Paul II, man "as a person [is thus] one who, even in his corporeality, is similar to God" (TB, 47). Animals and other creatures lack this close similarity to the Creator.

Summary

It is ironic perhaps that orthodox Catholic theology, once falsely perceived as a "despiser" of the body, is now the body's most ardent champion and defender. Critics like Nietzsche simply failed to appreciate the subtlety and depth of Aquinas's metaphysical anthropology. To be sure, the dualistic paradigm may be found in the thought of St. Augustine and in the writings of other neo-Platonists in early Christianity, who were under the influence of Plato's bias against the body and the realm of the physical. That prejudice, however, was incisively overcome by St. Thomas Aquinas. Beyond any doubt, he insisted upon the integral nature of the human person, who should be seen as an embodied spirit. But now new "despisers" of the body have emerged, advocates of a false "personhood theory," which sees the body as secondary and ancillary to conscious, rational awareness. The same could even be said of theologians like Karl Rahner, who followed Immanuel Kant and regarded the self as pure transcendence. According to this personhood theory, without cognitive capacity or consciousness, one is not a true person. Once again, this view is mistaken because it confuses functioning as a person with being a person. This mistake is not trivial, given the moral hazards that this flawed anthropology poses for embryos, fetuses, and even newborn infants, not to mention anyone in a coma or persistent vegetative state.

John Paul II writes at length on this topic, especially in *The Theology of the Body*. His exposition is a potent refutation of anthropological dualism. He will simply not accept the dualistic paradigm that denies that the body is an integral part of the human person: "human existence is characterized precisely by subjectivity which includes the meaning of the body" (TB, 41). For John Paul II this truth is found in a retrieval of the Thomistic notion of the human person as an embodied spirit, a unity of body and soul, a whole person free to act and achieve self-realization. According to John Paul II, "man is a person in the unity of body and his spirit" (LFam, 19). In Aquinas's terms, personhood implies presence to oneself in the act of understanding and in the mastery exercised over one's acts. John Paul II prefers the term "self-possession" to describe what it means to be a person. Personhood is never contingent on the person's actual state or his or her present functioning as a "rationally aware" or self-conscious being. Nor is personhood reducible to consciousness, which characterizes the person "only in the accidental order."[63] Rather, thanks to the soul, each human being *always* possesses a rational nature including the capacities for intellectual thought and free choice. According to Aquinas, "From the essence of the soul flow powers which are essentially different . . . but which are united in the soul's essence as in a root."[64] Because of these superior powers, each person is endowed with dignity and special intrinsic worth. Also, this "intrinsically valuable" human being comes into existence with a physical human body and "does not cease to be until that physical organism ceases to be."[65] All human beings, therefore, are entitled to be treated with dignity and respect, even if they lack consciousness or exist in an embryonic state.

John Paul II gives special prominence to the person as the self-aware subject who can say "I" and know what it means. In his view, this subjective dimension is shortchanged in Aquinas's philosophy. Yet a person's *lived experience* of deliberating, choosing, and carrying out one's choice is the basis for evaluating those choices. In all of his moral writings, therefore, John Paul II gives heed to the subjective and objective depth of the human person.

Finally, we can begin to appreciate the close interrelationship between ethics, anthropology, and metaphysics. In both his early and later writings John Paul II utilizes metaphysical categories borrowed from Aquinas in order to shed light on the nature of the person. Once we grasp the nature of the person, we can uncover and justify the norms found in the natural law that flows from this nature. As we have seen, this analysis of anthropological issues has special significance for our ethical deliberations. As Germain Grisez explains,

> If the person really is not his body, then the destruction of the life of the body is not directly and in itself an attack on the value intrinsic to the human person. The lives of the unborn, the lives of those not fully in possession of themselves—the hopelessly insane and the "vegetating" senile—and the lives of those who no longer can engage in praxis or problem-solving become lives no longer meaningful, no longer valuable, no longer inviolable.[66]

Now that we have a proper understanding of anthropology and an appreciation that humans must always be considered in their nondualistic wholeness, we can begin to unravel the natural law morality of John Paul II that is articulated in his encyclicals and other writings. The next chapter turns attention to this task.

Notes

1. For a fuller argument along these lines, see Patrick Lee, "Soul, Body and Personhood," *American Journal of Jurisprudence* 49 (2004): 87–125.

2. Friedrich Nietzsche, "Von den Verächtern des Leibes," in *Also Sprach Zarathustra* (Stuttgart: Philipp Reclam, 1962), 27.

3. Plotinus, *Enneads*, 6 vols., trans. A. H. Armstrong (Cambridge, Mass.: Harvard University Press, 1946), 1:249.

4. Robert O'Connell, S.J., *St. Augustine's Early Theory of Man* (Cambridge, Mass.: Harvard University Press, 1968), 185–186.

5. Karl Rahner, *Theological Investigations*, vol. 14 (London: Darton, Longman and Todd, 1976), 15–16.

6. George Weigel, *Witness to Hope* (New York: HarperCollins, 1999), 342.

7. Karol Wojtyla, "Thomistic Personalism," in *Person and Community: Selected Essays*, trans. Theresa Sandok (New York: Peter Lang, 1993), 169.

8. Joseph Fletcher, *Moral Responsibility: Situation Ethics at Work* (Philadelphia: Lippincott, 1967), 151.

9. Terri Schiavo was in a persistent vegetative state for a number of years. Her legal case received worldwide attention in 2005 when her husband won the legal right to remove her from a feeding tube despite the wishes of her parents.

10. Wesley Smith, "Human Non-Person," *National Review Online*, March 29, 2005, www.nationalreview.com/smithw/smith200503290755.asp (May 11, 2005).

11. Smith, "Human Non-Person."

12. Richard McCormick, S.J., "Moral Considerations Ill Considered," *America* 166 (June 1992): 210.

13. Wojtyla, "Thomistic Personalism," 170 (my emphasis).

14. Karol Wojtyla, *The Acting Person*, trans. A. Potocki, Analecta Husserliana, vol. 10 (Dordrecht, Holland: D. Reidel, 1979), vii.

15. Nietzsche, "Von den Verächtern des Leibes," 27.

16. Jean-Paul Sartre, *Existentialism and Human Emotions*, trans. Hazel Barnes (New York: Citadel Press, 1957), 50–51.

17. Jean-Paul Sartre, *Being and Nothingness*, trans. Hazel Barnes (New York: Philosophical Library, 1956), 516.

18. Karol Wojtyla, "The Person, Subject, and Community," *Review of Metaphysics 33*, no. 2 (December 1979): 277.

19. Wojtyla, "Person, Subject, and Community," 278 (my emphasis).

20. Quoted in Rocco Buttiglione, *Karol Wojtyla: The Thought of the Man Who Became Pope John Paul II* (Grand Rapids, Mich.: Eerdmans, 1997), 134.

21. See William May, "Philosophical Anthropology and *Evangelium Vitae*," 2002, www.christendom-awake.org/pages/may (December 12, 2005).

22. Patrick Lee, *Abortion and the Unborn Child* (Washington, D.C.: Catholic University of America Press, 1997), 122.

23. Ronald Tacelli, S.J., "Is Abortion Murder?" unpublished paper delivered at Boston College, November 12, 1992.

24. Karol Wojtyla, "The Human Person and Natural Law," in *Person and Community: Selected Essays*, 185.

25. St. Thomas Aquinas, *Summa Theologiae* I, q. 29, a. 3.

26. Wojtyla, "Thomistic Personalism," 167.

27. Norris Clarke, S.J., *Person and Being* (Milwaukee: Marquette University Press, 1993), 29.

28. Clarke, *Person and Being*, 29.

29. St. Thomas Aquinas, *Summa Theologiae* I, q. 12, a. 12.

30. The literal translation is "by body and soul one human being." This Latin phrase is taken from the Second Vatican Council document *Gaudium et Spes* (14), and it is clearly meant to endorse Aquinas's teaching on this matter.

31. St. Thomas Aquinas, *De Unitate Intellectus* III, n. 84.

32. St. Thomas Aquinas, *Summa Theologiae*, I, q. 75, a. 2.

33. St. Thomas Aquinas, *Super Epistolam Primam ad Corinthios Lectura*, commenting on 15.19.

34. St. Thomas Aquinas, *Summa Theologiae*, I, q. 29, a. 3; this conception of the person is derived from Boethius's definition: *persona est individua substantia rationalis naturae* (the person is an individual substance of a rational nature). See his *De Duobus Naturis*. Although Wojtyla accepted this basic definition, he did not believe that it adequately expressed the meaning of personhood. See Wojtyla, *The Acting Person*, 73–74.

35. Wojtyla, "Thomistic Personalism," 167.

36. Karol Wojtyla, *Love and Responsibility*, trans. J. J. Willetts (San Francisco: Ignatius Press, 1993), 22.

37. Quoted in J. Kupczak, O.P., *Destined for Liberty* (Washington, D.C.: Catholic University of America Press, 2000), 114.

38. St. Thomas Aquinas, *Summa Theologiae* I-II, q. 6, a. 2, ad. 2.

39. Karol Wojtyla, "The Personal Structure of Self-Determination," in *Person and Community: Selected Essays,* 194.

40. Clarke, *Person and Being,* 57.

41. Farley, "How Shall We Love," 318.

42. Kenneth Schmitz, *At the Center of the Human Drama: The Philosophical Anthropology of Karol Wojtyla/Pope John Paul II* (Washington, D.C.: Catholic University of America Press, 1993), 141–142.

43. Wojtyla develops this theme in both *The Acting Person* and a later essay, "The Person as Subject and as Community."

44. Wojtyla, *The Acting Person,* 96.

45. John Paul II, Homily at Capitol Mall (Washington, D.C.), *Observatore Romano,* November 5, 1979, 7.

46. Wojtyla, "Thomistic Personalism," 170–171.

47. Wojtyla, "The Personal Structure of Self-Determination," 191.

48. Wojtyla, *The Acting Person,* quoted in J. Kupczak, 111.

49. Aristotle, *Nicomachean Ethics,* trans. J. A. K. Thomson (New York: Penguin, 1976), Book III, 5:91.

50. See Karol Wojtyla, "The Structure of Self-Determination as the Core of the Theory of the Person," in *Tommaso d'Aquino nel suo VII Centennario* (Roma: Edizioni Domenicane Italiene, 1974). Also see Clarke's discussion of this topic in *Person and Being,* 54–56.

51. St. Thomas Aquinas, *Sent.* I, d. 4, q. 4, a. 4.

52. Karol Wojtyla, "The Problem of the Theory of Morality," in *Person and Community: Selected Essays,* 146.

53. Tracey Rowland, *Culture and the Thomist Tradition* (London: Routledge, 2003), 43.

54. Christopher West, *Theology of the Body Explained* (Boston: Pauline Books, 2003), 5.

55. West, *Theology of the Body Explained,* 101.

56. *Gaudium et Spes,* in *Vatican Council II: The Conciliar and Post Conciliar Documents,* ed. Austin Flannery, O.P. (Northport, N.Y.: Costello, 1975), 22.

57. Pope John Paul II, "Letter to President Clinton," *Origins* (1994): 760.

58. See John Finnis, *Historical Consciousness and Theological Foundations* (Toronto: Pontifical Institute of Medieval Studies, 1992), 24–25.

59. Wojtyla, "The Problem of the Theory of Morality," 155.

60. Peter Singer, "All Animals Are Equal," in *Social Ethics: Morality and Social Policy,* 5th edition, ed. Thomas Mappes and Jane Zembaty (New York: New York Review of Books, 1990), 441.

61. Lee, "Soul, Body and Personhood," 119.

62. Lucas Introna, "The 'Measure of Man' and the Ethics of Machines," in Proceedings of Computer Ethics Philosophical Enquiry (CEPE) Conference, ed. Richard Spinello and Herman Tavani, Boston College, June 2003, 128.

63. Wojtyla, "Thomistic Personalism," 170.

64. St. Thomas Aquinas, *Sent.* II, d. 26, q. 1, a. 4. This translation appears in John Finnis, *Aquinas* (Oxford: Oxford University Press, 1998), 179.

65. Lee, "Soul, Body and Personhood," 87.

66. Germain Grisez, *Living a Christian Life* (Quincy, Ill.: Franciscan Herald Press, 1983), 491–492.

CHAPTER 4

Freedom, the Good, and the Moral Law

NOW THAT WE have reviewed John Paul II's anthropology along with his notion of personhood, we are better able to understand the core principles of his moral theology. John Paul II's metaphysical anthropology is particularly important for its emphasis on our common humanity: all human persons, including those in the earliest stages of existence, are fundamentally alike, sharing the essential capabilities of intellect and free will. This common rational nature makes possible a universal moral law that applies to every single human person. John Paul II's anthropology is also vital for a proper understanding of human rights. Human beings have certain natural rights by virtue of the natural law that is based on their human nature. These rights are not contingent upon positive law or the caprice of the state.

Some critics of John Paul II have been troubled by his legalistic approach to moral theology that is also flawed by "physicalism." Those critics find fault with his moral vision because of its fidelity to the Catholic tradition of a natural law that should govern our actions. Part of the problem stems from confusing John Paul II's thought with certain strains of neo-Scholasticism, which have argued that moral goodness can be determined by simply comparing human actions with the structure of human nature.

But in this chapter we will demonstrate why John Paul II's thought is not vulnerable to these criticisms. He teaches that the natural law always directs us in relation to the fundamental goods of each person. It will become apparent that John Paul II's moral theology is not based on an abstract set of statutes, but on the dignity of the person as a bearer of goods, which are safeguarded by the precepts of the natural law. What John Paul II offers is a Christ-centered moral theology that skillfully orchestrates the themes of goodness, freedom, moral law, duty, human rights, moral choice, and conscience. This chapter and the following one will explore these themes and their interrelationship.

Being and Goodness

Chapter 1 focused attention on John Paul II's remarks in *Fides et Ratio* that the philosophical foundation of moral theology depends upon a "metaphysics of the good." John Paul II repeats this idea in his last work, *Memory and Identity*, where he calls for a retrieval of "Thomistic realism" in order to provide a proper grounding for ethics and moral theology (MI, 10). Indeed, it seems obvious from the analysis in the previous two chapters that such a retrieval is essential if we are to overcome the fatal mistakes of postmodernism and existentialism. Sartre and Heidegger, for example, are hostile to the metaphysical realism that regards beings (including the human person) as real active substances. Postmodern philosophers such as Gianni Vattimo celebrate the deconstruction of metaphysics and proclaim the need for a "postmetaphysical attitude."[1]

But, in John Paul II's view, this hostility to metaphysics contributes to a distorted conception of morality, since without metaphysics, ethics is without a stable foundation. Also, opting for moral theology with no metaphysical underpinnings means falling into the trap of "exchanging relevance for truth" (FR, 87). But exactly why is this Thomistic realism or metaphysics of the good so relevant to ethics? In order to answer this question, we must briefly review the salient elements of Aquinas's metaphysical system.

A major theme in Aquinas's work has been the concept of real being, a being that is actively present. An animal, a plant, a rock, a human person—each of these things is a real being, defined as "that which is" or as being "present" in some way. Action is an intrinsic property of every real being, since these beings act upon us by their very presence; they have an effect and make a difference in the world. Moreover, as we saw in the previous chapter, every being is by nature self-communicating: "It is the nature of every actuality to communicate itself insofar as it is possible."[2] As Etienne Gilson put it, "to be is to act."[3] For Aquinas, existence itself or being is the most basic perfection of real beings. Every real being possesses at its core an act of existence (*esse*), and as a result it tends naturally to overflow into action according to its essential form.

Furthermore, by virtue of their existence, all beings have the transcendental properties of unity or oneness ("to be is to be one"), goodness, and truth. According to Aquinas, "every being insofar as it is a being, is good."[4] Karol Wojtyla enunciates the same truth in an essay on the metaphysical basis of morality: "every being is good precisely because it has existence."[5] In *The Theology of the Body* John Paul II explains how the revelation of Genesis, "*ens et bonum convertuntur* (being and the good are convertible)," is "an unassailable point of reference and a solid basis for a metaphysic and also for an anthropology and an ethic" (TB, 29). All beings possess their being, their act of existence, by participating in the Pure Subsistent Act of Existence (*Ipsum Esse Subsistens*), the ultimate Good, God Himself. John Paul II wants to recapture this dynamic notion of *esse*, and most especially the convertibility of being and goodness, since these ideas have been obscured in contemporary philosophy and theology.

As John Paul II has observed, with the advent of modern philosophy the universe was no longer theocentric. John Paul II singled out the modern philosopher René Descartes for inaugurating "the great anthropocentric shift in philosophy" (CTH, 51). As philosophy turned away from God as creating cause, it also turned away from belief in the metaphysical goodness of His creation. Modern thinkers such as Descartes concentrated on the human subject, on the human as *cogito* (thinking being), who is the ground of his or her own certitude. Truth was no longer the conformity of the subject's knowing with an object in the real world. Philosophers like Kant, for example, rejected Aquinas's assumption that we can know real being that reveals itself by acting upon the knower. For Kant, action does not reveal the intrinsic being of things, so we can never know the "thing-in-itself." The mind can only know things under the condition of the a priori forms that it imposes.

Thus, the focal point became the knowing process itself, and not the objects of knowledge. According to John Paul II, "the objective truth of [human] thought is not as important as the fact that something exists in human consciousness" (CTH, 51). As a consequence, many philosophers became skeptical that truth, the "consonance between intellect and objective reality," was attainable (FR, 56). In addition, metaphysics gave way to transcendental philosophy focused on the boundaries of knowledge. According to John Paul II, after Descartes and Kant, philosophy "abandoned the investigation of being . . . [and] concentrated instead upon human knowing" (FR, 5). Nonetheless, Descartes' uncovering of the subjective was hailed as a major breakthrough by his successors. According to the German philosopher Hegel, "With [Descartes] we enter into an independent philosophy, which knows that it comes independently from reason and that self-consciousness is an essential moment of the true. . . . In this new period, the basic principle is thought, thinking that proceeds from itself."[6] In Hegel's estimation, Descartes' breakthrough is his perception that consciousness has within itself all that it needs to philosophize and comprehend the truth.

John Paul II, however, did not regard this so-called Cartesian revolution, this turning from real objects to exclusive focus on the thinking subject, as a salutary development. Even God Himself became an element of human consciousness. According to the Holy Father, "After Descartes, philosophy became a science of pure thought: all *esse*—both the created world and the Creator—remained within the ambit of the *cogito* as the content of human consciousness. Philosophy now concerned itself with beings *qua* content of consciousness, and not *qua* existing independently of it" (MI, 8–9). As a result, Thomistic realism, along with its assumption that God was the necessary ground of all created beings, was lost.

In Aquinas's theocentric world all beings were regarded in terms of their relation to God. Each being received its act of existence from God, the ultimate Source of all existence. Human beings, of course, had a privileged status among these creatures because of their autonomy and self-possession. But after the "Cartesian watershed" man himself becomes the ultimate reference point (MI, 10). Man takes God's place, and *he* determines the meaning and value of being.

In addition, thanks to the Cartesian revolution, the goodness of these created beings was no longer seen as naturally given. Being was depleted of its goodness. When God is rejected as the "source determining what is good" (MI, 12), nature is no longer regarded as innately good but as neutral, and it can no longer provide a secure reference point for morality. In a universe emptied of ontological goodness, being is penetrated by darkness and ambiguity.

For John Paul II, this intellectual development was the beginning of an anthropocentric liberty that would be portentous for ethics, since human beings began to see themselves as the center of the universe. Martin Heidegger aptly described the emergence of this "self-liberating man" who "guarantees for himself the certitude of the knowable" by grounding all knowledge and truth in his own self-certitude.[7] At the same time, in this new anthropocentric world man now "frees himself unto himself."[8] It is a short distance from Descartes' *cogito* to Nietzsche's *übermensch* (overman). If man can be the ground of his own truth, he can also be the ground and domain of his own moral values. Nietzsche was exhilarated at the prospect of this liberated *overman*, who *over*comes conventional morality in order to create or reinvent his own values. The overman is a creative force, "faithful to the earth," and the "highest hope" (*höchste Hoffnung*) for humanity.[9] But in John Paul II's estimation, this liberation from God, along with the "subjectivism" that commenced with Descartes, has only yielded a desolate nihilism. Moreover, as he explains, "the moral patrimony of Christianity was thus torn from [its] evangelical foundation" (CTH, 52).

It is vital, therefore, that we rediscover the inherent goodness of all being (*esse*) as an intelligible, objective reality. Wherever any being is found, there is a dynamic energy that overflows as a self-expression of that being's inner perfections (or goodness). For John Paul II, this is the real starting point of ethics and moral theology: the ontological goodness of all creation. Anything created by God is intrinsically valuable. As Scripture tells us, "For everything created by God is good, and nothing is to be rejected if it is received with thanksgiving; for then it is consecrated by the word of God and prayer" (1 Tim. 4:4–5). Thus, John Paul II explains in *Memory and Identity* that "if we wish to speak rationally about good and evil, we have to return to the philosophy of St. Thomas Aquinas, that is, to the philosophy of being" (MI, 12).

But what is wrong with subjectivism and subjective theories of the good that have displaced Thomistic realism? Is there really an objective universal good for all of humanity? Or is the good relative to different individuals and cultures? Is something considered good merely because we seek it, or do we seek it *because* it is good? After the Cartesian shift, some philosophers like Spinoza advocated a subjectivist value theory— things are good only because we seek them. Our desiring of those things makes them good or desirable. There is no objective value in anything; rather, value is a subjective property given to a thing because someone considers it valuable. If this subjectivist philosophy were merely arguing that nothing can be called good except in relation to a person who values that thing, it would be on reasonably firm ground. But if it claims that there is no objective basis for valuing something, then our experience of what is good is arbitrary and irrational. If what qualifies as "good" were purely subjective and contingent merely on people's wants and preferences, people could credibly value anything at all—grains of sand could be declared as beautiful as precious jewels and dry leaves as useful as edible food. This is contrary to both common sense and our human experience, however, since we value things precisely because we believe they will objectively fulfill us, perfect us in some way, and make us better off. As Aristotle reminds us in the *Metaphysics*, "we desire things because they seem good to us; it is not that they seem good to us because we desire them."[10] Desire alone cannot make something good-for-me or "perfective" of my nature.

John Paul II has consistently looked to Aquinas for a deeper understanding of the nature of this objective good. Inspired by Aquinas, he wrote early in his career that "the good as submitted to the will in the light of reason" is the "object of rational desire."[11] Aquinas himself defines the good as "that which is perfect in itself and perfective of another."[12] But what precisely does Aquinas mean by this? First, each being is ontologically good, good by virtue of its very nature, because it possesses some positive quality or "perfection." When we look at any being in isolation (an animal, a spider, a tree, a rock, etc.), that being in itself is good because it is an act of existence and so participates in the Supreme Act of Existence, God Himself. John Paul II, who unites being and goodness in *The Theology of the Body*, frequently cited the words of Genesis (1:31) to substantiate this metaphysical claim: "God saw all that he made and behold it was very good" (TB, 29). God clearly looked with favor on all of his creation.

Therefore, every being that exists, from a simple rock to a human person, shares in the basic perfection of existence and so belongs to the "absolute order of goods."[13] This is why we can say that "human life is good," "cat life is good," "water is good," and so forth. Moreover, because each created being is good, it is worthy of being desired or valued by another who is capable of desiring or esteeming that being. Thus, *goodness is being as valuable and desirable*. According to John Paul II, "in this metaphysical context of the description of Genesis 1, it is necessary to understand the entity of the good, namely, the aspect of value" (TB, 29).

As humans, thanks to what Aquinas calls our "appetitive dynamism," we consider many beings to be valuable and desirable. But as Father Norris Clarke observes, "the good does not have to be consciously valued or sought for, [since] any positive tendency toward something is enough to fulfill analogously the notion of appetite." Hence it makes sense to say that "water is good for a plant." We can appreciate this "relative order of the good," which enables us to make judgments such as "knowledge and art are good for human beings" or "raw meat is good for lions." We can also make more specific judgments such as "wine is good for most people, but it is not good for John who is an alcoholic."[14]

In the order of ontological goodness there are many kinds of good, since good is an analogous concept. Goods can be material, sensible, intellectual, aesthetic, and so on. In the relative order, there are two types of human goods: (i) instrumental or useful goods (such as a hammer), not valued in themselves but valued for their utility in achieving some end; and (ii) intrinsic goods, that is, goods that are inherently valuable for any human person. The latter category includes basic human goods such as life, friendship, and knowledge, goods that we value for themselves, not as a means to something else.

The corollary of this theory of the good is that evil is not a real being in itself. It can only be a *privation* of being, some absence or gap in good beings. Evil is not a positive mode of being since we do not discern the presence of evil until we find something missing, some deprivation or lack of some due good. Since all finite beings are created by God and participate in the plenitude of His Goodness, no being *in itself* can be evil. Thus, according to John Paul II, "evil is the absence of a good that ought to be present in a given being" (MI, 99). Deafness or blindness, for example, are forms of physical evil because they represent the absence of capabilities that all human beings should have. This conception of evil as a privation or "non-being" has its origins in the writings of St. Augustine, but it was fully assimilated into Aquinas's philosophy.

Thus, we must reject the notion that good and evil are purely subjective. In John Paul II's view, we must move beyond the popular misconception that goodness and value are not real but are imposed by human beings on a neutral and valueless reality. We must defer once again to "God *qua* creator," who is the ultimate source "determining what is good and what is evil" (MI, 12). The late Holy Father was keenly aware of the calamitous results that ensue when good and evil are no longer seen in relation to God: "If man can decide by himself, without God, what is good and what is bad, he can determine that a group of people is to be annihilated" (MI, 10). How easily mistakes in philosophy can engender "ideologies of evil," ideologies that declare one race or group of persons inferior to another and hence "unworthy" of life. Similarly, insidious ideologies support "legal extermination of human beings conceived but unborn" (MI, 11).

Only after we retrieve an ontology that supports the innate goodness of all creation along with a Supreme Being as its Source can we develop a coherent theory of moral goodness. We can uncover the meaning of moral goodness by turning to that Source: *"Only God can answer the question about what is good, because He is the Good itself"* (VS, 9). Of course, it is also possible to discover moral goodness in the order of nature, which reveals those goods that should be valued because they are perfective of human nature. Once practical reason appreciates what is truly worthwhile and good-for-us as human persons, it can recognize the self-evident, directive principles of the natural law. Surely, it is self-evident that I ought to desire and pursue whatever is really good for me (and anyone like me). This grounding of ethical duties in basic human goods is an essential feature of natural law morality.

Freedom for the Good

If we accept the basic premise of Aquinas and John Paul II that all created being is good, there will be implications for how we perceive the nature of human freedom and its role in the moral life. If goodness is given, if we are not *free* to create good and evil or to impose those values on a "valueless" creation, it is logical to assume that freedom must be subordinate to that good. Also, since we are not free to determine what is perfective of our human nature, and we ought to desire what is really good for us, the moral good must have priority over freedom. According to John Paul II, man "possesses an extremely far-reaching freedom . . . [b]ut his freedom is not unlimited: it must halt before the 'tree of the knowledge of good and evil'" (VS, 35).

Many contemporary philosophers, however, especially existentialists such as Sartre, reject this notion of freedom. They consider personal liberty as an unqualified good, and they elevate free action into a pure and absolute value in itself. Implicit in this conception of freedom is the premise that the value of freedom does not lie in the objects or ends freely chosen but in the openness of choice itself. According to this perspective, freedom is a formal principle with no real essence or material content. It does not favor truth versus falsehood, virtue versus vice, or good versus evil. Freedom is completely neutral when it comes to such choices. Once we begin to constrict freedom in any way by giving it some substance or insisting upon its subordination to truth, freedom begins to evanesce. If freedom is groundless and empty and respects only the indeterminateness of choice itself, then, according to this line of reasoning, freedom demands our respect and approbation regardless of its expression.

As chapter 2 discussed, John Paul II categorically rejects this conception of freedom as philosophically incoherent and inconsistent with moral common sense. He condemns those "currents of modern thought [that] have gone so far as to exalt freedom to such an extent that it becomes an absolute, which would then be the source of values" (VS, 32). Sartrean freedom knows no bounds, but boundless freedom is simply self-destructive. No one has the right to perpetrate evil deeds such as rape or murder against a neighbor merely because they are performed in the name of freedom. No society could survive if it supported that type of unfettered freedom, disconnected from what is true and good for humanity. Freedom that is not oriented toward the good is not authentic freedom, but license and anarchy.

John Paul II emphasized this theme with great clarity in his first encyclical, *Redemptor Hominis*:

> Nowadays it is sometimes held, though wrongly, that freedom is an end in itself, that each human being is free when he makes use of freedom as he wishes, and that this must be our aim in the lives of individuals and societies. In reality, freedom is a great gift only when we know how to use it consciously for everything that is our true good. (RH, 89)

John Paul II is arguing here that the true value of freedom does not lie in the act of free choice itself, but in the value of the goods or objects chosen in this free act. And since freedom is not an end in itself, it is not an absolute value or an unqualified good. Freedom is not even an intrinsic human good. Rather, it is an instrumental one. We value freedom precisely because it enables us to pursue true goods such as knowledge, religion, and friendship that perfect our nature. Thus, we do not value freedom just for its own sake but because it is *freedom for the good.*

Freedom, therefore, is a teleological principle, since it assumes its true worth and significance only when it is *for* the good. Freedom's value is not absolute but relative to the pursuit of the good life, a life predicated on intrinsic values such as knowledge, friendship, and the worship of God. In a speech on the topic of freedom that he gave during a visit to the United States, the late Holy Father spoke about an "ordered freedom," a freedom "channeled to the fullness of life, to the preservation of human dignity, and to the fullness of human life."[15] True freedom in his mind is never empty or unspecified but always oriented to what is good for humanity. John Paul II sums up this reality in the principle of "rightful autonomy," an autonomy ordained to and fulfilled by the good (VS, 40).

Natural Law and the Decalogue

Now that we understand the relationship between freedom and the good, we can grasp more fully the meaning of morality. According to John Paul II, "The morality of acts is defined by the relationship of man's freedom with the authentic good" (VS, 72). But how do we know this "authentic good," and, more specifically, how do we know which moral imperatives are consistent with that good? As we have observed, there are two sources of knowledge about moral goodness: the "book" of nature and the book of Revelation. God reveals the moral law directly through His Word and indirectly through our own human nature, which makes this law unmistakably human. According to John Paul II, "*The moral law has its origin in God and always finds its source in him*: at the same time, by virtue of natural reason, which derives from divine wisdom, it is a *properly human law*" (VS, 40).

Let us first consider what the "book" of nature reveals to us. God has told us what is good through the natural light of our human reason. According to John Paul II, God has given us an answer about the moral good "by *creating man and ordering him* with wisdom and love to his final end, through the law which is inscribed in his heart (cf. Rom. 2:15), the 'natural law'" (VS, 12). This natural law has a cognitive and normative character, so it is easily "accessible to human reason" (VS, 74). Thus, John Paul II approvingly cites Aquinas's definition of the natural law as "nothing other than the light of understanding infused in us by God whereby we understand what must be done and what must be avoided" (VS, 12).[16]

Although John Paul II does not articulate a natural law ethic in any great depth, it is evident that he subscribes to the main lines of Aquinas's philosophy. It is helpful, therefore, to follow the logic of Aquinas's analysis as a guide for understanding how John Paul II views this subject. According to Aquinas, all human beings are naturally disposed to understand some basic principles inscribed in their heart (Rom. 3:14–16). In philosophical terms, these principles are "self-evident."[17] The first practical principle is that "good is to be done and pursued and evil is to be avoided."[18] According to Germain Grisez, good refers not only to what is morally good but to what is "intelligibly worthwhile."[19] Intelligible choices are always oriented toward some fundamental human good such as life or health. John Paul II describes how "every choice always implies a reference by the deliberate will to the goods and evils indicated by the natural law as goods to be pursued and evils avoided" (VS, 67).

What are these goods? For Aquinas, people grasp as good the objects of their natural inclinations, and "all the inclinations of any part of human nature . . . as they are regulated by reason, belong to the natural law."[20] Thus, what practical reason understands as goods are what human beings have natural inclinations toward. John Paul II seems to be in agreement with this claim, since in *Veritatis Splendor* he refers to "certain goods towards which the human person is naturally inclined" (VS, 48). For example, we have the inclination to stay alive and remain healthy, and so human life (including health) is an intrinsic good. We have a natural desire to know the truth and to inquire about the world around us, and so knowledge is another intrinsic human good. And since it is natural for any human to "delight in the companionship of his fellow human beings,"[21] friendship, marriage, and the harmony of community life are also basic goods.

All of these fundamental goods are good-for-us since they perfect or enrich us in some way, and this is why they can be objectively esteemed by the valuer. Thus, the natural law identifies the human goods to be pursued through our own choices (such as life, friendship, knowledge, and so forth), and it tells us that it is worthwhile and fitting to pursue these goods. As we observed earlier, each one of us ought to desire and pursue that which is really good for us and anyone like us. According to Karol Wojtyla, the "ends" we seek must be "genuinely good, since the pursuit of evil ends is contrary to the rational nature of the person."[22] Of course, we must always pursue these goods in a fully rational way or in accordance with "right reason."

Moreover, we can infer from all this that the chief human good in this life is to be equated with human flourishing, or our fulfillment as persons. According to John Paul II, "natural inclinations take on moral relevance only insofar as they refer to the human person and his authentic fulfillment" (VS, 50). Such fulfillment takes place "only in human nature," and it is realized by participation in the basic human goods that we all value, such as life, knowledge, marriage, friendship, religion, and so forth (VS, 50). These goods, which are intrinsic aspects of human well-being and fulfillment, are the primary reasons for action and, as we shall see, the ultimate source of normativity, because what ought to be done is what is perfective of human nature.

This fundamental "practical principle," which precludes unchoiceworthy or purposeless actions, does not directly tell us what ought to be done. Rather, it provides a "foundation for practical thinking," a guide for how we can make sensible choices.[23] But how do we know what is a morally good choice? According to Aquinas, human beings are also naturally disposed to understand the primary *moral* principle that gives direction and coherence to our moral choices. Aquinas formulates this principle, which is "self-evident to human reason," in terms of charity: "one should do evil to no man," or "one should love one's neighbor as one's self."[24] The principle can also be specified by the Golden Rule: "do to others as we would have them do to us." For example, once I recognize that an intrinsic good such as life is perfective of my nature and worth pursuing, I realize that it is "perfective" of other human beings as well. If I expect them to respect my desire for and pursuit of life, consistency demands that I respect this same desire in others.

Similarly, John Paul II expresses this primary moral principle in terms of the imperative to love our neighbor as ourselves (VS, 76) or in terms of the "personalist norm" (see the next section). Quite simply, any person who loves his or her neighbor will not cause the neighbor harm and will seek the neighbor's good. For John Paul II, the fundamental goods, such as human life, "acquire a moral significance in reference to the good of the person, who must always be affirmed for his own sake" (VS, 50).

To be moral, then, means that we must avoid egoism and partiality, and we must will the good and well-being of our neighbor just as we will our own good. The normative principles of the natural law stipulate the need to accept the fulfillment of others as part of our moral responsibility, and this responsibility precludes unjust interference with our neighbor's participation in the basic human goods. We also realize that our own flourishing, our participation in goods such as life, knowledge, and community, can be achieved only in *solidarity* with others (SRS, 26).

From the fundamental human goods along with the practical and moral principles we can logically deduce more specific norms regarding the taking of innocent life, adultery, and so forth. Aquinas himself does not precisely deduce these norms or precepts, but the most basic ones are easy to discern. For example, once it is evident that human life is a basic human good to be preserved and "pursued," and that whatever damages or destroys life is to be avoided, we can infer that love for one's neighbor precludes the taking of someone's life, for "in every person, even the sinner, we ought to love the [human] nature . . . which is destroyed by killing."[25] Accordingly, we can formulate a specific precept of the natural law that forbids the intentional taking of an innocent human life. John Paul II articulates the same truth in simpler terms: since human life is a "fundamental good of man . . . it is always illicit to kill an innocent human being" (VS, 50).

The general moral principles, which are "self-evident to human reason,"[26] are also made known to us through revelation. According to John Paul II, the primary moral principle is summed up in Jesus's command to love God and to love our neighbor (VS, 12–13). Therefore, in addition to the principles of the natural law inscribed on our hearts, God directly reveals how we ought to behave "*in the history of Israel,* particularly in the 'ten words,' the *commandments of Sinai*" (VS, 12). The Decalogue can be regarded as a summary of the specific precepts of the natural law. John Paul II, following Aquinas, argues that the commands of the Decalogue are included in the natural law.[27] Thus, revelation and natural reason point to the same laws: the natural law is not opposed in any way to the law of the Old Covenant or the law of Christ.

Given the centrality of the Decalogue to the moral life, it is no surprise that it receives such prominence in *Veritatis Splendor* and in many of the Holy Father's other works. According to John Paul II, the Decalogue represents "ten principles of conduct, without which no human community, no nation, not even the international community, can function" (MI, 133). In Matthew's narrative of the rich young man (Matt. 19:16–21) that frames *Veritatis Splendor*, Jesus highlights the importance of following the commandments. When the rich young man asks Jesus, "what good must I do to have eternal life?" (Matt. 19:16), Jesus tells him that "if you wish to enter into life, keep the commandments" (Matt. 19:17). In this and other New Testament passages Jesus repromulgates these critically important commandments and thereby reconfirms their lasting validity.

John Paul II argues with great insistence about the intrinsic connection between human fulfillment and the Decalogue, "the Commandments of Sinai" (VS, 12), which are based on the two commands to love God and love our neighbor as ourselves. The reason for this is that the moral imperatives articulated in the commandments protect the "singular dignity of the human person" along with specific aspects of the human good (VS, 13). According to John Paul II, the commandments *"safeguard the good of the person, the image of God, by protecting his goods"* (VS, 13; my emphasis). Or, as he explains in *Memory and Identity*, "each of these commands from the Sinai code seeks to defend a fundamental good of human and social life" (MI, 133). In other words, the commandments protect the good and dignity of the human person by safeguarding those goods that perfect that person and allow him or her to flourish as a human being. For example, they demand the sanctity of life, protect the communion of marriage, and proclaim the need for truth. In the encyclical *Sollicitudo Rei Socialis*, John Paul II exclaims that "not to observe [the second tablet of the Ten Commandments] is to offend God and hurt one's neighbor, and to introduce into the world influences and obstacles that go far beyond the actions and brief lifespan of the individual" (SRS, 12). We love our neighbor and will his or her good when we do not interfere with those goods (life, community, etc.) that are perfective of him or her. And we do this by following the specific norms of the Decalogue about the taking of innocent life, lying, adultery, theft, and so forth. When any of these misdeeds are perpetrated against our neighbor, we are not willing his or her good.

Although the Decalogue is important, it does not represent the exclusive content of the moral law revealed by Sacred Scripture. Above all, we must bear in mind that leading a moral life is about following Christ. According to John Paul II, *"Following Christ is the essential and primordial foundation of Christian morality"* (VS, 19). The commandments help us to begin down the path to moral perfection that we seek as followers and imitators of Jesus. In the Sermon on the Mount, which John

Paul II calls the *"magna charta* of Gospel morality" (VS, 15), Jesus proclaims the Beatitudes, but he refers to the Decalogue as well (Matt. 5:20–48). Here we find the essence of the Gospel's moral message: the commandments "represent the absolutely essential ground in which desire for perfection can take root and mature" (VS, 17), while the Beatitudes "are a sort of *self-portrait of Christ,* and for this very reason are *invitations to discipleship and communion of life with Christ"* (VS, 16). Those who "walk by the Spirit" (Gal. 5:16) go beyond the minimal demands of the moral law and aspire to live the moral life to its fullest through heroic virtue, charity, and self-giving.

Finally, John Paul II reminds us that the precepts of the Decalogue, which attain perfection in the person of Jesus Christ, transcend history and culture. As a consequence, they "must be faithfully kept and continually put into practice in the various different cultures throughout the course of history" (VS, 25). Moreover, the task of interpreting these precepts has been entrusted by Jesus "to the Apostles and their successors" (VS, 25). When there are disputes over interpretation or the application of these precepts to new moral problems, the ultimate authority is the Magisterium of the Church.

The Personalist Norm

Although John Paul II never departs from adherence to Thomistic ethical principles, he has turned at times to Kant's philosophy in order to summarize the moral law, particularly for those who may not be attentive to the moral message of the Scripture. As we have seen, the key to morality for John Paul II is the need to sustain the good of the other person by respecting his or her goods such as life and health or friendship and marriage. One way to summarize this obligation is to use Kant's categorical imperative. Recall John Paul II's affinity for Kant's second formulation of that imperative: "Act so that you treat humanity, whether in your own person or in that of another, always as an end and never as a means only."[28] In *Love and Responsibility* Karol Wojtyla reformulated the Kantian principle in more precise terms: "whenever a person is the object of your activity, remember that you must not treat that person as only the means to an end, as an instrument, but must allow for the fact that he or she, too, has, or at least should have, distinct personal ends."[29] For example, when people tell lies, they treat the victim as a means by using his or her reason as an instrument for their advantage. Similarly, abortion treats the embryonic person in the womb merely as a means to some ulterior end such as the avoidance of an inconvenient pregnancy.

According to John Paul II, the primary category in this ethical formula is the person. Thus, the master principle of morality, which John Paul II sometimes calls the "personalist norm," is respect for the dignity of all persons, which is realized when we respect the person as an end, that is, as a bearer of goods, in every one of our actions. According to John Paul II, "the primordial moral requirement of loving and respecting the person as an end and never as a mere means also implies, by its very nature, respect for certain fundamental goods" (VS, 48). Following the specific commands of the Decalogue or the specific precepts of the natural law will bring about respect for these basic human goods such as marriage, truth, and life.

By turning to Immanuel Kant, who laid the foundation of a modern personalist ethic, John Paul II incorporates a dose of personalism into his moral system. In *Crossing the Threshold of Hope,* John Paul II explains that he formulated the personalist principle "to translate the commandment of love into the language of philosophical ethics" (CTH, 200–201). This personalist perspective helps to inoculate John Paul II's moral philosophy from charges of abstract legalism or "physicalism," because of its sharp concentration on the inalienable dignity of the person. Although the Holy Father's moral system never denies the validity of the natural law, it consistently demonstrates that the law exists to protect the unique dignity of each person. Aside from the imperative to love God, above all else we must respect the dignity of each human person, and we do this by respecting that person's goods (his or her marriage, life, etc.) as mandated by the moral law.

John Paul II, therefore, synthesizes the teleology of natural law morality with the deontology of Kant. This synthesis represents the distinctive philosophical ethics that can be disengaged from John Paul II's copious moral writings. The moral life must have a "teleological character since it consists in ordering human acts to the ultimate end of man" (VS, 73). Accordingly, John Paul II's moral philosophy is grounded in the fundamental human goods that perfect human nature, since they are the ultimate source of normativity. But that philosophy also has a deontological dimension since it is focused on a basic obligation or duty: to will the good of the other and to treat him or her always as an end.

According to John Paul II, "Kant rightly emphasized the obligatory character of man's moral choices" (MI, 37). Kant fails to adequately consider the objective criteria for those choices, the intrinsic human goods (or *bona honesta*), and so we need the natural law philosophy of Aquinas as a complement (MI, 34–35).

Kant also makes the mistake of identifying human nature with rationality. As we discussed in the previous chapter, however, for John Paul II, the human person referred to in Kant's ethical formula is an embodied soul with natural potentialities. And since *every human being*, from the moment of conception to natural death, is a potentially functioning *actual person*, he or she deserves never to be treated as a mere means but always as an end. This master moral principle or personalist norm, inspired by Kant, works only when supported by the right anthropology and a metaphysics of the good. John Paul II's personalism, therefore, is objective, teleological, and firmly rooted in the rich Thomistic notion of *persona*.

As John Paul II indicated, the Kantian imperative is a secular version of Christ's commandment to love our neighbor as ourselves. Kant's universal norm represents an antidote to utilitarianism and positivism, and so it offers an ethical foundation superior to rival systems based on the principle of utility. The Kantian principle is favored by John Paul II precisely because it directly contradicts proportionalism, which asserts that an action is right when it is the most efficient means of optimizing consequences in a given situation. According to proportionalism, the other can be treated only as a means if such treatment will yield the best state of affairs.

Although Kant's formulation is a philosophical expression of the Christian imperative to love one's neighbor, Kant did not fully interpret the commandment of love since that commandment "requires the *affirmation of the person as person*" (CTH, 201). And man affirms himself "most completely by giving of himself" (CTH, 202). An authentic Christian morality of love demands that I do not treat others as objects of pleasure. But it also requires the sincere gift of self. We might add that when the human person gives of himself or herself in this way, he or she fulfills his or her ontological destiny, since it is the nature of each substance to give itself in action.

Finally, although John Paul II does not subscribe to a virtue ethic, he puts great emphasis on the virtue of *solidarity*, which he defines as "a firm and persevering determination to commit oneself to the common good; that is to say to the good of all and of each individual, because we are all really responsible for all" (SRS, 38). Solidarity captures the spirit of the personalist norm, which also directs us to respect the common good of various human communities.

John Paul II repeatedly underscored the interdependence of all persons and communities, since he thoroughly appreciated that an individual's fulfillment can occur only within a common fulfillment, that is, in solidarity and cooperation with others. The person endowed with the virtue of solidarity has the willingness to promote and pursue the common good, the good of the community, which is necessary for his or her own fulfillment. Thus, the virtue of solidarity will help us to realize the ideal of the personalist norm.

Freedom and Moral Law

Now that we better understand John Paul II's moral vision, we must return to the theme of freedom. Despite our earlier remarks on this issue, the tension between man's freedom and the moral law still seems difficult to resolve. Isn't the human spirit constrained and fettered by the Decalogue or by the natural law precepts, as philosophers like Sartre and Nietzsche would have us believe? Even if we concede that freedom is not rational without the priority of the good, why not opt for the thinnest possible conception of the good so that one's horizon of free choices will be maximized without the hindrance of specific moral imperatives? In *Also Sprach Zarathustra*, Nietzsche metaphorically described the Christian era as the "age of the camel," since man was so burdened with the moral duties demanded by a higher level of reality.[30] In that age man was submissive: his "I will" (*Ich will*) was perpetually subdued by "Thou shalt" (*Du sollst*), an obvious allusion to the commands of the Decalogue.[31] Is there any validity to Nietzsche's popular claim? It would seem so, since obedience to external commands ("Thou shalt") is heterodoxy and the antithesis of human freedom.

How then do we reconcile our inner freedom with the alterity of law? How can I be free if I am required to follow a moral law that is apparently imposed upon me? For John Paul II, there is no conflict between free choice and the moral law. The moral law is not something arbitrarily imposed upon us to restrict our freedom. On the contrary, that law is inscribed in human nature as a gift of God in order to guide us toward the end of our own human flourishing and happiness. Paradoxically, therefore, we are most free when we follow those moral laws expressed in the Ten Commandments. The lawless person, on the other hand, is not free but is a slave to evil or compulsion, such as falsehood, envy, or lust, which is contrary to human nature.

John Paul II introduces the notion of "participated theonomy" to express the paradox that submission to the law of God is liberating. This is the case because our "free obedience to God's law effectively implies that human reason and human will participate in God's wisdom and providence" (VS, 41). The moral law is an "expression of God's wisdom," and by following that law each human person will make the "right" choices that perfect his or her human nature (VS, 41). The law is not meant to squelch spontaneity and creativity as the existentialists and postmodern philosophers have suggested. Rather, it gives order and direction so that creativity can flourish. A creative dancer must still follow the general rules of the dance. For example, a dancer cannot dance the tango if all the rules of that dance are broken. Only *within* the rules of the dance can the tango dancer be spontaneous and creative. Similarly, life without moral order is not creative or spontaneous; it is merely chaotic and undisciplined.

Thus, John Paul II would be in complete agreement with Aquinas's belief that real freedom exists when someone does the good that ought to be done for its own sake: "Whoever acts of his own accord acts freely. But one who is impelled by another is not free. He who avoids evil, not because it is evil, but because a precept of the Lord prohibits it, is not free. On the other hand, *he who avoids evil because it is evil is free.*"[32] Aquinas is describing the moral maturity that accompanies authentic freedom. The mature person makes choices in harmony with the natural law. He or she follows his or her own inclination to do what is right by seeking the good for himself or herself and for others. This person is free because he or she governs himself or herself in accordance with the moral laws of his or her own human nature and avoids the external influences or the blind impulses that are foreign to that rational nature. Thanks to his or her reason, the morally mature person apprehends what is objectively good and worthy of being chosen, and he or she makes this choice freely, without compulsion or impulse. The person knows that this choice is consistent with the moral law that is determined by principles constitutive of his or her essential nature. This is genuine *self-determination*, whereby the self shuns evil precisely because it is alien and unnatural, and follows the guidance of its own good human nature in the form of the first principles of morality. According to John Paul II, "by submitting to the law, freedom submits to the truth of creation" (VS, 41). True moral law is never alien to a human being, since it always directs him or her to those fundamental goods that perfect persons and communities.

Specific Moral Absolutes

The Decalogue, as well as the natural law, identifies specific acts (lying, taking of human life, adultery) that are forbidden because they are intrinsically evil (*intrinseca malum*). The act is wrong in itself, apart from context, intentions, or consequences. Circumstances or intention may attenuate one's subjective guilt, but they do not change the species of such an intrinsically evil act (VS, 62). The correlate of these forbidden acts are specific, exceptionless moral norms. This means that an exception to a norm such as "never intentionally assert what is false" is *always* morally excluded. The forbidden acts are specified not in moral terms but in terms of their content or object, such as "no sexual relations outside of marriage." According to John Paul II, "there are objects of the human act which are by their nature incapable of being ordered to God, because they radically contradict the good of the person made in His image" (VS, 80). Morality without such specific, exceptionless moral norms lacks the proper boundaries for moral deliberation and choice. Nonetheless, this teaching has been a bone of contention among John Paul II's critics, so we must understand the arguments he advances for the validity of these norms.

The substantial weight given to intrinsically evil acts in *Veritatis Splendor* is anticipated in earlier writings. In one of his apostolic exhortations, *Reconciliatio et paenitentia*, John Paul II affirms these specific moral norms, arguing that this dogma is "based on the Decalogue and on the preaching of the Old Testament, and assimilated into the kerygma of the apostles and belonging to the earliest teaching of the Church, and constantly affirmed by her to this day" (RP, 17). Throughout his papacy John Paul II focused particular attention on these specific moral norms because of their repudiation at the hands of some dissenting moral theologians. Recall that several contemporary theologians and philosophers have declaimed against the truth of specific moral absolutes with some insistence. They have argued that no act is intrinsically evil because it must *always* be assessed by its consequences or by the surrounding circumstances.

The genesis of this position can be traced back to dissenting views on artificial contraception that emerged in the wake of Pope Paul VI's *Humanae Vitae* encyclical. In the "majority report" of the Papal Commission for the Study of Population, the Family and Natality, several dissenting theologians made the following claim: "To take his or another's life is a sin not because life is under the exclusive dominion of God, but because it is contrary to right reason unless there is question of a good of a higher order. *It is licit to sacrifice a life for the good of the community.*"[33] Thus, even human life itself can be sacrificed for a greater or "proportionate" good.

Many proportionalists, following to one degree or another the moral philosophy of consequentialism, advocate a moral calculus, some consideration of comparative benefits and harms, as a criterion of moral judgment. Richard McCormick, S.J., follows the precedent of Father Fuchs, S.J., who taught that "the very 'meaning' of an action can only be gathered when all aspects of the action, especially its consequences, have been weighed as far as possible."[34] As we saw in chapter 2, some theologians advocate the use of proportionalism only in conflict situations where it is necessary to "choose the lesser evil."

On more than one occasion John Paul II has lamented the poverty of theological or philosophical analysis that leads to the unfortunate conclusion that these exceptionless norms are expendable. In his writings John Paul II elaborates upon a rationale for these norms that rests on three basic arguments: these norms can be logically deduced from the supreme moral principle (the personalist norm); they are necessary for social harmony and justice; and the notion of intrinsically evil acts is fully consistent with the Catholic tradition.

The first point is similar to Aquinas's claim that specific moral absolutes could be easily derived from formal moral principles such as "love one's neighbor as oneself." Similarly, John Paul II strongly implies that these requirements follow from the personalist norm, which forbids anyone from treating another person as a mere means. According to John Paul II, the "demands of the personal dignity of every man [are] protected by those moral norms which prohibit without exception actions which are intrinsically evil" (VS, 90). Among those absolutes the

Holy Father often singles out the injunction against intentional killing. Killing an innocent person is never morally acceptable even to safeguard other goods or to prevent a greater evil because it treats the victim as a mere means. Hence the moral absolutes that safeguard goods such as life, truth, and marriage clearly specify those acts that are not "ordered to God" because they damage the bearer of those goods and corrupt the acting person who performs them (VS, 80). As a result, "circumstances or intentions can never transform an act intrinsically evil by virtue of its object into an act 'subjectively' good or defensible as a choice" (VS, 81).

John Paul II argues that if we allow exceptions to norms that forbid the killing of an innocent person, it becomes impossible to uphold the personal dignity of *every* human being. If we excuse abortion under extenuating circumstances or in a "hard case," the right to life of a nascent human being, who is a person by virtue of his or her intellectual nature, is traduced for an ulterior end. Without absolute moral requirements we cannot protect each person's rights and dignity. The primary problem with competing ethical paradigms such as proportionalism is that basic rights are relativized and equal dignity is not always protected as it should be. Furthermore, in many cases the rights of the weak and the powerless (such as the unborn) are sacrificed by the more powerful (moral decision makers) for the sake of maximizing the balance of "premoral" goods.

Along the same lines, John Paul II maintains that these specific absolutes provide the real spine of any society's code of conduct. Just laws must be based on specific moral standards such as "it is wrong to intentionally take an innocent life," not on utilitarian standards that require us to maximize the overall net good. According to John Paul II, "In the end, only a morality which acknowledges certain norms as valid always and for everyone, with no exception, can guarantee the ethical foundation of social coexistence" (VS, 97). Once society permits exceptions for the overall net good, even in rare circumstances, the social fabric is frayed. The democratic ideals of "justice for all" or "equal rights" will become hollow, as basic rights are sacrificed in the name of pragmatism and efficiency.

The fundamental problem with proportionalism, then, is its insensitivity to the *universality* of human dignity and the *inalienable* rights that flow from that dignity, since basic rights such as the right to life can be compromised for the "greater good" depending upon the circumstances. For John Paul II, "protecting the inviolable personal dignity of every human being" is inconsistent with a philosophy that allows the rights of the weak to be sacrificed as part of a moral calculus (VS, 97).

Finally, John Paul II also observed that a moral philosophy denying moral absolutes departs too dramatically from the Catholic tradition. He writes that these theories "are not faithful to the Church's teaching, when they believe that they can justify, as morally good, deliberate choices of behavior contrary to the commandments of the divine and natural law" (VS, 76). In order to appreciate the incongruity of this approach with Catholic morality, it is instructive to provide a brief overview of the tradition to which the late Holy Father is referring.

To begin with, even some secular philosophers have enunciated the principle that certain actions are intrinsically evil (*intrinseca malum*), always wrong in themselves apart from circumstances or consequences. Certainly, Aristotle, who defined right or virtuous action as the mean between excesses, thought as much: "But not every action nor every passion admits of a mean; for some have names that already imply badness, e.g., spite, shamelessness, envy, and in the case of actions, adultery, theft, murder. . . . It is not possible ever to be right with regard to them; one must always be wrong."[35]

We find the same type of analysis in the thought of St. Augustine and St. Thomas Aquinas. John Paul II cites the works of both of these great saints to support his argument (VS, 81). Augustine, for example, proclaimed in the *Enchiridion* that lying is always wrong:

> Every liar says the opposite of what he thinks in his heart, with purpose to deceive. Now it is evident that speech was given to man, not that men might therewith deceive one another, but that one man might make known his thoughts to another. To use speech, then, in the purpose of deception, and not for its appointed end, is a sin. Nor are we to suppose that there is any lie that is not a sin, because it is sometimes possible by telling a lie, to do service to another.[36]

Augustine could not have been clearer—one can *never* lie even if doing so is for a good end.

In *Quaestiones de Quodlibet*, Aquinas proclaims that some kinds of acts "have deformity inseparably annexed to them, such as fornication, adultery, and others of this sort, which can in no way be done morally."[37] Similarly, Aquinas maintained that killing an innocent human being who has human dignity is evil in itself (*secundum se*) without exception: "In no case and in no way is it permissible to kill an innocent [person]."[38] Finally, it is worth noting Aquinas's response when confronted with a commentary on Aristotle's *Nicomachean Ethics* arguing that adultery would be morally acceptable if a woman slept with a tyrant so that he could be killed and the people liberated. Aquinas repudiates the commentator and writes that "the commentator is not to be followed in this matter; for one may not commit adultery for any good."[39]

At the same time, the presence of specific absolutes is repeatedly confirmed in Holy Scripture and in the writings of the early Church Fathers. In *Evangelium Vitae* John Paul II amply demonstrates Scriptural support for one of these absolute norms: direct and intentional killing of an innocent human being is always gravely immoral. Sacred Scripture presents this precept explicitly in the divine commandment "You shall not kill" (Exod. 20:13; Deut. 5:17) and more implicitly in Genesis (9:5): "From man in regard to his fellow man I will demand an accounting of human life" (EV, 53).

Specific moral absolutes were clearly acknowledged in the early Church. For example, in the *Didache* we read, "You shall not kill. You shall not commit adultery. . . . You shall not kill the child by corruption/destruction, nor kill it at birth."[40] The reference to the "corruption/destruction" of a child refers to abortion.[41] In addition, abortion was explicitly condemned in absolute terms by many of the Apostolic Fathers, including Clement of Alexandria, Tertullian, John Chrysostom, and Ambrose. John Chrysostom called it an act "even worse than murder."[42]

We also find unequivocal support for specific moral absolutes at the great councils such as Trent and among generations of moral theologians in the manualist tradition. William May explains that historians like John Noonan "clearly demonstrate that from the beginning of the Christian era Catholic theologians held as absolute norms proscribing adultery (understood as intercourse with someone who is not one's spouse), fornication, homosexual activity, and contraception."[43] Thus, John Paul II's reaffirmation of intrinsically evil acts is completely consonant with a long theological and philosophical tradition within the Catholic Church.

Unfortunately, some contemporary moral theologians have distorted this tradition by attempting to soften this teaching of moral absolutes. Some claim that philosophers like Aquinas do no more than offer us formal norms such as "love your neighbor," which function more like exhortations than real moral norms.[44] Others have proposed that Aquinas regards the precepts of the Decalogue as purely formal. According to John Finnis, they claim that these norms are exceptionless "only because they contain a tacit moral qualifier which makes them true tautologously— necessarily and therefore exceptionlessly."[45] According to this interpretation, "adultery is always wrong" is an exceptionless moral norm because adultery is defined as unjustified or "wrongful" extramarital intercourse.

But nowhere in the Catholic tradition do we find these intrinsically immoral acts defined as the proportionalists define them. Aquinas and others do not speak of "wrongful sex," but of adultery, and they do not equate the taking of innocent life with "unjust" or "disproportionate" killing. As we noted above, Aquinas explicitly says that certain acts have "deformity annexed to them, such as . . . adultery."[46] Aquinas never deviates from his teaching that a wrongful act is wrongful because it is directed toward the proximate object that the wrongdoer intends.[47] Adultery is always wrong precisely because it involves a choice by a married person to have sexual relations outside of marriage, and that choice is contrary to the good of marriage and cannot be ordered to God. John Paul II steadfastly resisted efforts to soften the principle of intrinsically evil acts, and he has unambiguously reaffirmed the essence of Aquinas's teaching on this matter.

Human Rights

John Paul II's insistence on exceptionless moral norms enables him to argue for inviolable human rights. If there is an absolute prohibition against taking the life of an innocent person, there must be a right to life that is also absolute. According to John Finnis, the language of rights permits us to focus on the question of what is just or unjust from the other person's perspective, "the viewpoint of the 'other(s)' to whom something is owed or due and who would be wronged if denied that something."[48] A natural right exists by virtue of the natural law, and it represents an entitlement required of others in justice. If there is a moral duty to refrain from taking what legitimately belongs to someone else, there must be a natural right to property.

John Paul II does not offer any comprehensive theory of human rights such as one might expect to find in philosophical or political treatises. But he certainly makes repeated reference to certain human rights, and we can also infer the existence of other rights from his general exposition. The corollary of specific absolute moral norms and the duties they impose are absolute human rights. We can infer, for example, that his emphasis on the absoluteness of the specific norms articulated in the Decalogue means that there are certain absolute rights such as the right to life. The basis of all human rights is our incomparable worth and dignity: "Human persons are willed by God; they are imprinted with God's image. Their dignity does not come from the work they do, but from the persons they are" (CA, 11). Thus, respect for human rights is tantamount to respect for the dignity and intrinsic worth of every human person.

The most basic right is the right to life. According to John Paul II, "for man, the right to life is the *fundamental* right" (CTH, 204). Natural law tells us that life is a fundamental human good, and since there is a duty not to destroy a basic human good such as life, there must be an absolute right to life. John Paul II insists upon this inviolable right in many of his writings, but most especially in *Evangelium Vitae*. He tells us that the commandment "thou shalt not kill" "has absolute value when it refers to the innocent person" (EV, 57). This qualification merely allows for "legitimate" self-defense or for the taking of life in a just war against an "unjust aggressor" (CTH, 206). For John Paul II, "the right to life means the right to be born and then to continue to live until one's natural end: 'As long as I live, I have the right to life'" (CTH, 205).

According to John Paul II, "the commandment regarding the inviolability of human life reverberates *at the heart of the 'ten words' in the covenant of Sinai*" (EV, 39). This right is absolute and sacrosanct, and it cannot be compromised for the sake of expediency, even for the sake of other conflicting rights. The sanctity of human life is also reinforced in other parts of the Scripture such as the book of Genesis. God's haunting question to Cain, "Where is your brother Abel?" is as compelling today as it ever was (Gen. 4:10). In this section of Genesis we are reminded that power over life belongs to God alone (EV, 39). This right to life applies to all persons, including those in the earliest stages of their existence. We must avoid the temptation to confine this right to life only to those who function as persons. Thus, the Holy Father concludes that "direct abortion, that is, abortion willed as an end or as a means, always constitutes a grave moral disorder, since it is the deliberate killing of an innocent human being" (EV, 62).

John Paul II certainly affirmed other inalienable rights besides the right to life. In *Redemptoris Missio* he argued for the importance of the right to religious liberty, which could become threatened in a world that "tends to reduce the human being to the horizontal dimension" (RMis, 8). According to the Holy Father, each human being has the right to religious freedom since all men and women are "bound by their human nature to seek religious truth" (RMis, 8). He reiterated the central importance of this right in his United Nations address in 1979, arguing that all nations must respect "the right to freedom of thought, conscience, religion, and the right to manifest one's religion either individually or in community, in public or in private."[49] The reason this right is so significant is that the "values of the human spirit" play such an indispensable role in the "development of civilization."[50]

During the dispute over population control at the time of the UN's Cairo Conference (1994), John Paul II took the opportunity to insist upon procreative rights of married couples. He reiterated the Church's position that married couples have the basic right to make their own decisions about procreation without the officious interference of the state. According to the "Charter of the Rights of Family," which was released by the Vatican in 1982, "spouses have the inalienable right to found a family and to decide on the spacing of births and the number of children to be born, taking into full consideration their duties toward themselves, their children already born, the family, and society."[51]

John Paul II also endorsed the UN's Universal Declaration of Human Rights (1948), and in that same UN speech he highlighted "the right to life, liberty, and the security of the person; the right to food, clothing, housing, sufficient health care, rest, and leisure; the right to freedom of expression, education, and culture."[52] In *Centesimus Annus* he developed an ethical rationale for many of these same rights, noting that "even in democracies [they] are not always respected" (CA, 47). The problem is that these rights have been severed from their roots in a proper anthropology. According to John Paul II, "the 1948 Declaration does not contain the anthropological and moral basis for the human rights that it proclaims."[53] Rights must be firmly grounded in our common humanity and in basic human goods that contribute to human flourishing. They cannot be thinly based on a dubious "social contract" or on some vague political consensus. As chapter 3 demonstrated, John Paul II's own anthropology, rooted in the Thomistic and personalist traditions, offers a firm foundation for universal human rights.

In *Centesimus Annus* and the other social encyclicals John Paul II called greater attention to some of the economic rights mentioned in the UN speech. The Holy Father was particularly concerned with the right to a just wage and decent working conditions that include "'human' working hours and adequate free-time" (LE, 20). We will consider those rights in more depth in chapter 6. John Paul II also affirmed a worker's right to strike so long as that right was not abused: "workers should be assured the right to strike, without being subjected to personal penal sanctions for taking part in a strike; while admitting that a strike remains, in a sense, an extreme means" (LE, 20).

Finally, one of the economic rights frequently mentioned by the Holy Father is the right to private property. He notes that "the church has always defended the right to private property, teaching at the same time that this right is not absolute" (CA, 30). Thus, property rights, unlike the right to life, are conditional, and so they can be constrained or overriden for the common good. Limitations on property rights might be necessary to deal with exigent circumstances such as hunger or an acute lack of housing. And in *Centesimus Annus*, Pope John Paul II seems to support the validity of intellectual property rights: "In our time, in particular, there exists another form of ownership which is becoming no less important than land: the possession of know-how . . . and skill" (CA, 32). The recognition of this right is a reflection of John Paul II's high regard for the worth of labor and creativity. His arguments echo John Locke's famous rationale for property rights, which presumes that the prospective owner (or creator) has the foundation of a property right within himself or herself in the form of the personal labor that he or she performs. Locke argued that labor on what is common and unowned engenders a property right: "As much land as a man tills, plants, improves, cultivates, and can use the product of, so much is his property. He, by his labor does, as it were, *enclose it from the common*."[54] Although Locke had in mind physical property such as land, scholars have plausibly argued that this theory is applicable to intellectual property as well.

In summary, John Paul II argues for the right to life as the most fundamental right, inalienable and indisputable. This right "necessarily concerns everyone," and unless it is taken seriously, society's commitment to other rights will lack sincerity and efficacy (EV, 101). In addition, he highlights the right to religious freedom along with the procreative rights of the family. These rights protect the basic human goods of life, religion, and marriage. Finally, he supports a broad set of economic rights such as the right to a just wage and decent working conditions that will ensure the priority of the person in the process of human work.

Summary

To some extent, the apprehensive tone of John Paul II's meditations on ethics springs from his dissatisfaction with the direction of moral theology and the urgent need for its revitalization. One can easily detect his restlessness over the strange drift of modern philosophy. After belief in God and certitudes of the faith vanish, human beings decide for themselves what is knowable and what is good. Self-assertion displaces submission to God's moral law given to us by the Creator Himself. This relativistic and godless philosophy has become the wellspring for the "ideologies of evil" that plague Western culture (MI, 5). In the wake of these dangerous ideologies, ethics must offer us more than advice about "coping with the flux" of modern life. If philosophy and theology are to remain credible, there must be an authentic retrieval of Thomistic realism, a reawakening of belief in God, the Creator and source of all goodness.

John Paul II lays the groundwork for this retrieval to take place among a new generation of moral theologians. In works such as *The Theology of the Body* he argues that ontological goodness is the only secure foundation for moral goodness. Once we know, for example, that human life is good (since it was created by God and participates in the basic perfection of existence), we can confidently make the moral claim that life is good for this ethnic group or for *this* particular person. One also finds in John Paul II a protest against mistaken notions of freedom, which have their roots in philosophies like Sartrean existentialism. Sartre and so many other contemporary thinkers celebrate the emptiness of freedom and assert its primacy over goodness and truth. According to this viewpoint, human beings are free to determine what is good or evil. But John Paul II argues vigorously that the opposite must be true: freedom is subordinate to the good, including the moral good that consists of the perfection of our human nature.

But what is the basis for discerning the objective human good and the norms that it implies? The answer to this question must be based on the metaphysics of human nature, which is oriented toward its own self-fulfillment. An objective good or value for a human person is what fulfills that person's natural potentialities in some way.[55] We can find those objective values by consulting either divine revelation or our own natural reason. Thus, we need look no further than our own human nature, given to us by God, to know what is good for us. What human beings understand as goods (life, knowledge, friendship) are what they have natural inclinations toward. These objective and fundamental human goods perfect our natures and lead to human flourishing. We are naturally disposed to pursue these goods and to eschew the partiality that interferes with the flourishing of others (Golden Rule). From the formal principles such as "love your neighbor as yourself," we can deduce specific exceptionless moral norms, whose absoluteness helps ensure that human dignity is always preserved even when it is inexpedient to do so. Moreover, we realize that our flourishing is achieved only in *solidarity* with others, and this realization is another incentive to will our neighbor's good, to respect those goods perfective of him or her.

Objective moral values are also given to us through revelation, especially in the Decalogue. The negative precepts of the Decalogue represent the conditions for the proper love of God and of one's neighbor. Like the natural law, these commandments are designed to protect the dignity of each person who is the bearer of basic human goods. Consider, for example, the good of life: "the commandment 'You shall not murder' becomes a call to an attentive love which protects and promotes the life of one's neighbor" (VS, 15).

John Paul II turned to Kant's categorical imperative to express morality's supreme principle in philosophical terms: always treat each human being as an end worthy of dignity and never only as a means. The personalist norm is the secular counterpart of Jesus's supreme command to love our neighbor. If there is one overriding principle that stands out in this ethic, it is John Paul II's consistent attempt to illuminate the dignity proper to humanity's nature. It is dangerous to reduce these meditations to a compact formula or a single phrase, but John Paul II's moral philosophy can be concisely characterized as *dignitarian humanism*, which asserts that the unconditional moral standard is the transcendent dignity of all human creatures. Dignity is not a social status to be bestowed because of one's accomplishments, but a universal human reality that cries out for proper recognition. For John Paul II, every person has dignity by virtue of his or her rational nature. The criterion for dignity is *being a person*, since a person has the radical capacity for intellectual thought and free choice. Moreover, that dignity can only be duly recognized and protected by means of absolute moral norms. Thanks to the *"moral norms prohibiting intrinsic evil, there are no privileges or exceptions for anyone"* (VS, 96).

Finally, from the exceptionless moral norms we can infer that certain basic human rights such as the right to life or religious freedom are inviolable. These rights are not derived from some sort of mutable or negotiable social contract. Rather, they are natural rights, "inscribed by the Creator in the order of creation" (CTH, 196). Hence, they cannot be discarded by the state for utilitarian reasons.

Notes

1. Richard Rorty and Gianni Vattimo, *The Future of Religion* (New York: Columbia University Press, 2005), 57.

2. St. Thomas Aquinas, *Quaestiones Disputatae de Potentia*, q. 2, a. 1.

3. Etienne Gilson, *Being and Some Philosophers* (Toronto: Pontifical Institute of Medieval Studies, 1952), 184.

4. St. Thomas Aquinas, *Summa Theologiae* I, q. 5, a. 3 ("omne ens, inquantum est ens, est bonum").

5. Karol Wojtyla, "On the Metaphysical and Phenomenological Basis of the Moral Norm," in *Person and Community: Selected Essays*, trans. Theresa Sandok (New York: Peter Lang, 1993), 74.

6. G. W. F. Hegel, *Vorlesungen über die Geschichte der Philosophie* III, in *Sämtliche Werke* XV, ed. G. Lasson and J. Hoffmeister (Leipzig: Meineer Verlag, 1905), 328.

7. Martin Heidegger, *Holzwege* (Frankfurt: Klostermann, 1950), 99.

8. Heidegger, *Holzwege*, 81 (". . . er sich zu sich selbst befreit"). See also William J. Richardson, S.J., *Heidegger: Through Phenomenology to Thought* (The Hague: Martinus Nijhoff, 1963), 321–322.

9. Friedrich Nietzsche, "Von der schenkenden Tugend," in *Also Sprach Zarathustra* (Stuttgart: Philipp Reclam, 1962), 69, 72.

10. Aristotle, *Metaphysics*, trans. R. Hope (Ann Arbor: University of Michigan Press, 1968), 1072a, 29. I am also indebted to Father Norris Clarke's lectures on metaphysics for these insights.

11. Karol Wojtyla, *Lublin Lectures*, quoted in J. Kupczak, O.P., *Destined for Liberty* (Washington, D.C.: Catholic University of America Press, 2000), 25.

12. St. Thomas Aquinas, *Sent.* I, d. 19, q. 2, a. 1.

13. Norris Clarke, S.J., *The One and the Many* (Notre Dame, Ind.: Notre Dame University Press, 2001), 269.

14. Clarke, *One and the Many*, 264.

15. John Paul II, "Address after Meeting with President and Mrs. Reagan," in *The Pope Speaks to the American Church* (San Francisco: HarperSanFrancisco, 1992), 142–145.

16. See also St. Thomas Aquinas, *Summa Theologiae* I-II, q. 94, a. 1.

17. St. Thomas Aquinas, *Summa Theologiae* I-II, q. 94, a. 2 ("principia per se nota").

18. St. Thomas Aquinas, *Summa Theologiae* I-II, q. 94, a. 1 ("bonum est faciendum et prosequendum, et malum vitandum").

19. Germain Grisez, *Christian Moral Principles* (Quincy, Ill.: Franciscan Press, 1983), 179.

20. St. Thomas Aquinas, *Summa Theologiae* I-II, q. 91, a. 2.

21. St. Thomas Aquinas, *Summa Theologiae* I-II, q. 94, a. 2.

22. Karol Wojtyla, *Love and Responsibility*, trans. J. J. Willetts (San Francisco: HarperCollins, 1981), 27.

23. Grisez, *Christian Moral Principles*, 179.

24. St. Thomas Aquinas, *Summa Theologiae* I-II, q. 100, a. 3.

25. St. Thomas Aquinas, *Summa Theologiae* II-II, q. 64, a. 6.

26. St. Thomas Aquinas, *Summa Theologiae* II-II, q. 64, a. 6.

27. See St. Thomas Aquinas, *Summa Theologiae* I-II, q. 108, a. 1–3.

28. Immanuel Kant, *Foundations of the Metaphysics of Morals*, trans. Lewis Beck (Indianapolis: Bobbs-Merrill, 1959), 16.

29. Wojtyla, *Love and Responsibility*, 28.

30. Friedrich Nietzsche, "Von den Drei Verwandlungen," in *Also Sprach Zarathustra*, 19.

31. Nietzsche, "Von den Drei Verwandlungen," 19.

32. St. Thomas Aquinas, *Super Primam Epistolam ad Corinthos*, commenting on 3.17–18.

33. "Documentum Syntheticum de Moralitate Nativitatum," in *The Birth Control Debate*, ed. R. Hoyt (Kansas City, Mo.: NCR Press, 1969), 69 (my emphasis).

34. Richard McCormick, S.J., "Notes on Moral Theology April–September 1971," in *Notes on Moral Theology, 1965–1980* (Washington, D.C.: University Press of America, 1981), 349–367.

35. Aristotle, *Nicomachean Ethics*, trans. J. A. K. Thomson (New York: Penguin, 1976), 1107a.

36. St. Augustine, *Enchiridion*, chapter 18 in *The Essential Augustine*, ed. Vernon Bourke (Indianapolis: Hackett, 1964), 169.

37. St. Thomas Aquinas, *Quaestiones de Quodlibet* 9, q. 7. a. 2.

38. St. Thomas Aquinas, *Summa Theologiae* II-II, q. 64, a. 6.

39. St. Thomas Aquinas, *De Malo*, q. 15, a. 1, arg. 5.

40. Quoted in Germain Grisez, *Abortion: The Myths, the Realities, and the Arguments* (New York: Corpus, 1970), 138.

41. See William May, *Moral Absolutes* (Milwaukee: Marquette University Press, 1989), 4.

42. May, *Moral Absolutes*, 6.

43. May, *Moral Absolutes*, 19.

44. See, for example, Josef Fuchs, S.J., *Christian Ethics in a Secular Arena* (Washington, D.C.: Georgetown University Press, 1984), 72.

45. John Finnis, *Aquinas* (Oxford: Oxford University Press, 1998), 165.

46. St. Thomas Aquinas, *Quaestiones de Quodlibet* 9, q. 7. a. 2.

47. St. Thomas Aquinas, *De Malo*, q. 72, a. 8. This text is cited and paraphrased in Finnis, *Aquinas*, 166.

48. John Finnis, *Natural Law and Natural Rights* (Oxford: Oxford University Press, 1980), 205.

49. John Paul II, "Address to United Nations General Assembly," sec. 13, *Origins* 9, October 11, 1979.

50. John Paul II, "Address to United Nations General Assembly."

51. The Vatican, "Charter of the Rights of the Family," 1982, sec. 3, www.vatican.va/documents (May 18, 2005).

52. John Paul II, "Address to United Nations General Assembly."

53. John Paul II, "Speech to the Vatican Diplomatic Corps," *Observatore Romano*, January 29, 1989, 1–3.

54. John Locke, *The Second Treatise of Government* (Indianapolis: Bobbs-Merrill, 1952), 20.

55. See Clarke, *One and the Many*, 268–269, for more elaboration on this theme.

CHAPTER 5

The Moral Person

N OW THAT WE understand the nature of freedom along with the natural law and the fundamental principles of morality, we must consider how moral choices are made. How is freedom exercised in a way that respects these principles? What does it mean to be a moral person in the eyes of John Paul II? Does it matter if one makes immoral choices so long as our inner relationship to God remains the same? Just how important are everyday free choices for our moral well-being and our salvation? And what is the role of conscience in moral decision making?

The tenor of these questions will suggest to the astute reader that we are moving into another area of moral theology in which there has been considerable confusion and dissent. New theories have emerged in the past several decades advocating a fundamental option, a choice at the core of one's being that orients the self toward good or evil. At the same time, erroneous accounts of conscience have proliferated. To some extent, the emergence of these problematic theories stems from a defective anthropology or a wrongheaded version of human action and freedom.

In *Veritatis Splendor*, however, John Paul II presents with remarkable clarity the Church's teaching on sin, moral choice, conscience, and the lasting significance of particular moral decisions. He draws from his earlier work on human action to illuminate the meaning of moral choice, but never deviates from Scripture or the Catholic tradition's sound approach to these issues. Before we take up his account of moral action, we must review the specious moral theory of the "fundamental option" that John Paul II addressed with noticeable vigor in *Veritatis Splendor*.

Fundamental Freedom and Morality

Some moral theologians have de-emphasized the role of free choice, preferring instead to focus on a "fundamental freedom." According to Josef Fuchs, this is a "deeper-rooted freedom, not immediately accessible to psychological investigation."[1] At this level one exercises a "fundamental option," a basic commitment for or against God. It is also described by some proponents, such as Karl Rahner, S.J., in terms of a basic or "transcendental" freedom. According to Rahner, this transcendental freedom "is the freedom of the subject towards itself in its finality and thus is freedom towards God, however *unconscious* this ground and most proper and original 'object' of freedom may be in the individual act of freedom."[2] According to another account, "man is structured in a series of concentric circles . . . [and] on the deepest level of the individual, at the personal center, man's freedom decides, loves, commits itself in the fullest sense." On the outer circle there is "peripheral" freedom, which lacks the same "stability as core freedom."[3] Through this peripheral freedom, one can perform good acts or evil ones, and yet still remain committed to God at the level of one's core freedom.

Advocates of this fundamental freedom seem to think that our individual choices are not really self-determining, since they are so limited in scope. These choices involve human goods such as knowledge or aesthetic experience. But how is my choice to read a certain book or attend a concert "self-determining"? According to John Paul II, "in the opinion of some theologians, none of these goods, which by their nature are partial, could determine the freedom of man as a person in his totality" (VS, 65). Our day-to-day free choices, therefore, lack any coherence and permanence. But through this deeper fundamental freedom a person disposes his or her self for or against God or the "absolute Good," and thereby provides a stable structure for this life (VS, 65).

Thus, John Paul II says that according to these theologians, "the key role in the moral life is to be attributed to a 'fundamental option' brought about by that fundamental freedom whereby the person makes an overall self-determination, not through a specific and conscious decision on the level of reflection, but in a transcendental and athematic way" (VS, 65). At the same time, particular acts that flow from one's commitment constitute only partial attempts to give it expression; those acts are only the "signs or symptoms" of one's commitment (VS, 65). As a result, this fundamental freedom differs from free choice since its exercise is not an action of some sort.

But this theory, while emotionally appealing, seems implausible and incompatible with how human beings make choices. This will become more apparent if we review some ambiguities in the fundamental option paradigm. First, the theory is predicated on a dualistic anthropology. It's not the human person as embodied spirit making the choice but some transcendental self at the core of one's being. According to John Paul II, "To separate the fundamental option from concrete kinds of behavior means to contradict the substantial integrity of personal unity of the moral agent in his body and in his soul" (VS, 67). Chapter 3 exposed the salient problems with this view of the human person, which separates personhood from its corporeal nature. In addition, if there are two levels of freedom, free choice and fundamental freedom, how do these two levels interact and relate to each other? If we suppose that our real freedom is fundamental freedom, how do we account for free choice? Does the peripheral freedom I enjoy in choosing different goods flow from or "participate in" my fundamental freedom? Or is fundamental freedom a condition of the possibility of free choice? In either case, what are we to make of those choices that contradict our fundamental option?[4]

Second, several proponents of this viewpoint say that some choices undermine one's fundamental option while others do not. But how do we know the difference? If a good person suddenly makes several disordered choices in the midst of a positive orientation toward God, do one or more of those bad choices signal a change at the innermost depths of one's freedom, which is apparently inaccessible to consciousness? A coherent theory must explain how and why certain malicious choices bring about the displacement of one's original option. Conversely, what if someone habituated to a life of sin suddenly began performing a few good deeds? How could anyone know whether this apparent change of heart at the "peripheral" level represented a reorientation of the will toward God at one's "personal center"? Proponents of the fundamental option cannot leave this process shrouded in mystery. Further, the theory does not account for the ambivalence and complexity that characterizes the moral life of many people who may manifest fidelity to certain aspects of God's Word while being alienated from God through serious sin. It would be hard to find in such a life a decisive orientation in one direction or another.

Third, the fundamental option theory is also too quick to dismiss the significance of individual choices, arguing that they are not truly self-determining. While some choices, such as the choice to watch a baseball game or the choice to eat a steak dinner, are trivial, others have great import. According to John Paul II, "certain choices 'shape' a person's entire moral life, and . . . serve as bounds within which other particular everyday choices can be situated and allowed to develop" (VS, 65). These choices, including the commitment to marry or to join the priesthood, are pivotal because they unify a person's life by integrating many of the lesser choices one makes. We can see therefore that some choices really are *self-determining*. The theory of fundamental freedom has been proposed because free choice cannot seem to account for self-determination. But given the enduring significance of many choices in one's life, it would seem that fundamental freedom is redundant.

A related problem with this theory is its inconsistency with the notion of the acting person and how actions affect the person. According to the fundamental option framework, individual choice performed at the level of one's peripheral freedom often has only a passing and transient effect on the person. Those choices simply have a different moral character than the fundamental option for or against God. The human self can even engage in sinful acts and yet remain insulated from the worst effects of those acts in some mysterious way.

On the contrary, the Holy Father has maintained that no sin or evil choice is extrinsic to the self: "Our evil choices do not pass alongside us; they do not exist before us; they do not pass through us as though they were events which do not involve us. Our evil choices, inasmuch as they are evil, arise within us, solely from us."[5] John Paul II has also insisted throughout his writings that individual choices, whether sinful or good, have deep and lasting effects on the person. A hallmark of his philosophical thought from those earliest days in Kraków has been a consistent belief in the *self-determining nature of individual choices*. Our free choices have existential, soul-making significance, especially those that give a person's life moral structure and unity. According to John Paul II, "freedom is not only the choice for one or another particular action; it is also, within that choice, *a decision about oneself* and a setting of one's life for or against the Good, for or against the Truth, and ultimately for or against God" (VS, 65).

We are determined in a lasting way by these choices, and it makes no sense to say that one can knowingly choose to perform a gravely evil act against God's will, while at the level of "transcendental freedom" one's commitment to God remains unaltered. Every act constructs the self in the moral order, some acts more decisively than others. We determine our being as moral persons through our particular actions and choices, not through the exercise of some basic freedom at the core of our being. The primary problem with the fundamental option theory, therefore, is that it severs the relationship between the person and his or her actions and "relocate[s] self-determination from *free choice* to an alleged 'fundamental' or 'transcendental freedom' deeper than free choice."[6]

John Paul II does not deny that people's lives exhibit a general orientation toward good or evil through the pattern of their free choices. But if someone exercises such an option to follow Christ there is a profound and explicit link between that choice and a person's "particular acts" (VS, 67). Moreover, that option is "revoked when man engages his freedom in conscious decisions to the contrary, with regard to morally grave matter" (VS, 67). For John Paul II, Scripture tells us that faith in Christ is a commitment to keeping the commandments of the covenant, and failure to do so when grave matter is involved breaks that covenant. It is inconsistent with Scripture to suggest that covenantal communion with God can be sustained even when one freely and knowingly commits sinful acts that are incompatible with the covenant.

There are also negative practical and pastoral implications involved in preaching the fundamental option theory as a basic tenet of moral theology. When the faithful hear this message, they will no doubt be falsely consoled, believing that they can commit sin through their peripheral freedom with virtual impunity, since such sin often does not disrupt their inner commitment to God. Moreover, there is no incentive to change, to repent, or to seek God's forgiveness in the sacrament of confession. Advocates of this view certainly do not intend to encourage moral irresponsibility. Preaching the fundamental option, however, could have the unintended effect of inuring sinners to their sin rather than fortifying their desire for repentance and conversion.

In the context of his critique of the fundamental option, John Paul II reiterates the Church's sound teaching on sin, moral evil that blocks human fulfillment through the deprivation or impairment of some due good. Sin disrupts harmony with God. The Holy Father strongly believed that sin was a matter of the heart and the will: "the relationship between man's freedom and God's law is most deeply lived out in the 'heart' of the person" (VS, 54). This is why if a woman is treated by her husband as an "object of pleasure," she becomes "in his heart an object of adultery" (MD, 14). This view of sin is founded on many scriptural texts. As God revealed to the prophet Ezekiel,

> I will give them a single heart and I will put a new spirit in them; I will remove the heart of stone from their bodies and give them a heart of flesh instead, so that they will keep my laws and respect my observances and put them into practice. . . . But those whose hearts are set on their idols and their filthy practices I will call to account for their conduct. (Ezek. 11:19–21)

The Catholic Church has long differentiated between mortal and venial sin. The validity of this teaching, rooted in Scripture and in the writings of the Church fathers, was affirmed at the Council of Trent. According to John Paul II, the 1983 Synod of Bishops "not only reaffirmed the teaching of the Council of Trent concerning the existence and nature of mortal and venial sins, but it also recalled that mortal sin is sin whose object is grave matter and which is also committed with full knowledge and deliberate consent" (VS, 70).

In direct contradiction of the fundamental option paradigm, John Paul II insisted that free and deliberate choice of grave matter severs one's relationship with God. Any person who has committed mortal sin needs the grace that comes from the sacrament of confession. A single act of this nature if done knowingly and willingly in defiance of God's love is enough to terminate one's fidelity. Thus, Holy Scripture calls upon us to "lay aside every weight and sin which clings so closely" (Heb. 12:1). The Church's traditional focus on particular acts rather than a fundamental option that transcends those acts has the great virtue of clarity and consistency. There is no confusion here about when or how one's commitment to God is subverted through specific concrete actions. And there is also perfect consistency with the teachings of Jesus, who constantly admonishes us to avoid sinful acts that violate the commandments.

Finally, the impact of sin in the world should not be underestimated or trivialized. According to John Paul II, "a soul that lowers itself through sin drags down with itself the Church and, in some way, the whole world" (RP, 16). The ill effects of sin reverberate through the human community, and that sin can sometimes take on a communal or structural character, as it becomes embedded in laws or in cultural institutions.

Moral Choice

In addition to the fundamental option theory, John Paul II also expressed concern in many of his encyclicals about the moral theory of proportionalism. As we have seen, one of John Paul II's major problems with proportionalism was its misunderstanding of human action and moral choice. Prudent and reasonable conduct is all about making good moral choices, but we must understand what it means to make a moral choice. Choices and the actions that execute those choices are complicated, and so the late Holy Father sought to be precise and thorough in explaining the nature of these acts. Hence there is an extensive treatment of this issue in *Veritatis Splendor* (71–81). Proportionalists sometimes conflate the morally significant differentiation between the immediate end, the intention, and the circumstances of an action. They also prefer to understand moral action by reference to the context of that action and the results achieved.

For example, Father Edward Vacek, S.J., criticizes the natural law tradition because it "locates morality not in behaviors, relationships, adequate attempts, or *results* but in attitudes and especially in the will." He cites the medieval example of the blind woman who intends to commit adultery but, unbeknownst to her, ends up sleeping with her husband. Vacek claims that the woman is not an adulteress even though she intended to commit adultery. She may be "subjectively" guilty, but there is no objective evil. Vacek and other proportionalists want to locate objective morality primarily in results and in the effectiveness of bringing about benefits and reducing harm. According to Vacek, "if we allow intention to suffice, our moral notions are stretched too far . . . and we [will] have adulteresses who have only had sex with their husbands."[7] Is Vacek right about this? Does it make sense to call this woman an adulteress if in reality she has not slept with any man but her own husband?

On the other hand, John Paul II, along with moralists such as Germain Grisez and John Finnis, have a different conception of moral action that is consistent with the tradition of Aquinas. First, in keeping with his views on personalism, John Paul II maintains that the identification and evaluation of the moral action (or choice) must be from the perspective of the *acting person*. It should not be from the perspective of the neutral or outside observer who uses a frame of reference that focuses primarily on causal relationships or the effects of one's actions. Second, unlike proportionalists, John Paul II wants to locate morality in the order of the will, not in the results or outcome of an action. One of his major criticisms of proportionalists is that they "do not take into sufficient consideration the fact that the will is involved in the concrete choices which it makes" (VS, 75). Revelation itself, according to John Paul II, has repeatedly confirmed the central importance of the "heart" or the interior depths of man as the source of moral actions (Mark 7:20–23; Luke 6:45).

This perspective is consonant with the work of philosophers like Aquinas who regarded acts as wrongful by virtue of the acting person's bad will. Aquinas defined what one wills or chooses as the "object of one's act."[8] In an important passage of *Veritatis Splendor* John Paul II elaborates on Aquinas's thesis:

> The morality of the human act depends primarily and fundamentally on the "object" rationally chosen by the deliberate will. . . . In order to be able to grasp the object of an act which specifies that act morally, it is therefore necessary to place oneself *in the perspective of the acting person*. The object of the act of willing is in fact a freely chosen kind of behavior. To the extent that it is in conformity with the order of reason, it is the cause of the goodness of the will; it perfects us morally, and disposes us to recognize our ultimate end in the perfect good, primordial love. By the object of a given moral act, then, one cannot mean a process or an event of the merely physical order, to be assessed on the basis of its ability to bring about a given state of affairs in the outside world. Rather, that object is the proximate end of a deliberate decision which determines the act of willing on the part of the acting person. (VS, 78)

This is a difficult and subtle text that invites several remarks. John Paul II is making the case that the morality of an action depends upon what one freely chooses. Germain Grisez's commentary on moral theology may provide some insight into the thrust of the Holy Father's analysis. Grisez claims that we can describe an individual's action properly by conceiving it as "the content of the proposal adopted by choice."[9] This is roughly equivalent to the "object of the action" in Aquinas, or "the object rationally chosen by the deliberate will" in John Paul II's text. The execution of what is decided or adopted completes the action. Thus, both the willing of this choice and its execution constitute a complete human act.

In Grisez's terms, there may be many eligible "proposals" before us, each one promising certain benefits to be achieved by some specific means. Choosing among them is an act of the will in which the moral agent ceases deliberating and adopts one proposal with a definitive intent. And that proposal incorporates an object or "proximate end," that is, the immediate goal or the end intrinsic to that choice. In making this willful choice the moral agent usually intends some intelligible benefits that are to be achieved through this choice, so the proximate end is also a means. These expected benefits explain the motivating goal or ultimate purpose of the agent. For example, if someone chooses to drive a friend to church, the proximate end is getting the person to this destination, but the motivating goal or purpose may be to win the person's favor.

The moral agent then executes or carries out the choice (or proposal) at some point, unless, of course, prior to the execution the agent changes his or her mind and reverses the original choice. Finally, a moral act includes accidental as well as essential features such as the foreseen side effects of carrying out the act. For example, Sam's choice to go to the baseball game with his friends is morally permissible, unless he skips work to attend the game despite his boss's warning and finds himself out of a job and unable to support his family. Given these foreseeable side effects, the act of going to the baseball game takes on a new moral character.

It is obvious that John Paul II does not make the mistake of some neo-Scholastic philosophers or classical moral theologians who regarded the "object of the act" as referring merely to the external physical action itself, unrelated to deliberation and choice. Instead they should have concentrated on the acting person's relevant willing and on the morally relevant description of the proposal adopted by one's choice. The reason for this is based on Aquinas's argument that acts can be the same in the natural (or physical) order but differ in the moral order:

> Sexual intercourse . . . can be considered in two ways: either according to the genus of nature and then matrimonial sexual intercourse and fornication do not differ in species, and their natural effects are the same in species; or they can be considered as they relate to the genus of morality, and then their effects differ in species, as to merit or demerit.[10]

When seen in this light, we appreciate that two acts of killing another person, while the same in the natural order (*in genus naturae*), can differ in the moral order (*in genus moris*) if there is a difference in what the will wills. For example, let's assume that Joe shoots George out of revenge and anger, but Paul shoots Mike because Mike is approaching him with a knife and Paul will be killed unless he fires the deadly shot. The external act of killing is identical in both of these scenarios, but the acts are morally different—the first act is an act of murder where the will wills the killing of an innocent person, and the second act is killing in self-defense where the will wills the impediment of the attacker. When the "object of the act" is recast in John Paul II's more nuanced terms, "the proximate end of a deliberate decision which determines the act of willing," we can appreciate the moral distinction between these two acts. It lies in the difference between what the moral agent deliberately chooses or wills—in one case the "proximate end" is the death of an innocent person, while in the other it is stopping the attacker. As Finnis points out, describing acts *in genere moris* "enable[s] the peculiarly moral predicates to be accurately applied to them."[11]

Thus, every moral act should be evaluated by focusing precisely on what the moral agent directly wills. An action is defined by what is intended, by the proposal one adopts by choice. John Paul II is in full accord with Aquinas that acts are specified by their object or proximate end. According to Aquinas, "we know the act through its object."[12] Along the same lines, John Paul II writes that it is possible "to qualify as morally evil according to its species—its 'object'—the deliberate choice of certain kinds of behavior or specific acts, apart from a consideration of the intention [ultimate end] for which the choice is made" (VS, 79).

To be thorough, however, the evaluation of a moral action must include the deliberate choice (*electio*), one's immediate purpose in making this choice (the proximate end or *finis proximus*), the ultimate end (*finis ultimus*), which is sometimes called the intention, and even the foreseen side effects of one's choice. The operative principle that John Paul II endorses at least implicitly is *bonum ex integra causa, autem malum ex quocumque defectu*, that is, the moral goodness of an act comes from the whole set of factors, but the badness comes from a defect in any one factor. In order to be morally acceptable, all the relevant factors must be good. It is significant that in his Lublin lectures Karol Wojtyla approvingly mentions that this high standard, first articulated by the medieval philosopher Pseudo-Dionysus, forms the basis for Aquinas's whole moral system.[13]

This analysis enables us to appreciate more clearly the scope of John Paul II's disagreement with the proportionalists. Even if an action has a good ultimate end or purpose, if the choice itself is to do some sort of evil as a means to that end, the action is morally wrong. According to John Paul II, "circumstance or intention can never transform an act intrinsically evil *by virtue of its object* into an act 'subjectively' good or defensible as a choice" (VS, 81). For example, a married couple freely chooses to use contraception, a choice that has the impeding of procreation as its object or proximate end (*finis proximus*), but they make this choice for a "higher" purpose or ultimate end (*finis ultimus*): to improve their unstable financial situation so they can properly care for their children. However, the noble purpose of this couple does not validate the immoral nature of this choice, because the will aims at deterring procreation. As we noted in the last section, some actions (or choices), such as adultery, are intrinsically immoral and cannot be justified by any proportionate reasons or ultimate end. Thus, from the perspective of the acting person, the goodness or badness of one's action is determined by the goodness or badness of one's will, what one chooses and willfully tries to do, perhaps as a means to some ultimate end.[14]

Vacek and other proportionalists deviate from the tradition because they will not judge a course of action to be morally wrong purely on the basis of its "object," the choice and its proximate end, or what the acting person chooses and attempts to do, since the ultimate end (*finis ultimus*) or the "context" may justify that action. Yet for John Paul II, "the primary and decisive element for moral judgement is the 'object' of the human act" (VS, 79). Even if what the will wills is harmful in some way, proportionalists want to consider factors such as the agent's ultimate end (or motivating purpose), along with the context, when they evaluate a moral decision. In the contraception case, most proportionalists would regard the proximate end of impeding procreation as insufficient grounds for rendering a definitive moral judgment. The couple's ultimate goal of improving their financial status and other contextual factors must also be taken into account. John Paul II objects to this line of reasoning since it permits an immoral means, the impairment of human goods such as marriage, to justify a good end. The good thereby becomes the enemy of the right and the just. On the contrary, moral acts are objectively determined by one's deliberately choosing or willing and by what people believe they are doing in making a particular choice. What is of primary moral relevance for John Paul II is not outcomes or results, but the choice made in the acting person's heart and his or her relevant willing.

Also, since morality is about *the self-determining choices of the will*, even if that choice (or proposal) is not carried out, there can still be objective immorality. Consider this hypothetical example. Let's say that Jeff begins to flirt with Jane, the clerk at the pro shop where he plays golf every Saturday. Jeff is married, but he is angry at his wife, whom he suspects of cheating. The more he flirts with Jane, the more responsive she becomes. On one Saturday morning he makes a willful moral choice— he chooses to ask Jane to sleep with him at the nearby motel. Aside from sexual gratification, he is motivated by the desire to get even with his wife. He heads to the golf course to execute that choice. However, when he gets there he finds that Jane has quit her job, and so he cannot carry out his plan. The point here is that Jeff has made an objectively immoral choice: to commit the grave sin of adultery by sleeping with another woman. Even though there is no carrying out of this choice and no physical adultery occurs, he has done something gravely wrong in the objective moral order by willing to engage in adultery. What happened here goes beyond his subjective intentions, if intention is understood as some provisional resolution to sleep with this woman if the opportunity might arise. In this context, Jeff arrived at a definite decision and made a willful choice to commit adultery. That choice, that willing in the depth of his heart to commit adultery with Jane, changes Jeff's character (along with the relationship with his wife) decisively for the worse.

This notion that interior choice and willing (rather than behavior or results) matters profoundly in moral affairs is consistent with the Scriptural tradition. Recall Jesus's striking but hard words in Matthew (5:27–28): "You have heard that it was said that 'You shall not commit adultery.' But I say to you that everyone who looks at a woman lustfully has already committed adultery with her in his heart." Thus, the person who chooses to commit adultery, who has a lust in his heart that he willfully indulges, has committed adultery even if the physical act of sleeping with another's spouse is absent. We might borrow a common idiom used to describe activities in the realm of cyberspace and call this "virtual adultery," in order to differentiate this form of adultery from adultery that includes the physical act itself. Virtual acts are real and have a significant impact—they just don't happen to occur in the physical world of "meat space." Thus, the type of adultery committed by our friend Jeff involves a deliberate act of the will. Even though the choice is not consummated physically, the adultery is real nonetheless. It occurs in the space of his own heart and soul, but with real negative effects on himself and on others.

In the above citation from *Veritatis Splendor* John Paul II refers to the "acting person," an obvious allusion to the book he wrote as Karol Wojtyla called *The Acting Person*, where these issues are treated in great philosophical depth. In that book and in a number of related essays he emphasizes moral subjectivity and the need to understand the moral act from within. According to Wojtyla, "human beings are subjects," and subjectivity "takes on a distinctive inwardness of activity and existence."[15] It is important to adopt this inward perspective when assessing a moral action *in genere moris*, under its morally relevant description. Otherwise, one cannot provide an adequate description of the moral act that is relevant, true, and objective. All rational moral agents know the proposals they are deliberately adopting. They know their intentions, the foreseen side effects, and what they are choosing as a proximate end. This interior knowledge, which is not always transparent in one's external behavior or in the outcome, is vital for understanding a moral action and assigning blame or culpability.[16]

Also, in those same writings John Paul II repeatedly refers to the intransitive nature of moral actions and choices. Our willing has an "intransitive significance in the human person," since the object of my willing has a lasting impact on the self. Thus he describes "the persistence of an action in the person" because of that action's "moral value."[17] He continues to highlight this theme in encyclicals like *Veritatis Splendor*, in which he quotes from Gregory of Nyssa to reinforce his argument: *"we are* in a certain way our own parents, creating ourselves as we will, by our decisions"* (VS, 71). Our choices, whether we execute them or not, have a lasting effect on our character. According to Wojtyla, "the will is not only an efficient power, a power that gives rise to action, but also a kind of ability to become."[18] As we noted in chapter 3, the need to consider both the external and internal effects of one's choices has been a recurrent theme in John Paul II's writings. Jeff's character is indelibly changed by his choice, his willing embrace of this adulterous relationship, even though his plan was thwarted by a twist of fate. The choice leaves upon him a lasting mark or trace. And since the subject-oriented and object-oriented aspects of an act are distinct but inseparable, we can be sure that because of the real effect on his character, this deliberately willed choice, though not executed, is objectively immoral.

We see more clearly now why John Paul II eschews the reasoning of the fundamental option proponents, who downplay free choice in favor of one's basic orientation to God attributed to our fundamental freedom. On the contrary, John Paul II gives full primacy to free choice, which is always a choice to do something, to be virtuous or vicious. Only specific choices create our identity, not some opaque inner commitment of full self-disposal. Those specific choices are self-determining and sometimes embody commitments that shape our character and future choices. Choices last both as dispositions to act in the same way in similar situations and as an evolution of the existential self. According to Wojtyla, "through self-determination the person becomes more of a 'someone' in the ethical sense, although in the ontological sense the human being is a 'someone' from the very beginning."[19]

Conscience

Given the lasting significance of our choices, we need to choose prudently. But how do we know how to make the right choice? Moral quandaries abound in one's personal and professional life. Fortunately, each human being has a moral conscience, a "secret sanctuary," where he or she can find refuge and where "God's voice echoes" (DV, 43). This voice of conscience comes in stillness and silence, in the depth of our souls. Conscience enables us to resolve moral dilemmas and to formulate a moral judgment from among the alternative choices (or "proposals") we are considering. In *Veritatis Splendor* and in *Dominum et Vivificantem* John Paul II devotes considerable attention to this topic. This attention seems needed, given the tendency in today's culture to equate "following one's conscience" with subjectivism or to confuse conscience with a superego-like awareness of conventional norms. John Paul II is quite clear that conscience "is not an independent and exclusive capacity to decide what is good and what is evil" (DV, 43). Rather, conscience is awareness of moral truth, of what is the right thing to do.

John Paul II's conception of conscience is squarely in line with the Thomistic tradition. Aquinas regarded conscience as an intellectual act of judgment. For Aquinas and for John Paul II, the work of conscience begins with awareness of the guiding principles of morality. These principles include Christian moral norms, such as the norms of the Decalogue, which are derived from the natural law and through divine revelation. Conscience is a "witness for man: a witness of his own faithfulness or unfaithfulness with regard to the law" (VS, 57). What follows is the application of these moral norms to a particular, concrete situation. One reasons from principles to a practical conclusion, which is expressed as a command of our conscience or practical reason: "This action is morally right and should be carried out," or "This action is wrong and it should be avoided." We can choose either to agree or to disagree with this practical judgment of conscience. As Germain Grisez puts it, "Conscience is one's last and best judgement concerning what one should choose."[20] Finally, conscience continues its work by inducing us to compare the actual choice with one's judgment regarding the choice one should have made.

Catholics believe that the Church, through the Magisterium, offers moral guidance that must form their consciences. No one who professes to be a faithful Catholic can ignore that guidance. Moreover, given the unerring charism of the Church in matters of faith and morals, that guidance is equivalent to the moral truth. Thus, a judgment of a well-formed conscience cannot conflict with the Church's teaching since that teaching embodies the moral truth. According to John Henry Cardinal Newman, before revelation, conscience operated on the natural level as an "inward guide." But in the aftermath of revelation, conscience becomes "the voice of Scripture, or of the Church, or of the Holy See."[21] Thus, "Christians have a great help for the formation of conscience *in the Church and her Magisterium*" (VS, 64).

John Paul II warns against confusing the mandate to follow one's conscience with subjective morality. Unless one's conscience follows Christian moral principles and the Church's moral teaching, it will only have subjective standards to follow. We must also beware of those who advocate some creative latitude for conscience so that it can make exceptions to moral principles. According to this viewpoint, conscience makes independent "decisions" instead of formulating "judgments." According to John Paul II, "In their desire to emphasize the 'creative' character of conscience, certain authors no longer call its actions 'judgments' but 'decisions': only by making these decisions 'autonomously' would man be able to attain moral maturity" (VS, 56). But conscience is the capacity to know and apply moral truth, so there is no room for such "creative" reasoning.

Although everyone is obliged to follow his or her conscience, a conscience could be erroneous. Conscience is "not an infallible judge" (VS, 62). But one must still follow one's conscience even when it is mistaken. An error of conscience could be the result of "invincible ignorance"; in this case, one is not culpable for following a conscience that is in error (VS, 62). In other circumstances a person could be culpable for following an erroneous conscience if the error is that person's fault. This could happen through deliberately willed ignorance, an unwillingness to investigate the norms or moral issues that should have a bearing on one's choice. We have a responsibility to form conscience correctly so that our judgments will conform with the moral truth.

Above all, conscience can never make intrinsically evil actions good or morally acceptable. If we accept the premise that conscience is awareness of moral truth, then it follows that just because some course of action *seems* right to a person's conscience, it does not mean the action *is* right. For example, if someone with a deformed conscience comes to the conclusion that slavery in modern society is morally permissible, we would not tolerate such an error and allow this person to sell people into bondage just because he or she claims that his or her conscience says that slavery is perfectly fine. Thus, although conscience is an individual's personal apprehension of moral truth, that truth has its own objective existence apart from the individual's conscience. The same moral truth exists for others to grasp as well. Consider a soldier who reaches a judgment that "it is wrong to kill this group of innocent civilians" since doing so violates the moral norm that it is wrong to take innocent human life. That soldier does not construct this moral truth but reaches it by reasoning, by applying a general norm ("one cannot intentionally kill an innocent human being") to this concrete situation. He can be sure that many others will be disposed to see the same truth through the personal, intellectual vision of their own consciences.

John Paul II observes in *Dominum et Vivificantem* that the Holy Spirit is the interior guide to our conscience. The Holy Spirit will sharpen our conscience so that it is sensitive to discovering and comprehending sin: "humanity is ignorant of the 'mystery of iniquity' . . . and cannot be convinced of these dimensions except by the Holy Spirit" (DV, 32). The Holy

Spirit also helps us see that "imprinted" on our conscience is the "principle of obedience" to the objective moral norms. For example, with the Spirit's help the upright conscience perceives clearly that whatever is opposed to life, such as murder, abortion, genocide, euthanasia, or willful self-destruction, is always wrong (DV, 43).

It is enlightening to compare John Paul II's orthodox views on conscience with those of great theologians such as Cardinal Newman. Consider the prophetic tone of Cardinal Newman's famous remarks:

> Conscience has rights because it has duties, but in this age, with a large portion of the public, it is the very right and freedom of conscience to dispense with conscience, to ignore a Lawgiver and Judge, to be independent of unseen obligations. It becomes a license to take up any or no religion, to take up this or that and let it go again, to go to church, to go to the chapel, to boast of being above all religions and to be an impartial critic of each of them. Conscience is a stern monitor, but in this century it has been superseded by a counterfeit, which the eighteen centuries prior to it never heard of, and could not have mistaken for it, if they had. It is the right of self-will.[22]

This true meaning of conscience has become even more concealed today, since conscience is conceived even by some moral theologians as this "right of self-will," a right to create one's own norms. But John Paul II, like Newman, regards conscience not as the "right of self-will," but as the capability to know with confidence the moral truth. Everyone is responsible for forming his or her conscience by being aware of the principles of morality and by acquiring the necessary factual knowledge so that one can make the right choice among the available moral options.

Finally, it is worth noting Newman's claim that the active presence of this "inner voice" operating as an unconditional imperative and standing as a judge of our actions can only have God as its sufficient reason, since He is the giver of the eternal law. For where else does this voice come from? How else to explain the alterity of this voice that resonates so strongly and clearly within us? For Newman, this voice points us directly to the existence of God. John Paul II would undoubtedly agree. Like Newman, he appreciated the transcendent dimension of conscience, where we find "a dialogue of man with God, the author of the law, the primordial image and final end of man" (VS, 58).

We can debate the validity of Newman's argument for God's existence, based on the articulate dialogue of our moral conscience with a Being beyond itself. But we cannot debate the power and impeccable reliability of this inner voice when it is properly guided by the Holy Spirit.

The Challenge of the Moral Life

One constant theme in John Paul II's writings is that those who aspire to make the right choices in accordance with the moral truth will have a difficult time, particularly in a society that prizes relativism, pluralism, and tolerance. Of course, this notion should come as no surprise since "Christ forewarned us, telling us that the road to salvation is not broad and comfortable, but narrow and difficult (cf. Matt. 7:13–14). We do not have the right to abandon that perspective, nor to change it" (CTH, 173).

Thanks to the lasting effects of original sin, there is a moral frailty and undulant darkness that permeates our spiritual being. The moral life is full of challenges, and there are always temptations to compromise and to "cut corners." These temptations can arise for people in both their professional and their personal lives. Perhaps the allure of proportionalism and consequentialism is its pragmatic and open-ended approach to moral problems. This way of thinking certainly paves the way for some of these compromises and makes the moral life a little easier. In the mind of some proportionalists, the broad prospects of enhancing satisfaction or "alleviating pain" might even become a proportionate reason for making exceptions to basic moral norms.[23]

But, as we have been at pains to insist in this book, John Paul II's moral vision is based on firm Christian principles, not pragmatic compromise. Thus, it sometimes calls on people to make sacrifices on behalf of the moral truth. In one of his general audiences John Paul II proclaimed:

> One thing is certain—the life which Jesus Christ, and the Church with Him, proposes to man is full of *moral demands* which bind him to what is good even to the heights of heroism. It is necessary to observe whether, when one says *"no to the Church,"* in reality one is not seeking to escape these demands. Here more than in any other case the *"no to the Church"* would be equivalent to a *"no to Christ."* Unfortunately, experience shows that this is often the case.[24]

Many philosophers before John Paul II have elaborated upon the same theme. Aristotle, for example, also recognized the demands of pursuing the right path, since it is so much easier to succumb to moral failure:

> Again, it is possible to fail in many ways (for evil belongs to the class of the unlimited as the Pythagoreans conjectured, and good to that of the limited), while to succeed is possible only in one way (for which reason also one is easy and the other difficult—to miss the mark easy, to hit it difficult); for these reasons also, then, excess and defect are characteristic of vice, and the mean of virtue; for men are good in but one way, but bad in many.[25]

Although Aristotle is talking primarily about the challenge for practical reason to locate the mean of virtue and discern the right course to follow, John Paul II is more worried about weakness of will when the right course is evident. The moral life requires fortitude and resoluteness, which is so often lacking in our lax and permissive culture. We must look to the saints, the martyrs, and other heroes for the faith, who can inspire us through their moral commitment so we can avoid "missing the mark." According to John Paul II,

> The Church proposes the example of numerous Saints, who bore witness to and defended the moral truth even to the point of enduring martyrdom, or who preferred death to a single mortal sin. In raising them to the honor of the altars, the Church has canonized their witness and declared the truth of their judgement, according to which the love of God entails the obligation to respect his commandments, even in the most dire of circumstances, and the refusal to betray those commandments even for the sake of saving one's own life. (VS, 91)

In the Old Testament we find Susanna's willingness to accept death rather than succumb to the illicit passions of two unjust judges (Dan. 13:22–23). This act of courage typifies the uncompromising moral commitment John Paul II is exhorting us to follow. St. Thomas More's willingness to accept death rather than lie under oath about Henry VIII's marriage represents another powerful example of principled behavior and moral rectitude. John Paul II applauds St. Thomas More for being "unwavering in this rigorous moral stance."[26] St. Maria Goretti's moral fortitude and her convincing witness to the worth of chastity also come to mind. Or more recently, we find the selfless love of St. Gianna Molla, who was willing to risk her own life for the life of her unborn child. According to John Paul II, St. Gianna "gave witness in her daily life to the demanding values of the Gospel."[27] The lives of these saints and many others represent an inspiration and a challenge for all of us—to adhere to the moral truth at any cost, even if this must mean living on the edge and sometimes risking all for the sake of the Gospel.

But despite the challenge of leading a moral life, there is no reason for despair. At the conclusion of *Veritatis Splendor*, John Paul II commends us to look to the Blessed Mother for inspiration: "Mary is the radiant sign and inviting model of the moral life. . . . Mary lived and exercised her freedom precisely by giving herself to God and accepting God's gift within herself" (VS, 120). She bears witness to the great beauty that accompanies the life of virtue. Mary's conscience was always conformed to the teachings of God, and yet no living person enjoyed more freedom. Mary, therefore, is "the model of all of those who hear the word of God and keep it" (VS, 120). Those who waver in seeking that authentic freedom that comes from following the moral truth should look to Mary for the fortitude to do what is right.

According to John Paul II, as soon as we are created, we are called to the moral life since we are oriented to desire and pursue the good through our own human nature. But living the moral life fully, responding to God's invitation to "have eternal life," requires the gift of God's grace that comes through prayer and the sacraments. With the help of that grace, we too can always "hear the word of God and keep it."

Summary

According to John Paul II, we must always consider the person's moral actions from the perspective of the acting person. The goodness or badness of the acting person's behavior depends on what that person wills and chooses, because the moral character of that act is determined by its species *in genere moris*, that is, in the order of willing and choosing.[28] The acting person's willful choices have an objective effect as well as a subjective one: they cause a result outside of the self, but they also leave an enduring mark within. Unlike proportionalists, John Paul II has consistently underscored the reflexive character of human actions, which "once performed do not vanish without a trace, [but] leave their moral value."[29]

John Paul II's insightful discussion on the subjective dimension of moral action represents a notable contribution to current moral discourse. The Holy Father takes quite seriously "the person as a subject experiencing its *acts*," along with the character-shaping import of those acts.[30] Proportionalists give great weight to the overall net good; what counts is not what we will and choose but the results attained by our choice. Other theologians suggest that the moral life can be explained in terms of a fundamental option for good or evil. This "free determination of oneself with regard to the totality of existence" transcends our particular choices.[31] But John Paul II insists on the lasting significance of our individual moral choices. There is no mysterious determination of the self in its "totality," only specific choices for true love or self-love. Those choices create our identity. Thus, by choosing life for one's unborn baby instead of abortion, a woman creates herself as someone who respects human life and upholds the law of God.

Since choices last within us, we cannot afford to make the wrong choice. Fortunately, we can depend on our conscience for guidance. Conscience is the place where a person experiences the call of moral duty, the call to live up to the requirements of the personalist norm. According to John Paul II, the function of conscience is "to apply the universal knowledge of the good in a specific situation and thus to express a judgement about the right conduct to be chosen" (VS, 32). Conscience, therefore, summons us to follow our last and best judgment about what is right, and we are always obliged to follow our conscience. Conscience must be properly formed, and, for Catholics, this means listening to the voice of Scripture and the Magisterium.

Because of original sin we have a fallen nature, an ineradicable finitude that impedes our aspirations to follow the demands of morality. It is easy to fail but difficult to "hit the mark" and do what is right. Hence the need for prayer, diligent moral judgment, God's grace, and the inspiring example of the martyrs and other moral heroes who have had the courage to do what is right despite the sacrifice or adverse consequences. The martyrs are especially inspiring since they manifest to us a transcendent good that is worth dying for. We should also turn our attention to Mary as a sign and exemplary model of the moral life, who "lived and exercised her freedom by giving herself to God" (VS, 120).

Notes

1. Josef Fuchs, S.J., *Human Values and Christian Morality* (Dublin: Gill, 1970), 93.

2. Karl Rahner, S.J., "The Fundamental Option," *Theological Investigations*, vol. 6 (New York: Seabury, 1964), 181–188 (my emphasis).

3. John Glaser, S.J., "Transition between Grace and Sin: Fresh Perspectives," *Theological Studies* 29 (1968): 261–262.

4. See Joseph Boyle, "Freedom, the Human Person, and Human Action," in *Principles of Catholic Moral Life*, ed. William May (Chicago: Franciscan Herald Press, 1980), 237–266.

5. John Paul II, "General Audience," March 14, 1984, in *L'Osservatore Romano*, March 20, 1984, 1.

6. William May, "Free Choice," 2003, www.christendom-awake.org/pages/may/free-choice.htm (November 8, 2005).

7. Edward Vacek, S.J., "Contraception Again—A Conclusion in Search of Convincing Arguments: One Proportionalist's [Mis?]Understanding of a Text," in *Natural Law and Moral Inquiry*, ed. Robert George (Washington, D.C.: Georgetown University Press, 1998), 50–81 (my emphasis).

8. St. Thomas Aquinas, *Summa Theologiae* I-II, q. 18, a. 2.

9. Germain Grisez, *Christian Moral Principles* (Quincy, Ill.: Franciscan Press, 1983), 233.

10. St. Thomas Aquinas, *Sent.* II, q. 1, a. 1, ad. 4.

11. See John Finnis, "Object and Intention in Moral Judgements According to Aquinas," *The Thomist* 55 (1991): 17.

12. St. Thomas Aquinas, *De Anima* II, lect. 6 ("per objecta cogniscimus actus").

13. See Jaroslaw Kupczak, O.P., *Destined for Liberty* (Washington, D.C.: Catholic University of America Press, 2000), 54.

14. See Finnis, "Object and Intention in Moral Judgements," 1–27.

15. Karol Wojtyla, "The Person: Subject and Community," in *Person and Community: Selected Essays*, trans. Theresa Sandok (New York: Peter Lang, 1993), 227.

16. See John Finnis, Germain Grisez, and Joseph Boyle, "'Direct' and 'Indirect': A Reply to Critics of Our Action Theory," *The Thomist* 65 (2001): 1–41.

17. Karol Wojtyla, *The Acting Person*, trans. A. Potocki, Analecta Husserliana, vol. 10 (Dordrecht, Holland: D. Reidel, 1979), 160–161.

18. Karol Wojtyla, "Human Nature as the Basis of Ethical Formation," in *Person and Community: Selected Essays*, 99.

19. Karol Wojtyla, "The Personal Structure of Self-Determination," in *Person and Community: Selected Essays*, 192. See also Grisez, *Christian Moral Principles*, 52–53.

20. Grisez, *Christian Moral Principles*, 76.

21. John Henry Cardinal Newman, *An Essay on the Development of Christian Doctrine* (New York: Longmans, Green, 1949), 80.

22. John Henry Cardinal Newman, *Certain Difficulties Felt by Their Anglicans Considered: A Letter Addressed to the Duke of Norfolk* (London: Longmans, Green, 1897), 250.

23. See, for example, John Giles Milhaven, *Toward a New Catholic Morality* (Garden City, N.Y.: Doubleday, 1970).

24. John Paul II, "General Audience," July 24, 1991, in *L'Osservatore Romano*, July 25, 1991, 4.

25. Aristotle, *Nicomachean Ethics*, trans. J. A. K. Thomson (New York: Penguin, 1976), 1106b.

26. John Paul II, "Apostolic Letter Proclaiming Saint Thomas More Patron of Statesmen and Politicians," issued Mont Proprio, October 23, 2000.

27. Pietro Molla and Elio Guerriero, *Saint Gianna Molla* (San Francisco: Ignatius Press, 2004), 88.

28. St. Thomas Aquinas, *De Malo*, q. 2, a. 4, ad. 7.

29. Wojtyla, *The Acting Person*, 151.

30. Karol Wojtyla, "Subjectivity and the Irreducible in the Human Being," in *Person and Community: Selected Essays*, 213.

31. Richard McCormick, "The Moral Theology of Vatican II," in *The Future of Ethics and Moral Theology*, ed. Richard McCormick (Chicago: Argus, 1968), 12.

CHAPTER 6

Ethics for Modern Life

I T SHOULD BE apparent by now that John Paul II has articulated a
clear and convincing moral vision, centered on the transcendence of
universal human dignity. That vision will be fully realized only when
all human beings, including those in an embryonic state and those facing
imminent death, are treated with equal respect and properly recognized
for who they are and who they are capable of becoming. Underlying this
moral imperative to respect human beings because of their inalienable
dignity is John Paul II's rich conception of the human person—each individual person exists and acts as an embodied spirit, a unity of body and
soul, with an intrinsic power of self-possession.

In the past, great evils have been perpetrated due to corrupt ideologies "rooted in the history of European philosophical thought" (MI, 7).
Philosophy abandoned Christianity "as a source of philosophizing,"
and the "very possibility of attaining to God was placed in question"
(MI, 10). Some nominalist philosophers have impugned the idea of an
objectively given species or class of beings, and so they repudiate the
ontological equality that comes from the membership of each single
human person in the human species. The rejection of this metaphysical
principle along with any notion of a human soul has spawned new
philosophies supporting radical individualism and positivism. Once such
ontological equality is denied, the propagation of a "master race" philosophy or an *übermensch* (superman) mentality becomes a realistic possibility. After all, if man is not equal in this fundamental way, if each one
of us forms a unique sort of being, why couldn't one group of individuals or race of people declare itself to be superior to others based
on some arbitrary criteria? The "ideologies of evil," rooted in these

specious theories, have produced calamitous results for the world throughout the twentieth century: wars, ethnic cleansing, the Holocaust, and similar horrific tragedies (MI, 7).

As a remedy, John Paul II calls for the swift revival of the intellectual tradition of "Thomistic realism" (MI, 10). As chapter 4 revealed, Aquinas's philosophy deals with real beings and rests upon the mystery of God, who is their ground and source of goodness. Thomistic realism is equipped to answer questions such as "What accounts for the fact that many distinct individuals share a certain similarity or essential mode of existence?" Or, more simply, "Why are all human beings the same and yet different?" Through careful reasoning it unfolds the sublime metaphysical truth that all humans are equal members of the same human species thanks to the fact that they share the same essential form, which makes something *this specific kind of being* and not another. That form is the soul by which bodily matter is actualized as an active subject. Revelation confirms this philosophical insight. Genesis (1:26–27) describes how each human being is created *in the same way*, that is, in God's "image and likeness."

John Paul II's moral vision is firmly grounded in these metaphysical principles, which provide the underpinnings for his normative discussions about dignity and equal human rights. In this chapter we seek to apply that moral vision to some common moral problems and to show more concretely how it can be a formidable intellectual force for dealing with the new and more subtle "ideologies of evil" that are gaining ascendancy in areas such as bioethics. We will seek to apply John Paul II's personalistic version of natural law to several controversial moral issues and expand on our earlier discussion about human rights. Although our aim is to demonstrate how John Paul II addresses these problems using the tools of reason and revelation, we will try to highlight the special relevance of his *moral philosophy*. As we have seen, that philosophy is rooted in the personalist norm, and it is worth considering the specific obligations that follow from this norm.

We first reflect on the grave threat posed to humanity by some types of technology that officiously tamper with human nature itself. Thanks to advances in biotechnology and computer technology, the integrity of human nature is now in some jeopardy. Yet those who question this technological progress are usually branded as Luddites. Can these technologies be used in a morally proper way? Does John Paul II's exposition on morality give us the tools to make the necessary moral distinctions so that we can ascertain such a proper use? We will also consider the efficacy of John Paul II's moral framework in two areas of applied ethics: corporate responsibility and bioethics. What are the basic rights of workers in this new economy, and how can moral theology address the growing turmoil in the field of biotechnology? We will demonstrate that John Paul II's person-centered approach to morality has a definite relevance for both of these areas of concern. Finally, we briefly review John Paul II's moral teaching on marriage and family, which has been eloquently stated in several important works including *Familiaris consortio* and *Letter to Families*.

Technology and Morality in the Twenty-First Century

The German philosopher Martin Heidegger was fond of describing the contemporary culture as the epoch of technicity (*die Technik*). His notion of technicity is not to be equated with technology, however. The meaning of technicity is something more primordial: how men and women experience all beings (including themselves) as objects that can be submitted to their control.[1] According to Father William J. Richardson, technicity "is the fundamental attitude in man by which all beings, even man himself, become raw material for his . . . (self)imposing comportment with beings."[2] Modern biotechnology or computer technology is simply the latest manifestation of this attitude, which is a dangerous impediment for moral reflection. Inhabitants of this world of objects can easily become oblivious of their identity as persons or human subjects endowed with rights and dignity by the Creator.

To some extent, this problem originates in the retreat from Thomistic metaphysics and the denial of nature as good and true. When created beings, including humans, are no longer seen as intrinsically valuable, they become neutral "stuff," subject to manipulation. The innate goodness of the natural order no longer serves as a reference point for morality or a constraint on technology. Rather, nature is valued only for its usefulness. These beliefs pave the way for science's intervention in order to make improvements, to make natural beings "better off" through the wonders of technology.

John Paul II appreciated the plight of modern man in this epoch of technicity, and he clearly echoed the concerns of Heidegger in this admonition: "The danger is that while making advances in its dominion over things, humanity might be subjected to the world, becoming the slave of things" (RH, 16). Immersed in technicity and its concomitant materialism, our ear can easily be dulled to the appeals of traditional morality or God's humanizing Word.

What is increasingly worrisome is the ultimate objectification of human beings. This occurs through technologies whose aim is to transform the human body into something better or different. In this context, the human person becomes an object in the most literal sense. What better proof of our slavery to technicity than the submission of humans to experiments that tamper with the integrity of the human body and even human nature itself? For example, the mapping of the human genome poses a threat that people will be reduced to their genetic identities, which can be manipulated for good or ill. In Heideggerian terms, humanity becomes its own object.

Thus, the indiscriminate use of genetic engineering and even some forms of computer technology to enhance the human species represents a tremendous challenge for morality. What will happen if human beings one day manufacture themselves in factories? And what are the ramifications if genetic engineering succeeds in recalibrating the boundaries of our humanity and changing in a substantial way the human essence upon which the natural law is based?

Similarly problematic is the transformation of humans into "cyborgs" through the implantation of computer chips designed to enhance human capabilities. When human beings become platforms for computer applications, they become cybernetic organisms, part human and part computer. Implanted chips inserted under the skin that track the whereabouts of children or visual bionics represent examples of this evolving technology. Some of these computer implants, especially those with a therapeutic application, are welcomed advances since they can correct physiological deficiencies (such as blindness and deafness). On the other hand, some applications aim at the fusion of the robotic and the human in order to achieve greater longevity or even near immortality.

But when these technologies are deployed for such radical enhancement purposes, there should be cause for alarm. For example, when enhancement technologies instill into human beings certain virtues such as courage or impart the fruits of human accomplishment, individuality and freedom will be materially compromised. How can a semirobotic existence, perhaps a cyborg programmed to know no fear, be authentically human? We strip away from these beings the most precious possession of human self-determination, since they have no opportunity to *choose* courageous acts and thereby freely cultivate the virtue of courage. Recall from chapter 3 that personhood as self-possession included the capacity of self-determination by which we become unique individuals with different skills, talents, virtues, and traits. Through computer-based or genetic self-enhancement, however, we become products instead of persons, objects instead of subjects.

Consider also the ramifications of using technology to "enhance" human beings with traits that make them exceptionally self-sufficient. In this case there is a danger that human receptivity, the ontological complement of a being's self-communicative power, would be eradicated. Without this capability, there could be no mutual love, since it would be impossible for someone to receive love or other personal gifts. There is no giving without receiving. To be sure, the secular world might regard receptivity as an imperfection, signifying an interior lack or a need for another. But as John Paul II has repeatedly indicated, we find fulfillment as persons-in-communion, and so both giving and receiving must be positive aspects of our nature. Receptivity, therefore, must be seen as a positive ontological perfection.[3] This judgment is confirmed in the light of other Christian doctrines. Receptivity is not confined to human persons since we find it even in angelic persons and Divine Persons. Christ the Son, the second person of the Blessed Trinity, receives love from God the Father and so must possess receptivity or the capability to receive that love. But by tampering with various aspects of the human body to effect some sort of self-sufficient being, the innate receptivity of human personhood, this positive dimension of human love, could be imperiled. We see how the enhancement of people in order to overcome some purported imperfection could come at great expense—the effacement of a necessary attribute of personhood.

In some prescient remarks made many years ago, C. S. Lewis cautioned that this sort of experimentation could well mean the end of authentic human freedom:

> [A]s soon as we take the final step of reducing our species to the level of mere nature, the whole process is stultified, for this time the being who stood to gain and the being who has been sacrificed are one and the same. . . . But once our souls—that is, our selves—have

been given up, the power thus conferred will not belong to us. We shall, in fact, be the slaves and puppets of that to which we have given our souls.[4]

Regrettably, some philosophers see no problem in engineering new "boundaries" for humanity. Jane Flax applauds postmodernists who "wish to destroy all essentialist conceptions of human being or nature, [since] man is a social, historical, linguistic artifact, not a noumenal or transcendental being."[5] Her hope is that technology will liberate humans from the servitude of biology and nature, including the "servitude" of sexual identity. The question for Elaine Graham is finding a proper vision of what it means to be human in the postmodern era—how do we judge which vision "is more or less desirable, authentic, or sustainable"?[6] The implication is that human nature is now "up for grabs." The only question is how we want it to evolve. But to answer this provocative question we cannot appeal to any preconceived notion of "human nature" as a benchmark, since the notion of a shared human essence has been nullified. How then do we judge which vision for the future of man is "desirable, authentic, and sustainable"? How do we know what is authentically human if we have no idea what humanity is?

One wonders, of course, what moral standards can emerge in this void in order to help direct human nature's alleged "progress." How can we judge what is a good direction in which human beings can evolve if we no longer know what it means to be human? If ethical values are grounded in humanity and if human nature becomes unstable, the possibility for a stable morality is effectively negated. Also, as we have seen, the moral order must be grounded in the metaphysical order. As human beings, we belong to the same species with the same rational nature, allowing us to assert with confidence that *by nature all human beings are equal and deserve certain rights*. But if we are regarded merely as material "artifacts," as some transhumanists have contended, who can stop a government or institution from discrimination or from shaping those artifacts for its own political or social purposes?

The complexity of these moral problems is dizzying even to the professional ethicist. But do we find our bearings in the writings of John Paul II for how to deal with this latest aggrandizement of science? While John Paul II does not address all of these problems explicitly, he does offer important admonitions about the adoption and deployment of technology. First, his whole moral philosophy, epitomized in the personalist norm, is oriented toward rejecting the objectification of human beings whether this happens in the sexual sphere or in the laboratory. Such objectification, whether it takes the form of lustful or technological manipulation, violates the dignity of the person as embodied spirit who deserves to be treated always as a thinking and free subject, and never as an object. According to the late Holy Father, "when the human body . . . comes to be used as *raw material* in the same way that the bodies of animals are used—and this actually happens for example in experimentation on embryos and fetuses—we will inevitably arrive at a dreadful ethical defeat" (LFam, 19).

Second, society must be wary of technology and use it wisely and prudently. Sometimes infatuation with science and technology induces us to assume that technological innovation is inherently beneficial. We place our faith in technology's ability to solve humanity's problems. We hope that technology can eliminate poverty and hunger, and maybe one day abolish our mortality. Thus, we idealize technology and rarely challenge it. It is highly imprudent, however, to promote or support technological innovation without careful ethical reflection. That reflection must ponder the harm and risk of harm associated with any form of technological progress.

Ethics, properly practiced, must always take precedence over technology, which should never be used to compromise the transcendent dignity of the human person. John Paul II clearly enunciates this principle: "Scientific and technical progress, whatever it be, must then maintain the greatest respect for the moral values that constitute a safeguard for the dignity of the human person." And yet "the development of moral ethics seems not to keep in step with the progress of technology" (RH, 15). Elsewhere in the same encyclical, *Redemptor Hominis*, he articulates an unambiguous benchmark for directing science and technology. While man rightly perceives his *dominion* over nature, he cannot take it upon himself to *dominate* the earth through sheer willpower and logic such that all beings (including himself) become raw material for his projects. On the contrary, man must never forget his proper place as a being created by God with a constant human nature that orients him to understand the priorities of the Creator. According to John Paul II, "The essential meaning of this 'kingship' and 'dominion' of man over the visible world, which the Creator himself gave man for his task, consists in the priority of ethics over technology, in the primacy of the person over things, and in the superiority of spirit over matter" (RH, 16). The message is clear: human beings must never allow themselves to be subservient to the forces of technology. Rather, technology must serve the aims and values of humanity and support those fundamental human goods that enable human beings to flourish.

Obviously, the principles articulated in *Redemptor Hominis* are consistent with John Paul II's dignitarian humanism, which absolutizes human dignity and the need to regard each human being as an end. Human beings have intrinsic worth and equal dignity, which means that they cannot be treated in an instrumental fashion. But transforming human beings into "products" or cybernetic creatures designed to be fearless or to excel in mathematics contaminates the human essence by taking away a person's dominion over himself or herself as *dominus sui*. We compromise the person's capacity for self-determination—the acting person is constrained and programmed to act in certain ways, and so does not truly create himself or herself. This direct interference with our freedom can only be construed as an attack aimed at the core of personhood.

Early on in his papacy, John Paul II singled out genetic manipulation for moral scrutiny. In an address to the World Medical Association in 1983, he expressed concern about whether this practice, which appeared on the distant horizon at that time, could be reconciled with the innate dignity of humanity. John Paul II argued that science must respect humanity's biological nature and appreciate that changes to the body deeply affect the whole person. There is a biological basis to our common humanity, since we are all embodied spirits. A dualistic framework must be rejected for the reasons we articulated in chapter 3. Hence science must steadfastly "avoid manipulations that tend to modify genetic inheritance and to create groups of different men at the risk of causing new cases of marginalization in society."[7] Such manipulation is a manifestation of technology's hubris as it refuses to cede authority over created beings to their Creator. In John Paul II's words, it "exposes the individual to the caprice of others."[8]

However, John Paul II did not oppose "a strictly therapeutic intervention" whose aim is "the healing of maladies" that originate in defective genes. Such intervention is acceptable so long as "it is directed to the true promotion of the personal well being of man."[9] With these remarks, Pope John Paul II seemed to be joining many other ethicists who embrace this distinction between therapy and enhancement as a key basis for moral decision making about genetic manipulation.

Although John Paul II does not address the phenomenon of cyborgs, the therapy/enhancement distinction can also serve as a principle for how to curtail unnecessary computer implants. Like genetic manipulation, computer implants that endow individuals with freakish powers would tamper with our biological nature, which should remain "untouchable." The deployment of these cybernetic devices is incompatible with John Paul II's metaphysical anthropology, which regards embodiment as an essential feature of humanity, not as an accident or a temporary phase of the evolutionary process. Moreover, the human body has been created by God in a certain way in order to enable the intellectual powers of the soul. The human body is not simply an artificial "prosthesis" to be replaced or improved upon with other prostheses as if they were just "natural extensions" of the human self.[10] As John Paul II remarks, "the biological nature of each person is untouchable,"[11] so radical enhancement or alteration of natural bodily functions is proscribed. But repairing those natural functions by fixing a defective gene or by the use of nanotechnology is morally acceptable. A bionic eye that restores one's vision is fine, but an implant that gives someone infrared vision cannot be justified according to this line of reasoning.

Critics argue that the therapy-enhancement dichotomy is unclear since it can be difficult sometimes to distinguish between therapy and enhancement. There may be some merit to this objection, but Dr. Hook offers a reasonable guideline for drawing this distinction: "allow as healing that which may return a given function to a level normal for the species, not to exceed the capability of the fittest members of the species, trained in the most rigorous fashion."[12] A much more problematic objection voiced by some ethicists is that abiding by this rule imposes an arbitrary limit on our freedom. After all, they contend, why not give people the freedom to experiment with their bodies, to transform themselves into freakish, cybernetic creatures if they freely and willingly submit to those experiments? But the freedom argument would have little merit for John Paul II. As he has been at pains to insist, freedom is always limited by the good, which includes the good of one's bodily integrity, our distinctive biological nature, and our essential capabilities. No one should presume the freedom to tamper with the human body or to change the boundaries of humanity in the name of science. Scientists who see themselves as "gods" overlook technology's potential to sow the seeds for human calamity.

John Paul II has often spoken about the "great mystery" of man, who "with regard to his deepest, metaphysical dimension . . . remains to a great extent a being unknown to himself" (LFam, 19). But modern rationalism and science "does not tolerate mystery" and aims to overcome it whenever possible (LFam, 19). Instead of accepting the mystery of human development, some scientists adopt the following attitude: why not transform John and Jane into intelligent and self-sufficient individuals, rather than wait to see how they develop through their own God-given talents and free decisions? Once we lose sight of God, a God who calls us to share in the "great mystery" of life, we fear our own freedom. We would rather confine human possibility and live in conformity than face an uncertain future.

The key insight that should guide this discussion is that human nature for John Paul II is not arbitrary or contingent. Human nature, man as embodied spirit, is unalterable, and hence technologies that alter nature must be strenuously resisted. The prospect of "human self-design" should frighten all sensible persons even if they do not believe in a Divine Creator. Hence the need to limit forms of genetic manipulation or the embedding of certain types of computer transplants that will alter human nature, perhaps even in a substantial or irrevocable way. Once our distinct human identity is engineered out of existence, it will be impossible to safeguard any semblance of human dignity. Beyond any doubt, human self-design is an affront to John Paul II's philosophy of dignitarian humanism. All human beings must realize that their ultimate destiny does not lie in the illogical technological imperative, or technological progress for its own sake, but in authentic human flourishing and openness to the "great mystery" of God and human existence.

Dignitarian Humanism in the Workplace

One of John Paul II's earliest encyclicals, *Laborem Exercens*, was devoted to the theme of labor. John Paul II asserts here that if we want to appreciate the value of work and its importance in human life, we should turn once again to the opening chapters of Genesis:

> Work means any activity by man, whether manual or intellectual,
> whatever its nature or circumstances; it means any human activity
> that can and must be recognized as work, in the midst of all the
> many activities of which man is capable. . . . Man is made to be in
> the visible universe an image and likeness of God himself (Gen.
> 1:26), and he is placed in it in order to subdue the earth (Gen. 1:28).
> From the beginning therefore he is *called to work*. (LE, Preface)

Work is a mandate from God to subdue the earth and to cooperate with God's divine action.

In that same encyclical John Paul II argued for the priority of labor over capital: "human work comes before what we have begun to call capital" (LE, 12). Capital in this context represents the means of production, including the world's natural resources given to us by God along with the tools and implements constructed by previous labor. Unfortunately, the economic system of capitalism tends to value things produced by human labor more than the laborers themselves.

The full meaning of John Paul II's conception of work cannot be resolved here. But let it suffice to say that John Paul II was not expressing some thinly disguised Marxist view of labor. Rather, he was stipulating that labor, the cooperative activity of managers and workers, has objective priority because it entails personal dignity. Capital, on the other hand, has only the limited value that we assign to material objects. Human workers have a dignity that machines and other forms of capital can never have.

Work, therefore, has a moral purpose "linked to the fact that the one who carries it out is a person, a conscious and free subject, that is to say a subject that decides about himself" (LE, 6). Work is human action that affects not only the world but also the individual worker. The acting person shapes himself or herself through work. Accordingly, we must "recognize the pre-eminence of the subjective meaning of work over the objective one" (LE, 6). It is always "man who is the purpose of the work" (LE, 6). Labor's external effects, such as the tilling of land or the construction of a building, are far less important than the way labor affects the development and self-realization of the worker. Thus, the dignity of work is to be found in its subjective dimension, that is, within the worker rather than the objects produced by the worker.

If we fail to appreciate the priority of human labor, we fall into the trap of "economism" or "practical materialism," whereby the worker is treated not as the "subject of work" but as "just another factor in production . . . a mere tool" (LE, 13). But for John Paul II, the priority of labor over capital, along with the preeminence accorded to the subjective meaning of work, has moral and social justice implications that are spelled out in the encyclical. Above all, the worker is entitled to certain fundamental rights. Also, in light of this analysis it becomes necessary to reevaluate certain economic issues such as the nature of ownership and the suitability of economic systems such as capitalism.

John Paul II's treatment of these questions is not confined to *Laborem Exercens*. It is taken up again in two other encyclicals devoted to social issues: *Sollicitudo Rei Socialis* and *Centesimus Annus*. In both of these encyclicals he builds on the themes of *Laborem Exercens* but with even greater focus on worker rights. Also, *Centesimus Annus* directly addresses the moral character of capitalism. John Paul II endorsed a "free economy," an economic system "which recognizes the fundamental and positive role of business, the market, private property and the resulting responsibility for the means of production, as well as free human creativity in the economic sector" (CA, 42). While we cannot consider the nuances of Pope John Paul II's social teaching, we will examine in more depth two issues: what are the most prominent worker rights that logically follow from John Paul II's views on labor, and can the insights in these encyclicals form the basis for a tenable ethic of corporate social responsibility?

Worker Rights

The moral priority of labor over capital, the notion that humans are always the source and purpose of work, along with the general dignity of the human person, clearly imply that workers are entitled to certain basic human rights. John Paul II contends that the commitment to the "development of the whole person . . . implies and presupposes a lively awareness of the rights of all and of each person, the right to life at every stage of existence, the rights of the family as the basic social community, *justice in labor relations*, political rights and religious freedom" (SRS, 32–33; my emphasis).

According to John Paul II, in the economic sphere these rights should include just pay and decent working conditions, including "humane working hours and adequate free time to be guaranteed, as well as the right to express one's personality at the work-place without suffering any affront to one's conscience or personal dignity" (CA, 15). Chapter 4 reinforced that worker rights also include the right to strike as a last resort. Workers should also have the right to share in the responsibility and creativity of the work process, and they should be assured some degree of autonomy so that the individual worker does not become "a cog" within some impersonal, bureaucratic apparatus. These rights logically follow from the "primacy of the person over things" (LE, 13). John Paul singles out the moral right to a just wage in many of his writings. He writes that "the justice of a social and economic system is finally measured by the way in which a person's work is rewarded" (LE, 19). He explains in *Laborem Exercens* that "the just wage for an adult responsible for a family is one that allows for the establishment of a family, its proper maintenance, and provision for the security of its future" (LE, 19). Elsewhere a just wage is defined as the right to a wage "sufficient to support [the worker], his wife, and his children" (CA, 8).

In this era of globalization, the overriding importance of this issue of just remuneration for work cannot be denied. The problem of a just wage most often arises when companies determine salaries and working condition for their laborers in developing countries. In many situations, companies will pay market wages, which barely allow for the subsistence of one person, let alone a whole family. A case in point:

> Employees of a maquiladora in Ciudad Acuna, Mexico, owned by the Aluminum Company of America (Alcoa), calculated that to buy the most basic food items needed by a factory worker—items such as beans, tortilla, rice, potatoes, onions, and cooking oil, and excluding such "luxuries" as milk, meat, vegetables, and cereal—cost U.S. $26.78 per week. At the time, weekly wages at the plant ranged only from $21.44 to $24.60.[13]

This company did not pay a just wage. Rather, it treated work as a mere commodity to be purchased at the lowest cost possible. There was no moral priority given to labor, which was callously regarded as "just another factor of production" (LE, 13).

According to the personalist norm, however, a corporation would be morally responsible only if the humanity of its employees was treated as an end and never as a mere means. Treating the worker as an end, not just as a material *means* of production, requires acknowledging and honoring that worker's self-respect. In the workplace, self-respect is honored primarily through the wages paid to employees. Those wages should always reflect a fair and reasonable reward for the work performed. At the same time, treating the worker as an end means taking into account his or her material well-being along with the well-being of the family members he or she supports, since their well-being depends upon those wages. Hence, responsible corporations cannot be indifferent to a worker's self-respect or to his or her physical welfare. At a minimum, they must provide their workers with a living wage as defined by John Paul II, even if the labor markets in a particular industry price labor below the living wage level. Markets fail, and sometimes they embody certain structural injustices. Thus, just because the market permits unjust labor practices and rock-bottom wages, companies should not blindly accept this outcome. If corporations like Alcoa refuse to pay a just, living wage that covers the basic cost of food, clothing, and shelter, they are exploiting their workers as tools (or means) and not treating them as fellow human beings (ends) deserving of the highest respect. When a viable corporation refuses to pay a just, living wage, it transgresses the personalist norm.

Critics have rightly condemned the proliferation of unjust labor practices thanks to transnational companies that operate throughout the world. Those practices have led to strident protest and discord. Many of these protesters condemn globalization as an example of unbridled Western capitalism and as an oppressive and impoverishing force. We cannot enter into this heated debate about the benefits and harms of globalization and economic integration. But it seems safe to conclude that while globalization is not inherently sinister, transnational companies cannot simply regard their overseas operations as incremental markets and convenient sources of low-cost labor. They must instead come to see all their laborers as deserving of the rights delineated by the late Holy Father, most particularly the right to a just wage and a decent work environment. And they must appreciate that the interdependence that makes globalization possible has a moral character that John Paul II refers to as "solidarity." Hence these corporations have a responsibility to support laborers and other stakeholders in their networks of productivity through just practices.

In *Sollicitudo Rei Socialis* John Paul II devotes attention to another right of all workers that is implied in his view of labor: the right of economic initiative. According to the late Holy Father,

It should be noted that in today's world, among other rights, *the right of economic initiative* is often suppressed. Yet it is a right which is important not only for the individual but also for the common good. Experience shows us that the denial of this right, or its limitation in the name of an alleged "equality" of everyone in society, diminishes, or in practice absolutely destroys the spirit of initiative, that is to say the *creative subjectivity of the citizen.* As a consequence, there arises not so much a true equality as a "leveling down." In the place of creative initiative there appears passivity, dependence and submission to the bureaucratic apparatus. (SRS, 15)

John Paul II is criticizing forms of socialism that deny such initiative by organizing the whole economy in a way that deprives individuals of any economic freedom. Such systems, moreover, tend to spawn repressive bureaucracies. This right of economic initiative follows from John Paul II's views that through the activity of labor people realize themselves as acting subjects. Therefore people should have the right to choose the work they prefer, to be entrepreneurs if they believe that this is how they should carry out God's command to "subdue" the earth (Gen. 1:28). Each person should have the right to choose *how* he or she will achieve self-realization through the intrinsically valuable activity of work. If we deny this right, we stand in the way of the "creative subjectivity" of the worker. As a result, instead of initiative and energy, there will be inertia and passivity.

The Socially Responsible Corporation

In *Veritatis Splendor* John Paul II postulates that respect for human dignity requires the cultivation and practice of three virtues in economic affairs: temperance, justice, and solidarity (VS, 100). He quotes the *Catechism of the Catholic Church*, which explains these virtues in more detail:

In economic matters, respect for human dignity requires the practice of the virtue of temperance, to moderate our attachment to the goods of this world; of the virtue of justice, to preserve our neighbor's rights and to render what is his or her due; and of solidarity, following the Golden Rule in keeping with the generosity of the Lord.[14]

John Paul II goes on to cite theft, fraud, unjust wages, and excessively high prices as examples of economic activities "contrary to human dignity" (VS, 100).

While John Paul II has in mind individuals who must abide by the virtues of temperance, justice, and solidarity, we could also claim with some plausibility that corporations should possess these virtues as well. Corporate activities too should manifest the virtues of moderation, justice (or fairness), and solidarity. The basis for this claim lies in John Paul II's argument that "subjectivity" is not confined to individual persons. We find it also at the level of communities or voluntary associations. Subjectivity expresses itself in those associations "including economic, social, political and cultural groups which stem from human nature itself and have their own autonomy" (CA, 13). The corporation, then, as a "voluntary association," is a subject with its own autonomy. As a subject, it has moral responsibility for the impact of its activities on others, and it deserves to be treated with respect by others.

Thus, it is logical to claim that justice, solidarity, and temperance are corporate virtues as well as individual ones. If practiced, they will instill in corporations respect for the basic human goods that natural law requires us to preserve and pursue. The virtue of justice, for example, demands respect for the good of knowledge, and it forbids exploiting a buyer's ignorance when there is an asymmetry of information in a business transaction whereby the seller knows much more than the buyer. In chapter 4 we discussed the principal role of solidarity in John Paul II's moral vision. Solidarity is a "determination to commit oneself to the common good"; it is "squarely opposed to greed and the thirst for power" (SRS, 38). By fostering solidarity, corporations can come to realize that their interests cannot be disengaged from the interests of their stakeholders and the global community. As the *Catechism* suggests, solidarity is equivalent to acting in accordance with the Golden Rule by treating others as you would like to be treated.

We cannot explore the many forms of corporate misbehavior that have been rampant in the past several decades, but let's single out one problem that will exhibit the relevance of the virtues of solidarity and temperance. Far too many corporations operating within the capitalist framework have manifested a lack of temperance, an inability to moderate their behavior. Capitalism is predicated on the principle of self-interest, as its intellectual founder, Adam Smith, has reminded us: "It is not from the benevolence of the butcher, the brewer, or the baker that we expect our dinner, but from their regard to their own interest." Yet, Smith goes on, "by pursuing his own interest [man] frequently promotes that of society more effectually than he really intends to promote it."[15] The challenge is to curb that self-interest so it does not lead to excess without suppressing the individual initiative that is at the wellspring of capitalism.

Corporations, for example, sometimes go to extremes in the quest for profits by engaging in fraud or unfair competition. The tendency is to see competition in bellicose terms according to which one's rival is the "enemy." Business textbooks frequently refer to the ongoing "cola wars" between Coke and Pepsi or the "postal wars" between FedEx and UPS. Embattled companies believe that in order to overcome the "enemy," wide latitude must be given for aggressive strategies and predatory tactics that will ensure success at almost any cost.

But if companies aspire to be socially responsible, they must make every effort to behave ethically, and that means respect for basic human goods and for virtues such as temperance and solidarity. Solidarity in this context implies that companies must compete fairly or positively, that is, they must engage in competition without negativity. At a minimum, they must respect the basic "rules of the game" without which there could be no competition. Negative competition that breaks those rules undermines trust, erodes the bonds of community, and hence impairs solidarity. Also, when competition turns ruthless, it often becomes exploitive of others. Thus, a corporation's competitive efforts must be based purely on the merits of its products or services. This norm of *positive competition* precludes sabotage and related activities that subvert a competitor's efforts to sell its goods in the marketplace.[16] Attacks on reputation, exclusionary deals, theft of trade secrets, retaliation against those who deal with one's competitors—these are all examples of such subversion.

This norm is clearly compatible with the natural law principles and the Golden Rule, since no reasonable company would want its operations to be unjustly sabotaged by one of its competitors. As we have seen, in John Paul II's estimation, the corporation is a subject, a voluntary association and an embodiment of the basic human good of community. Hence a deliberate and calculated effort to drive a corporation out of business represents the destruction of the good of community and cannot be justified. When that happens, there is likely to be substantial injury to key stakeholder groups such as suppliers, employees, customers, and share-holders. But if a company aspires to "positive competition," its intention is to win in the marketplace by providing a superior product at a low price. If my product prevails in a fair contest, rivals might be eliminated, but this is a side effect of my success and it is not the intention of my actions. Such a strategy is different from one that predatorily causes the elimination of competitors. Corporations with organizational integrity, endowed with the virtues of temperance and solidarity, will respect this norm of positive competition and avoid excessive behavior.[17]

It should be evident that one can find in the moral philosophy of John Paul II the seeds of a coherent model of corporate social responsibility. The natural law framework linked with the antiutilitarian personalist norm, mandating that all human beings be treated as an end and never only as a means, can easily serve as a reliable moral compass for today's managers. This approach should have a privileged place in ethical decision making in corporate America. A business ethic predicated on acknowledgment of the basic human goods and the Kantian obligation to respect the transcendent dignity of the person provides a clear focal point for moral judgment.

Second, a business ethic consonant with John Paul II's moral vision would also stress the primacy of labor and unconditional rights for the worker such as the right to a just wage and decent working conditions. It will not support exploitation of workers or their treatment as just another "factor of production."

Third, the responsible corporation will endorse the consistent and conscientious practice of three key virtues: moderation, justice or fairness, and solidarity. Solidarity is of special importance because it encourages corporations not to lose sight of the communitarian nature of the human person and what Martin Luther King Jr. called the "inescapable network of mutuality."[18]

Thus, John Paul II, the moral philosopher, presents a viable approach to moral problems that surface in the corporate realm based on the standard of dignitarian humanism or the personalist norm. This norm, supported by the principles of the natural law, is centered on the interconnected ideas of *personal dignity* and *communal solidarity*. It can certainly provide a firm grounding for a corporate ethic that will be far superior to the framework of utilitarianism. Many corporations and managers either pay scant attention to ethical concerns or rely exclusively on utilitarian reasoning, despite its many deficiencies. As we have seen, utilitarianism is flawed due to its impracticality and its insensitivity to justice and human rights issues. Also, as John Paul II makes clear, utilitarianism "ignores the first and fundamental dimension of good, that of the *bonum honestum*" (MI, 35). But from the richness of John Paul II's writings, we can disengage a methodology for applied ethics based on the personalist norm supported by the intrinsic goods of the natural law. This distinct moral perspective avoids the liabilities of utilitarianism and the incompleteness of Kant's single deontological standard.

Bioethics and Human Dignity

Developments in biotechnology and health science have thrown into disrepute traditional approaches to medical ethics compliant with the Hippocratic oath. As the Holy Father reminded us, that oath "requires every doctor to commit himself to absolute respect for human life and its sacredness" (EV, 89). And yet in the "culture of death," health-care professionals "are strongly tempted at times to become manipulators of life, or even agents of death" (EV, 89).

John Paul II was deeply concerned about these pivotal issues and hence wrote an entire encyclical, *Evangelium Vitae*, dedicated to the topic of life. The fundamental problem is that the incomparable worth of the human person is no longer recognized. This is due to philosophical confusion and false assumptions about the nature of the human person. We have already addressed in depth John Paul II's views on anthropology, which can go a long way to clarifying some of this confusion. But, anthropological issues aside, the problem of lack of respect for life is an acute one for many reasons. John Paul II voiced apprehension regarding a "new cultural climate," one that "gives crimes against life *a new and—if possible—even more sinister character*" (EV, 4).

As proof, consider recent events in the Netherlands. This country has become notorious for its practice of euthanasia. In 2005 the Groningen Protocol was introduced. This law would essentially legalize infanticide in cases of disability. The law permits the killing of a newborn baby under certain conditions, "including whether the child would be able to live independently, experience self-realization (being able to hear, read, write, labor) and have meaningful interpersonal relations."[19] Even in other countries such as the United States there has been a subtle undercurrent of approbation for this insidious practice. There have also been discussions in prestigious medical journals offering muted praise for those involved in the effort to develop norms for infanticide.

This protocol, along with many other similar initiatives, affirms John Paul II's concern about the diffusion of a new "Promethean attitude" that encourages people to assume "that they can control life and death by taking decisions about them into their own hands" (EV, 15). Hence the need for unambiguous moral teaching that will address these threats to life and expose the invalid arguments put forth to justify abortion, infanticide, and other acts of violence against humanity.

As we discussed in chapter 4, the right to life is the most fundamental of all rights. John Paul II is at pains to insist that "life is always a good" (EV, 34). Why? There are many reasons, but the foremost is that "in man there shines forth a reflection of God Himself" (EV, 34). And the sanctity of life as a gift from God and bearing the image of God "gives rise to its inviolability written from the beginning in man's heart" (EV, 40). John Paul II was committed to the defense of every life, and he spoke frequently about the evil of abortion: "the legalization of the termination of pregnancy is none other than the authorization given to an adult, with the approval of an established law, to take the lives of children yet unborn and thus incapable of defending themselves" (CTH, 205).

This inviolability of the right to human life and the unity of the human person as an embodied spirit (as discussed in chapter 3) are perhaps the most important premises for a bioethic based on John Paul II's moral theology. Bioethics is a vast and complex area of study, so we cannot provide an in-depth analysis of all the main hot-button issues. Instead, we must be more selective, so we will focus on two representative issues that involve the sanctity of life: therapeutic cloning for embryonic stem cell research and euthanasia.

Embryonic Stem Cell Research

At the time of John Paul II's death in April 2005, the debate over embryonic stem cell research was reaching a fever pitch in countries like the United States. Despite opposition from the Catholic Church, California voters passed Proposition 71, which both legalized and funded cloning for this type of research. States like Massachusetts and New Jersey have passed similar legislation that endorses research methods involving the cloning of human embryos for the purpose of embryonic stem cell research. The architect of this legislation in Massachusetts, Senate President Robert Travaglini, said that he hoped the new law would "send a very clear message that we are serious about removing the cloud over this type of research."[20]

But should this cloud be removed? Is this type of research as benign or morally neutral as its supporters claim? In order to appreciate the ethical nuances of this debate, it is first necessary to review some basic elements of biology. Cells are the building blocks of each person's body. While most cells are specialized (for example, skin cells), stem cells are undifferentiated, that is, they have the capacity to become any kind of cell, such as a brain cell, a skin cell, or a bone cell. These undifferentiated stem cells are found in a blastocyst, which is a one- or two-week-old embryo. But those stem cells can only be obtained by disaggregating the embryo. The hope is to use these stem cells as the basis for cures for certain degenerative diseases, such as multiple sclerosis or Parkinson's disease. It should be pointed out that adults also have a supply of stem cells, but adult stem cell research is considered ethically acceptable and is not the bone of contention in this debate.

The moral difficulty with embryonic stem cell research is twofold. The first problem is the need to clone embryos so there is an adequate supply for the treatment of these degenerative diseases. The cloning of human beings for such purposes, a process sometimes referred to as therapeutic cloning, is disrespectful of human life, which is brought into existence as a product. When human beings are produced for the express purpose of harvesting their body parts, human life is commoditized and human dignity is grotesquely compromised.

The second problem, of course, is the need to destroy the human embryo (produced through fertilization or cloning) in order to obtain the stem cells. Predictably, proponents of this research see no problem with this action since they consider the human embryo to be a clump of cells rather than a human being. But there is something desperately wrong with this way of thinking. Human life begins upon conception or, in the case of asexual reproduction, "upon the activation by an electrical charge of an egg cell from which the original nucleus has been replaced by one taken from a 'somatic' or body cell."[21] From that moment we have a human being with the intrinsic power to achieve the self-possession characteristic of personhood. This human being has the capability *within itself* to direct its own integral functioning and its evolution into full person-hood. This embryo's nature as a human being is determined from the moment it came to be, and it will never change. According to John Paul II, "from the first instant there is established the program of what this living being will be: a person, this individual person with his characteristic aspects already well determined" (EV, 60).

One counterargument, proposed by some dissenting moral theologians, is based on the claim that an embryo younger than two weeks (before implantation in the uterus) is actually nothing more than a "pre-embryo," without the moral status of being a human embryo.[22] The mainstream media disingenuously refers to this incipient human being as a "precursor" to the embryo. These terms, however, are quite misleading, because in the world of biology there is no such thing as a pre-embryo. If one consults a standard textbook, such as *Human Embryology and Teratology*, one finds that the authors categorically reject this terminology because it is "ill-defined," "inaccurate," and "unjustified," since "the accepted meaning of the word embryo includes all of the first 8 weeks."[23] Even the youngest embryo has the unity, identity, and uniqueness of a human person. Professor Jerome Lejeune, a geneticist at the University of Paris, testified to this same conclusion before the Louisiana state legislature: "Each of us has a very precise starting moment, which is at the time at which the whole necessary and sufficient genetic information is gathered inside one cell, the fertilized egg, and this moment is the moment of fertilization. We know that this information is written on a kind of ribbon which we call DNA."[24] That fertilized egg or embryo can propel itself into full being and selfhood if no one interferes with its development process.

Many in the scientific community acknowledge the commonsense fact that the one- or two-week-old embryo, which will be destroyed for its cells, is a living human being in the earliest stages of its existence, capable of becoming a loving, thinking, and willing person. It is no surprise therefore that John Paul II condemns this practice in the strongest moral terms: "the use of human embryos or fetuses as an object of experimentation constitutes a crime against their dignity as human beings who have a right to the same respect owed to a child once born, just as to every person" (EV, 63). Once again, it seems, thanks to science that makes pawns of human beings in the first stages of life, we have technicity in full bloom.

The critical moral issues at stake here are the moral status of the embryo and the basic good of human life at each stage of existence. If we are to accord *all* human beings dignity, we cannot deny that dignity to those in the first two weeks of their existence by allowing these individuals to be used for spare parts and then be casually destroyed. As chapter 3 reiterated, all human beings share in the same common human nature, and so each one deserves to be treated with equal respect from the moment of conception. If medical textbooks describe an embryo in morally neutral terms as a human being, then it belongs to the human species and should be treated accordingly. That embryo is a human person in its incipient stages of development from active potency toward actual "self-possession." Human life is continuous from the first moment of the embryo's existence until death. It is impossible to pick a point on that continuum where life begins to assume value and worth without being completely arbitrary. Thus, the destruction of the human embryo for the purpose of research cannot be morally justified. It continues the "conspiracy against life," which has progressed without interruption for the past several decades (EV, 12).

It follows that the recommended fourteen-day cutoff point is a purely arbitrary one, even though the claim is made that "life begins at implantation" (on the uterus), which typically takes place about ten days after fertilization. But there is no essential difference between a one-week-old embryo and a one-month-old embryo. Although implantation provides a safer environment for the embryo, it does not change its rational nature. Life begins at conception, and conception begins at the time of fertilization, as science affirms. One wonders, of course, how long the fourteen-day cutoff point codified in states like Massachusetts would last if researchers determined that it would be beneficial to extend that period. If harvesting body parts from older embryos or fetuses might yield a rich research harvest, why not do so if there is even a modest hope of a "therapeutic" payoff? Once the principle of respect for human life is compromised, we always seem to find ourselves on a slippery slope where it becomes increasingly difficult to find the breaking point, particularly as people become gradually desensitized and convinced that the potential therapeutic benefits far outweigh the costs. As a result, embryonic research will most likely proliferate into more serious abuses than the exploitation of two-week-old embryos.

The moral wrongdoing in the act of disaggregating a one- or two-week-old embryo for its body parts or stem cells is the destruction of the intrinsic good of life for utilitarian reasons. There is never a sufficient reason to destroy innocent human life, no matter what the outcome. Such destruction violates the personalist norm because it treats a human being as a mere means to an ulterior end. It also violates the Pauline principle, which states that we cannot choose evil or unjust means for the sake of a good end. In this case, we cannot choose the unjust means of destroying an embryo even for a worthy objective such as scientific research. As we noted, at the core of John Paul II's humanistic philosophy is the principle that "life is always a good, even the life of a one or two week old embryo" (EV, 34). Moreover, the late Holy Father cites passages from both the Old and New Testaments to confirm "the indisputable recognition of the value of life from its very beginning" (EV, 45).

Lamentably, advocates of embryonic stem cell research, who usually ignore the promising developments in adult stem cell research, fall under the seductive spell of unadulterated utilitarian reasoning, which gives precedence to efficiency over absolute rights. They are willing to tolerate the destruction of incipient life for the sake of technological progress, with only the vaguest sense of the full consequences of such a decision, which can hardly be foreseen or calculated accurately. In *Fides et Ratio* John Paul II referred to the moral myopia of modern science: "lacking any ethical reference point, certain scientists are in danger of losing the human person as the center of their concerns" (FR, 46). The rush to therapeutic cloning, the creation and destruction of human life, as a means of furthering research is further evidence of this mentality.

But John Paul II's "gospel of life" stands firm as a bulwark against the continuing encroachment of unreflective and amoral science on the intrinsic goodness of life. That gospel reminds us that every person at whatever stage of his or her development is imprinted with the image of God. Thanks to this message, the debate over embryonic stem cell research will rage on, and the cloud engulfing this research will not soon disappear, no matter what the politicians say.

Euthanasia and Physician-Assisted Suicide

It is not surprising that the "culture of death" warmly embraces the prospect of euthanasia and physician-assisted suicide. Those who favor the legalization of euthanasia typically base their moral justification on broad autonomy rights. They contend that those individuals who are in the throes of death or who suffer from a debilitating terminal illness should have the prerogative to hasten their own death, to die with "dignity," that is, on their own terms. Once again, presumably out of respect for autonomy, the Dutch have been in the forefront of recognizing this so-called right.

John Paul II defines euthanasia "as an action or omission which of itself and by intention causes death, with the purpose of eliminating all suffering" (EV, 65). What is most important for classifying an action as "euthanasia" is "intention of the will" and the methods used (EV, 65).

Many scholars in the legal community, such as Ronald Dworkin, advocate legalization of euthanasia as long as this is done with care and balance. According to Dworkin, "once we understand that legalizing no euthanasia is itself harmful to many people . . . we realize that doing our best to draw and maintain a defensible line . . . is better than abandoning these people altogether."[25] We must overcome, he goes on to say, a tyrannical law that criminalizes merciful behavior of doctors toward dying patients.

But, like embryonic stem cell research, euthanasia and physician-assisted suicide cannot be morally acceptable, since the act of choosing or willing the death of a person is equivalent to the direct destruction of the fundamental good of human life, even if the ultimate purpose (alleviation of pain) appears to be worthwhile. Both Sacred Scripture and natural law confirm that innocent human life cannot be destroyed for any reason.

All reasonable people are sympathetic to the pain of someone struggling through his or her last days with cancer or some other type of debilitating illness. The impulse to bring an end to this suffering is understandable. But even when motives are unselfish, euthanasia represents a "false mercy, and indeed a disturbing 'perversion' of mercy" (EV, 66). On the contrary, according to John Paul II, "true 'compassion' leads to sharing another's pain; it does not kill the person whose suffering we cannot bear" (EV, 66). Thus, euthanasia is another bad means to a good end, the termination of someone's suffering.

As discussed in chapter 4, natural law and revelation converge on the same specific moral absolute: "the direct and voluntary killing of an innocent human being is always gravely immoral" (EV, 57). There is *never* a sufficient reason to actively participate in the destruction of a human being's life. This does not imply that doctors should ignore the suffering of terminally ill patients. Rather, they must aggressively treat the pain to minimize suffering. Occasionally, the problem of pain may be utterly intractable. But this problem is far more rare than proponents of euthanasia admit. John Finnis cites the work of Oxford doctors who present evidence that "the proportion of such cases where mastery of pain is difficult for skillful practitioners is of the order of 1%."[26]

Some may object that aggressive pain killing will eventually cause death, so why not permit euthanasia in the first place? But, unlike John Paul II, they fail to see the proximate end of what is being willed, the alleviation of pain. There is a substantial moral difference between administering drugs with the intention of alleviating pain and giving someone a lethal injection with the intention of deliberately ending that person's life. As John Paul II underscored in *Veritatis Splendor*, a moral act is measured by what one wills or the object of that act freely chosen. For example, there is no problem when the end intended is the suppression of severe pain and the means is a heavy dose of painkillers even if one foresees the likely consequences of a more imminent death. According to John Paul II, "it is licit to relieve pain by narcotics, even when the result is a decreased consciousness and a shortening of life; in such a case, death is not willed or sought" (EV, 65). Nor is there any need to keep a dying person alive by extraordinary means. These distinctions between euthanasia and the forgoing of disproportionate means of treatment are quite pertinent, yet they are often glossed over or dismissed in legal arguments justifying a "right to die."

Proponents of euthanasia often argue that human life is not always a good for those who are terminally ill, especially if they are semiconscious or in an altered mental state. For example, let's suppose that Jill's father is a victim of Alzheimer's disease. He also has physical ailments that confine him to a hospital bed. His condition steadily worsens to the point where Jill says, "That's not my father!" She reasons that while it's wrong to kill a person, this individual in the hospital bed is no longer the father she once knew, no longer an authentic person. Rather, he is a suffering human organism engulfed in dementia. What would be so wrong with ending his pitiful existence? If only euthanasia were legal, Jill concludes, she could prevail upon the doctors to put her father out of his misery.

But this reasoning is predicated on a dualistic anthropology, rejected by John Paul II (see chapter 3). As Patrick Lee explains, if Jill's father is not the human organism sitting in that hospital bed, "then he must be either a spiritual subject somehow associated with a human organism, or a series of experiences—a nonsubstantial consciousness sustained or embodied somehow in this organism during certain stages of existence."[27] The problem, therefore, with Jill's rationalization for euthanasia is that it implicitly denies that we are essentially corporeal beings. It assumes that the person is a conscious "I," but when that conscious "I" is no longer functioning, what remains is an empty shell, a personless organism. According to John Paul II, "the body is no longer perceived as a properly personal reality, . . . [but] is reduced to pure materiality" (EV, 23). But if we accept the Christian anthropology proposed by John Paul II, we know that the human person is a unity of body and soul, so each human being is always a person, no matter what may be his or her physical or mental condition. Each person always possesses a rational nature, including the natural human capacities of thought and free choice, although a physical impediment may interfere with the actualization of those capabilities. As chapter 3 observed, we are always *potentially functioning actual persons*.

This Manichaean duality, embraced by so many euthanasia advocates, rejects the notion that human life, the life of the person as embodied spirit, is inherently good, a gift of the Creator. Besides their implicit acceptance of dualism, they discard the "metaphysics of the good" that underscores the convertibility of being and goodness. Chapter 4 stated that human life must be seen within the whole horizon of created being as an intrinsic good, which, like all goods, has "its foundation in God alone" (MI, 15). The perfection of human life is objectively valued by human beings whose will and intellect are naturally oriented to respond to all being as good and true. The Manichaean paradigm does not regard human life as an intrinsic good but as neutral or "premoral." Hence, when the quality of that life is diminished through illness or dementia, it is no longer valuable or "good" in any way. As the philosopher Peter Singer points out, the lives of those who are not "self-conscious rational, or autonomous . . . have no intrinsic value; their life's journey has come to an end."[28] If one accepts this set of assumptions, euthanasia might indeed seem morally permissible.

This spurious line of reasoning is a perfect illustration of why it is so essential to retrieve a metaphysics of the good in order to ground morality and to avoid the mistakes of contemporary philosophy. Once we retrieve an understanding of the intrinsic worth of human life within God's natural order of objective goods, the project of euthanasia loses all credibility.

Finally, if Catholics and Christians are not persuaded by philosophical arguments, they might be moved by more spiritual ones. The Christian ideas about death and suffering contradict the prevailing secular viewpoint. The Christian realizes that life is a gift and that the power to end life should not be usurped by the forces of science. Instead, we must submit to God's will and live out our lives in holiness and humility. The secularist wants to avoid the humiliation of pain and suffering that often accompanies the last days, and perceives suffering only as a degradation of human dignity. On the contrary, practices like euthanasia and physician-assisted suicide represent a denial of the dignity that is due to all human beings even in the midst of their deepest suffering.

As John Paul II writes in his apostolic letter *Salvifici doloris*, "Down through the centuries and generations it has been seen that in suffering there is concealed a particular power that draws a person interiorly close to Christ; . . . the individual discovers the salvific meaning of suffering [and] above all becomes a completely new person" (SD, 26). Of course, Christ himself voluntarily shared in human suffering to reveal its significance in the life of every human being: *"The cross with Christ* is the great revelation of the meaning of suffering and of the value which it has in life and in history."[29] But just as a suffering Jesus looked forward to the joy of resurrection, so too can we anticipate future glory.

Marriage and Family

John Paul II's prophetic vision of marriage was often misrepresented in the media, which chose to narrowly focus on his opposition to artificial contraception or sexual relations outside of marriage. There was usually little or no explanation of the pope's elaborate reasons behind these well-founded moral convictions. To some extent, this should not be surprising, given the complexity of John Paul II's thought. In order to understand John Paul II's vision of human sexuality, one must appreciate the basic elements of his anthropology, which was presented in chapter 3. John Paul II has written extensively about this topic, but we can do little more than provide a terse overview of his marital and family ethic.

Recall that the human person, as embodied spirit, always reveals himself or herself through the "language of the body." The body has a nuptial meaning, since our sexual differences reveal that God made man and woman for each other. When man and woman are united in the "conjugal covenant," they become one flesh. They complete each other through marital self-donation. As chapter 3 noted, John Paul II conceives of the marital covenant as the consummate gift of self:

> Every man and woman fully realizes himself or herself through the serious gift of self. For spouses, the moment of conjugal union constitutes a very particular expression of this. It is then that a man and woman, in the "truth" of their masculinity and femininity, become a mutual gift to each other. All married life is a gift; but this becomes most evident when the spouses, in giving themselves to each other in love, bring about that encounter which makes them "one flesh" (Gen. 2:24). (LFam, 12)

The clear implication is that marriage is an intrinsic good, not an instrumental one. John Paul II certainly implies as much in this reading of Genesis, as he explains how man and woman realize their true selfhood by overcoming "original solitude" and existing *for someone*. According to Grisez, "the contrast between man's initial loneliness ('not good') and the fulfillment of marriage that motivates him to leave his father and mother implies that marital communion is in itself good."[30] This viewpoint is consistent with the teaching of Vatican II, which describes marriage as an "intimate community of conjugal life and love."[31] Bearing and raising children perfects marital communion.

Jesus Himself confirms the uniqueness of marital communion: "they are no longer two, but one flesh; therefore what God has joined together, let no one separate" (Mark 10:8–9). Marriage requires permanence or indissolubility and exclusivity ("one flesh"). For this reason Jesus also teaches that remarriage after divorce is adultery (Mark 10:11–12). According to John Paul II, "In the light of these words of Christ, Genesis 2:24 [the two become 'one flesh'] sets forth the principle of the unity and indissolubility of marriage as the very content of the Word of God set forth in the most ancient revelation" (TB, 26). In summary, the moral implications are quite evident: divorce and remarriage is impossible, and any sexual relations outside of marriage violate the marital covenant. As observed in chapter 4, in John Paul II's view, the sixth commandment, against adultery, is not an arbitrary restriction; rather, it protects the fundamental good of marriage.

For John Paul II there are other ways besides adultery in which the "truthful sign" of the marital covenant can be violated. The Holy Father calls attention to the truth because the language of the body "is subject to the demands of truth . . . [and] to objective moral norms" (RHV, 32). The fundamental problem with artificial contraception is its betrayal of the language of the body. According to John Paul II, "the innate language that expresses the total reciprocal self-giving of husband and wife is overlaid, through contraception, by an objectively contradictory language, namely, that of giving oneself totally to the other" (FC, 32). The dual aspects of the conjugal union, the unitive and the procreative, cannot be artificially separated without undermining the conjugal act itself.

Hence John Paul II, following his predecessors, unequivocally rejects artificial contraception. He is in full accord with the principles articulated so clearly by Pope Paul VI in *Humanae Vitae*. When the procreative potential of the conjugal act is eliminated through artificial means, the married couple destroys the integration of physical fertility and marital commitment. The natural rhythm method, on the other hand, "involves accepting the cycle of the person, that is, the woman, and thereby accepting dialogue, reciprocal respect, shared responsibility, and self-control" (FC, 32).

Of course, "free love," sexual relations prior to or outside of marriage, is also a betrayal of the body's sacramental language. Such actions presume that the body is to be "used" for pleasure. They fail to acknowledge that the sexual act has an intrinsic moral structure that aims toward true unity and procreation. In sexual relations outside of marriage, the person is reduced to an object, a means to the end of sexual satisfaction and desire. This violates the personalist norm, the central principle of John Paul II's philosophical ethics. Even mutual sexual pleasure is problematic because it is not true love. When two people engage in sex for pleasure, the relationship is expendable. When the pleasure ceases for one party, so does the relationship. But conjugal love aims at unity as the two become one in spirit and flesh. In *Love and Responsibility*, Wojtyla wrote:

> Carnal love born of carnal concupiscence alone lacks the value which love for the person must contain. It substitutes for what should be the object of love, the person, a different object, namely, "the body and sex" of a person. The sensual reaction, as we know, does not relate to the person *qua* person, but only to "the body and

sex" of a concrete person, and to these specifically as "a possible object of enjoyment."[32]

The ethic of individualism and hedonism that contributes to the popularity of sexual promiscuity and "free love" has greatly impaired the welfare of the family. We cannot separate sexuality from commitment, marriage, and love without grave consequences. The Holy Father echoes the concerns of many spiritual leaders as he describes the modern family under siege:

> [S]igns are not lacking of a disturbing degradation of some fundamental values: a mistaken theoretical and practical concept of the independence of the spouses in relation to each other; serious misconceptions regarding the relationship of authority between parents and children; the concrete difficulties that the family experiences in the transmission of values; the growing number of divorces; the scourge of abortion; the ever more frequent recourse to sterilization; the appearance of a truly contraceptive mentality. At the root of these negative phenomena there frequently lies a corruption of the idea and the experience of *freedom*, conceived not as a capacity for realizing the truth of God's plan for marriage and the family, but as an autonomous power of self-affirmation, often against others, for one's own selfish well-being. (FC, 6)

Thus, a false conception of freedom as an end in itself is at the origin of many family problems. As John Paul II has been at pains to insist, real freedom is always subordinate to the good and to truth. Society's misplaced emphasis on autonomy for its own sake undermines the commitment needed for the stability of marriage and family life. It devalues sexual fidelity and exalts the individual over the human perfection of persons-in-communion. In this context, freedom must be directed by the good of marital commitment and sexual fidelity, which demands self-discipline, responsibility, and self-constraint for this higher purpose.

The stability of the family is also put at risk by government officials willing to promote abortion, artificial contraception, and even infanticide under the auspices of "population control." This mentality was in evidence at the UN's Cairo Conference on Population in 1994. As George

Weigel points out, the draft document of that conference "was full of Orwellian euphemisms: coercive state family planning policies became 'fertility regulation'; abortion on demand was transmuted into 'safe motherhood' and 'reproductive rights.'"[33] Despite the Catholic Church's Herculean efforts, coercive population control is still practiced by the United Nations. For example, aid programs in Peru have "included bribes of food and clothing to poor women who submitted to sterilization."[34]

In response to the deployment of controversial methods of population control, John Paul II affirmed the family's right to decide for itself the number and spacing of its children. He also affirmed the sovereignty of the family and rebuked those states seeking to limit the procreative rights of families through coercive family planning. According to John Paul II,

> [A]ny violence applied by [state] authorities in favor of contraception or, still worse, of sterilization and procured abortion, must be altogether condemned and forcefully rejected. Likewise to be denounced as gravely unjust are cases where, in international relations, economic help given for the advancement of people is made conditional on programs of contraception, sterilization, and procured abortion. (FC, 30)

As John Conley, S.J., has observed, procreative rights differ greatly from "reproductive rights." According to Conley, "First, the decision to procreate is proper only to a duly married couple ('the spouses'), not to individuals or to cohabiting couples; second, the right is inalienable—that is, intrinsic to the very structure of the human person."[35] As a result, this right cannot be usurped or infringed upon by the state for utilitarian purposes.

If states must honor these procreative rights, the family must also exercise this right responsibly. The family is the primordial community of persons and, as such, constitutes the foundation of human society. The family is called by God to serve life through both the transmission of life and the education of offspring. That education is "before all else a reciprocal offering on the part of both parents: together they communicate their own mature humanity to the newborn child" (LFam, 16).

Families have other tasks that take the form of moral obligations. Since the family is "the fundamental 'cell' of society," it must contribute to society's development and flourishing (LFam, 13). The family must also participate as fully as possible in the life and mission of Christ's Church. Children must be educated in the faith, and the whole family must take part in the Church's sacramental life, which will give the family the graces needed to thrive in a world that is so antifamily. The family—mother, father, and children—is of the utmost importance for the welfare of society and the future of the Church. As the Holy Father reminds us, "The history of mankind, the history of salvation, passes by way of the family" (LFam, 23).

Summary

John Paul II was a profound optimist, but he was not blind to the unpleasant tendencies of this new millennium, nor was he a stranger to the range of questions investigated in this chapter. Like Heidegger, he recognized the attitude of "technicity" as a subtle menace for modern man. But what can be done about the burgeoning of these dangerous new technologies that objectify humanity by turning the person into a research object or a platform for implants and robotic appendages? How do we deal with globalization and ensure that workers' rights are respected? How can we assure a version of bioethics that reinforces the true value of our humanity, that does justice to the self as embodied spirit and protects human beings when they are most vulnerable? And how do we protect the intrinsic good of marriage in an age of hedonism?

We can find answers for these questions in revelation or by relying on the light of reason. John Paul II clearly draws from both sources. He carefully blends philosophy and theology as he tackles the vexing moral dilemmas of contemporary human beings. Thus, it should be evident from our analysis that his moral philosophy can provide a reliable moral compass for addressing these dilemmas. Through the prism of the transcendent personalist norm, with its focus on the dignity of the human subject, John Paul II presents an unambiguous remedy for the growing tendency of humanity to objectify itself. That personalist norm requires the treatment of each human as an end and never only as a means; it implies that the goods of each person (such as life or marriage) must be protected and that inalienable rights such as the right to life have no exceptions. John Paul II applies this fundamental moral principle in all areas of morality. This norm also implies that the work performed by laborers embodies personal dignity and so takes priority over capital. This chapter has also demonstrated the interrelationship between moral philosophy, realist metaphysics, and a nondualistic anthropology.

John Paul II's personalist approach, combined with natural law's focus on intrinsic human goods, is surely superior to the postmodern ethical frameworks that were critiqued in chapter 2. And it is far superior to proportionalism, which introduces a soft relativism into moral reasoning that often diminishes the value of intrinsic goods such as bodily life and marriage. As we have seen, many proportionalists opt for a dualistic view of the person, which leads to questionable solutions to the daunting problems that now dominate the area of bioethics. John Paul II's framework, on the other hand, incorporates a sound Christian anthropology that does not fall prey to the pitfalls of Manichaean dualism.

John Paul II's moral theology, which insists upon absolute principles and absolute rights, is a powerful antidote to the "scientistic mentality." Those who adopt this mentality choose to live "outside the parameters of good and evil, outside the context of values derived by God" (MI, 48). In order to overcome this mode of thinking, John Paul II points to the natural law, which reveals moral truths that can lead us to the true path of happiness and fulfillment.

Finally, John Paul II constantly reminds us that while the human person has a privileged place in this world, that person is still a humble creature. Thanks to what Charles Taylor calls an "eclipse of the transcendent," many people forget this fact.[36] We cannot succumb to the temptation of "technicity" and regard all of creation as objects for our manipulation or enjoyment, so that even the person himself or herself becomes raw material for the imposition of another's will-to-power. Rather, we must rediscover the metaphysical subjectivity of each human creature who is brought into being and sustained by the Creator. The only complete humanism is one that is thoroughly theocentric: it must go beyond the purely human dimension and recognize humanity's absolute dependence on God. Without this docility we will be further menaced by a Promethean hubris that has already begun to take root in our morally destitute modern culture.

Notes

1. Martin Heidegger, *Vorträge und Aufsätze* (Pfullingen: Neske, 1954), 277.

2. William J. Richardson, S.J., *Heidegger: Through Phenomenology to Thought* (The Hague: Martinus Nijhoff, 1963), 395.

3. See Norris Clarke, "Reply to Steven Long," *The Thomist* 61 (October 1997): 617–624.

4. C. S. Lewis, "The Abolition of Man," in *Philosophy and Technology*, ed. Carl Mitcham and Richard Mackey (New York: Free Press, 1972), 147.

5. Jane Flax, quoted in Seyla Benhabib, "Feminism and Postmodernism: An Uneasy Alliance," *Feminist Contentions* 18 (1995): 25.

6. Elaine Graham, "Politics of the Post/Human," paper presented September 3, 2003, at Yale University, Technology and Ethics Working Research Group.

7. Pope John Paul II, "Dangers of Genetic Manipulation," address to members of the World Medical Association, October 29, 1983.

8. Pope John Paul II, "Dangers of Genetic Manipulation."

9. Pope John Paul II, "Dangers of Genetic Manipulation."

10. C. Christopher Hook, "Techno Sapiens," in *Human Dignity in the Biotech Century*, ed. Charles Colson and N. de S. Cameron (Downers Grove, Ill.: InterVarsity Press, 2004), 87.

11. Pope John Paul II, "Dangers of Genetic Manipulation."

12. Hook, "Techno Sapiens," 94.

13. Pamela Varley, ed., *The Sweatshop Quarterly: Corporate Responsibility on the Global Frontier* (Washington, D.C.: Investor Responsibility Research Center, 1998), 63.

14. *Catechism of the Catholic Church* (New York: Doubleday, 1995), no. 2407.

15. Adam Smith, *The Wealth of Nations* (London: Cannan, 1876), 423.

16. See L. S. Paine, "Ideals of Competition and Today's Marketplace," in *Enriching Business Ethics*, ed. Clarence Walton (New York: Plenum, 1990), 91–110.

17. For a more in-depth treatment of this topic, see Richard A. Spinello, "Competing Fairly in the New Economy: Lessons from the Browser Wars," *Journal of Business Ethics* 57 (2005): 343–361.

18. Martin Luther King Jr., *Letter from a Birmingham Jail* (San Francisco: Harper, 1992), 17.

19. Wesley Smith, "Pushing Infanticide," *National Review Online*, www.nationalreview.com/smithw/smith200503220759.asp (May 22, 2005).

20. Scott Greenberger, "Senate OK's Research on Stem Cells," *The Boston Globe*, March 30, 2005, A1.

21. William Saunders, "The Human Embryo in Debate," in *Human Dignity in the Biotech Century*, ed. Charles Colson and N. de S. Cameron (Downers Grove, Ill.: InterVarsity Press, 2004), 115–135.

22. Saunders, "Human Embryo in Debate," 127.

23. Ronan O'Rahilly and Fabiola Muller, *Human Embryology and Teratology* (New York: Wiley-Liss, 2001), 187.

24. Quoted in Deal Hudson, "Does Life Begin at Implantation?" *The Window*, May 15, 2005, 2–3.

25. Ronald Dworkin, *Life's Dominion: An Argument about Abortion, Euthanasia and Individual Freedom* (New York: Knopf, 1993), 217.

26. John Finnis, "Euthanasia, Morality and Law," *Loyola of Los Angeles Law Review* 31 (June 1998): 1139 n. 55.

27. Patrick Lee, "Personhood, Dignity, Suicide, and Euthanasia," *The National Catholic Bioethics Quarterly* (Autumn 2001): 112.

28. Peter Singer, *Practical Ethics*, 2nd ed. (New York: Cambridge University Press, 1993), 395.

29. John Paul II, "General Audience," March 30, 1983, *Observatore Romano*, April 5, 1983, 4.

30. Germain Grisez, *Living a Christian Life* (Quincy, Ill.: Franciscan Press, 1993), 556.

31. *Gaudium et Spes*, in *Vatican Council II: The Conciliar and Post Conciliar Documents*, ed. Austin Flannery, O.P. (Northport, N.Y.: Costello, 1975), 48.

32. John Paul II, *Love and Responsibility*, trans. J. J. Willetts (San Francisco: HarperCollins, 1981), 150.

33. George Weigel, *Witness to Hope* (New York: HarperCollins, 1999), 720.

34. Mary Jo Anderson, "The Collapse of the United Nations," *Crisis* (October 2005): 13.

35. John Conley, S.J., "Demographic Ethics," in *Prophecy and Diplomacy: The Moral Doctrine of John Paul II*, ed. John Conley, S.J., and J. Koterski, S.J. (New York: Fordham University Press, 1999), 190–203.

36. Charles Taylor, "Die Immanente Gegenaufklärung," in *Aufklärung Heute* (Stuttgart: Kett-Cotta, 1991), 60–61.

CHAPTER 7

Conclusions

W E HAVE COVERED many difficult topics in this book, and this final chapter will give us an opportunity to climb upon higher ground in order to gain some perspective. Although we have sacrificed some of the subtleties of John Paul II's thought for the sake of conciseness and clarity, his key arguments on conscience, moral law, moral choice, intrinsically evil acts, freedom, and goodness have been presented in considerable depth. In order to appreciate the cogency of John Paul II's moral thought, it will be instructive to briefly review and synthesize his basic arguments. So in these final pages we will simply present a summary along with a modest assessment of John Paul II's moral theology.

Anyone who reads John Paul II's prayerful writings with an open mind cannot help but be impressed by his prodigious effort to confront the moral challenges of the early twenty-first century. He provides a consistent philosophy for resolving the complex problems that arise in bioethics and other areas of applied ethics. As we have demonstrated, his moral vision represents a striking contrast to the glaring deficiencies of postmodernism along with the pitfalls of proportionalism and utilitarian reasoning. John Paul II rejects the pragmatic notion that a good end can justify the use of unjust means. He presents a moral theology that is faithful to the Catholic Church's traditional teachings, but he disassociates himself from those neo-Scholastic versions of the natural law that see moral action purely in physical terms. John Paul II argues for a natural law grounded in fundamental objective goods that direct our actions.

At its deepest level, John Paul II's work is an effort to reinvigorate essential Catholic teachings, which remain in danger of being obscured by the revisionist work of some contemporary moral theologians. The Holy Father has turned to St. Thomas Aquinas for this task, but his reappropriation of Thomistic morality is infused with the insights of personalism and its emphasis on human subjectivity, personal dignity, and communal solidarity.

One will notice in this synopsis frequent references to John Paul II's last book, *Memory and Identity*, published shortly before his death in 2005. In this book, consisting of contemplative musings on a range of philosophical topics, the Holy Father interrogates the meaning of several key moral themes such as freedom and responsibility. While John Paul II expresses himself on these matters with a slightly different nuance, the unity and continuity of his body of work remains unmistakable. As a result, this final meditation represents a valuable perspective on his moral theology, ratifying the vision first made manifest in encyclicals such as *Veritatis Splendor*.

Two Pathways to Moral Truth

This book began with an affirmation that moral truth is accessible through divine revelation or through natural reason. Knowledge of God and of His Word unfolds in a process of "faith seeking understanding" (*fides quaerens intellectum*). Since there is one truth, John Paul II presents a compelling vision of an integrated moral wisdom in which faith and reason are perfectly complementary. This vision is fully compatible with the moral teachings of Vatican II, which maintain that there is a "natural and Gospel law" (*lex naturalis et evangelica*).[1]

In his encyclicals and letters, John Paul II clearly explains that one way we can bear witness to the moral truth is by following the Gospel. He consistently reminds us of the moral relevance of Scripture along with "the intrinsic and unbreakable bond between faith and morality" (VS, 4). Accordingly, his moral theology is heavily Christocentric: Christ is the summation and center of morality. According to John Paul II, "People need to turn to Christ once again in order to receive from him the answer to questions about what is good and what is evil" (VS, 8). Christ is the Incarnate Word of truth, who shows us the right way to live when we encounter Him in the Gospel. Thus, the meaning of the moral life is revealed in the moral norms presented in Christ's teachings.

Among those teachings is the Decalogue that Jesus explicitly repromulgates: "From the very lips of Jesus, the new Moses, man is *once again* given the commandments of the Decalogue" (VS, 12; my emphasis). The Holy Father underscores the "centrality" of the Decalogue (VS, 13), which is based on the prefatory words "I am the Lord your God" (Deut. 6:5). These commands are not a burden for man. Rather, they are "God's gift" in which God makes Himself known as the "model" of moral action in accordance with His command "You shall be holy; for I the Lord your God am holy" (Lev. 19:2; VS, 10). The commandments, therefore, are fundamental to the moral life not because they proscribe certain activities, but because they reveal what is truly valuable and worthwhile. The commandments teach us about our humanity and our relationship with our neighbor, who is also created in God's image. They reflect "the complex of 'personal goods' which serve the 'good of the person': the good which is the person himself and his perfection" (VS, 79). Those fundamental human goods such as life, truth, and marriage are "safeguarded by the commandments, which, according to St. Thomas, contain the whole natural law" (VS, 79).

The Decalogue is not the only moral teaching of Scripture. We find in other parables concrete moral norms such as the mandate to feed the hungry and visit the sick or the imprisoned (Matt. 25:31–46). In *Veritatis Splendor* the Holy Father also devotes considerable attention to the Sermon on the Mount, which "demonstrates the openness of the commandments and their orientation toward the horizon of the perfection proper to the Beatitudes" (VS, 16). Of course, we must also turn to the tradition of the Church and to the Magisterium for moral instruction that bears on contemporary issues that are not specifically addressed in the Scripture.

Moral truth is also accessible through natural reason, since God has inscribed that moral truth within our human nature. According to Wojtyla, "the source of norms is found in natural law, which is not a written law."[2] Through practical reason, human beings discern that certain goods such as knowledge or the harmony of friendship perfect their natures and promote their flourishing as humans. People grasp as basic human goods the forms of human fulfillment to which they are naturally inclined. For example, we are naturally inclined to enjoy the companionship of others, so friendship is a basic human good. The first practical principle of the natural law tells us that these goods are to be desired and pursued and anything bad is to be avoided.

This plurality of fundamental human goods (*bona honesta*), the reasons for action that direct all intelligible human choices, is the logical starting point for our practical reflections about morality (MI, 37). The primary *moral* principle of the natural law is the imperative to love one's neighbor as oneself (Matt. 7:12; VS, 76). This formal principle requires us to respect our neighbor's basic goods such as life, knowledge, and marriage, since those goods perfect our neighbor and lead to his or her flourishing. Moreover, as Aquinas points out, from this formal standard we can derive with "little reflection" (*modica consideratione*)[3] exceptionless moral norms that forbid dignitary harms interfering with the human flourishing of ourselves and others; these norms parallel the commandments and include prohibitions against adultery, lying, or the taking of innocent life. The protection of human nature's unity and dignity requires such specific and permanent moral precepts.

John Paul II borrows from Kant's philosophy to express this first principle of morality, the imperative to love one's neighbor as oneself, in more secular terms. He derives the *personalist norm* from Kant's second formulation of the categorical imperative: "Act so that you treat humanity, whether in your own person or in that of another, always as an end and never as a means only."[4] According to John Paul II, "Kant could be said to have laid the foundations for modern personalist ethics" (MI, 36). This personalist norm, which asserts that we must treat the other as an end by respecting his or her goods, accentuates the inalienable dignity of every human person. Kant wrote that this formulation of the categorical imperative was "the supreme limiting condition in pursuit of all means."[5] Thus, the personalist norm stands in sharp contrast to proportionalism, since it asserts that there are some acts (or means) that can never be justified by any end or purpose. Although proportionalism sometimes allows for the rights of the weak and disenfranchised (for example, the unborn) to be sacrificed for the overall net good, the personalist norm forbids the rights of *any* person from being displaced for an ulterior end. According to John Paul II, "it makes no difference whether one is the master of the world or the 'poorest of the poor' on the face of the earth; before the demands of morality we are all absolutely equal" (VS, 96).

John Paul II recognized the inadequacy of Kant's master principle, unless it is complemented with the account of the fundamental human goods found in the natural law. The problem with Kant and contemporary ethicists is that they have abandoned a metaphysics of the good, which asserts that being and goodness are convertible and that all beings created by God are objectively good. Without God, man arbitrarily decides "what is good and what is bad" (MI, 10). John Paul II also finds fault with Kant's impoverished notion of the person, which reduces humanity to rationality, that is, to the "accidental" feature of conscious thought. John Paul II, on the other hand, understands "humanity" in terms of the Thomistic notion of personhood: each human person is an embodied spirit, a natural unity of body and soul, who must always be regarded in his or her nondualistic wholeness. Our physical life is not an instrumental or "ontic" good, as some theologians have presumed, since this would imply that the body is a reality distinct from the rest of the self. Rather the body is an integral part of the person. For John Paul II, the concept of a common universal human nature includes *all* human beings in every stage of existence because each human person is endowed with a rational nature and the active potency for intelligent and free action.

John Paul II's blending of personalism and Thomism is also evident in his description of moral action. We must always evaluate moral action from the perspective of the acting person. Proportionalists contend that we cannot know whether an action is right or wrong unless we know the context and the ultimate purpose or intention. But for John Paul II, the moral rightness or wrongness of an action is determined by what the acting person wills or chooses and by the object or proximate intention (*finis proximus*) of that choice. Unless the act's object is capable of being "ordered to God," it is always wrong (VS, 82). Lying even for a good end or purpose (*finis ultimus*) is wrong by virtue of the choice to assert what is false and the proximate intention (or the object), such as deception of another person. Thus, John Paul II completely agrees with Aquinas that "the primary and decisive element for moral judgement is the object of the human act" (VS, 79).

In summary, John Paul II speaks to us as both a theologian and a philosopher. His writings, which sought to reconcile faith and reason, sometimes oscillate between the mystical or the poetic and dense philosophical analysis. He exhorts us to turn to Christ, who inspires us to live an authentic moral life, for "in Christ, man is called to a new life" (MI, 25). He eloquently reminds us that the dialogue of conscience is not within the subject but rather represents an opening to the divine light of transcendence. He evokes the simplicity of the moral life as he beckons us to contemplate the example of Mary, who is "the radiant sign" of moral rectitude (VS, 120). In contrast to the "beguiling doctrines [of] philosophy and theology," the solution to many moral dilemmas becomes transparent when we follow "Mary's command given to the servants at Cana during the wedding feast: 'Do whatever he tells you' (John 2:5)" (VS, 120). At the same time, there is no dearth of metaphysical analysis as John Paul II sets out to correct flawed conceptions of freedom and human action. John Paul II deeply admired the rational synthesis of Aquinas. He even finds accommodation with philosophers like Kant "to oppose Anglo-Saxon utilitarianism" (CTH, 201). But whether we follow a more mystical path, guided by the Incarnate Word of truth and the example of Mary, or we turn to the rational ideal of the personalist norm, *we encounter the same moral reality.*

A Comprehensive Moral Theory

It becomes clear that we can disengage from John Paul II's writings the broad lines of a philosophical ethics, an ethical paradigm based purely on the light of reason. As discussed in chapter 1, philosophical ethics cannot be separated from metaphysics and anthropology. What we find, therefore, is a creative interplay between these three disciplines. The distinctive elements of this moral philosophy can be summarized as follows:

- First, a metaphysics of the good serves as a foundation for John Paul II's moral philosophy, since the natural goodness of all things (including life itself) comes from the Creator. All created beings are good to the extent to which they possess actuality, while evil is the privation of some due good. Morality is firmly grounded in fundamental human goods (*bona honesta*), which are grasped by practical reason as goods to be done and pursued. Practical reason recognizes that fundamental human goods such as life or marriage, whether instantiated in oneself or in other human beings, are worth preserving and pursuing. John Paul II's version of the natural law takes on a different stripe due to the incorporation of personalism, but it is essentially faithful to the Thomistic tradition. Although the Holy Father does not give us an elaborate moral system, the sinews of a teleological, natural law philosophy are certainly evident in his writings, including *Veritatis Splendor* and the essays assembled in *Person and Community*.

- Second, John Paul II's moral philosophy has a distinct deontological strain thanks to its emphasis on moral duty as summed up in the personalist norm: treat each human person as an end and never as a mere means. Since the person becomes the center of morality, we must understand the nature of the person. Hence the need for a well-conceived metaphysical anthropology that clarifies that each human person has a rational nature (thanks to the soul) that comes into existence when the physical body comes into existence.

- Third, it logically follows from the personalist norm that there must be intrinsically evil acts (*intrinseca mala*) specified by their object or proximate intention (for example, a married person's extramarital intercourse). Specific moral norms such as "direct killing of the innocent is always wrong" cannot be rationally compromised without treating the victim merely as a means. These specific, absolute norms protect the inviolable dignity of each person. John Paul II's philosophy is radically antiutilitarian: human actions receive their moral character from their object, from what the moral agent adopts as a choice, not from their end or the results achieved.

- Fourth, in order to be able to grasp the object of the act, which determines that act's moral character, it is necessary "to place oneself in the perspective of the acting person" (VS, 78). The goodness or badness of an action depends primarily on what the acting person wills and chooses, including his or her immediate purpose (*finis proximus*). Given the obvious importance of the moral subject's deliberation and intention, we cannot neglect "the person as subject experiencing its acts and inner happenings."[6]

- Finally, John Paul II's philosophy underscores the intransitivity of moral choice. Through moral actions I decide not only what should be done, but also what kind of person I should be: "freedom is not only the choice for one or another particular action; it is also, within that choice, a *decision about oneself*" (VS, 65). Our choices continue to affect our identity long after they have been executed unless a contrary choice is made.

This last feature of John Paul II's philosophy deserves special mention, since it has been so neglected by moral theologians and philosophers who are far too results-oriented. According to Wojtyla, "efficacy" does not tell the whole story about personal subjectivity, since "not only am I the agent of the action . . . and of its effects, but I also determine myself."[7] Those who argue for the proportionately greater good as the criterion for moral decision making often overlook the actual choice made by the moral agent. Within that framework, a courageous choice on behalf of the sanctity of life is unimportant in itself. What matters is whether or not the overall net good is achieved. But John Paul II calls attention to the singular importance of what the acting person wills and chooses and how that person's character is shaped by those choices. As a result, he elevates the significance of each moral choice, which quite often influences future choices and attitudes, perhaps by engendering within the self a disposition to act in the same way in similar situations. A businessperson may rationalize a single act of deception because she believes that it is her "professional" duty to avoid the greater harm. Her action may be "efficacious" and benefit her company's stakeholders in the short run. But what is at stake for this individual *as a person*? Will she be compelled to perpetuate this dishonesty or to commit other misdeeds to follow up her original act of deception? What does deception do to the deceiver? Will it breed deviousness that spills over into her personal life?

We have suggested that John Paul II's *moral philosophy*, a creative synthesis of natural law and personalism, could be described as dignitarian humanism because of its concentration on "the transcendent dignity of the human person" (VS, 99). Respect for human dignity is the unconditioned and supreme norm of morality, and that dignity is accorded to all human beings by virtue of their human nature. For Aquinas, dignity "signifies something's goodness for its own sake."[8] Since each person is endowed from conception with a rational nature, he or she deserves special intrinsic worth. That worth is vitiated by intrinsically evil acts that thwart human flourishing through the destruction or impediment of fundamental human goods.

Many commentators on John Paul II's moral reflections have called attention to his synthesis of natural law and personalism, and they have rendered different opinions about whether he gives priority to one school of thought or another. According to Kevin Schmiesing, "the debate centers on which school holds primary importance in the pope's view."[9] But given John Paul II's comments in *Memory and Identity* about the primacy of Thomism and the need for a retrieval of Thomistic realism, there is little doubt that the natural law approach is more basic than phenomenology for the development of a coherent ethical system. Similarly, while John Paul II's anthropology incorporated a personalist element, it is essentially faithful to the metaphysical anthropology of Aquinas. According to Wojtyla, we need that "metaphysical terrain" for understanding "the personal subjectivity of the human being."[10] The person is both substance and subject. To be sure, John Paul II's understanding of the subjective side was influenced by philosophers like the German phenomenologist Max Scheler. But throughout his long career as a moralist, theologian, and philosopher there seems little doubt that "Thomism prevails" when it comes to John Paul II's understanding of personhood and morality.[11]

Evaluation: John Paul II contra the Dissenters

John Paul II's moral theology has had several vocal critics, who emerged in the wake of the publication of *Veritatis Splendor* to defend their own positions and to point out how they had been misinterpreted. A recent book by Father Charles Curran, *The Moral Theology of John Paul II*, summarizes many of the criticisms of the dissenters in the course of its exposition.[12] Curran's thoughtful but trenchant critique deserves attention. Most of the problems he cites with John Paul II's moral theology are shared by other dissenters, whom we have already discussed in this book. Our contention throughout this book has been that John Paul II's moral theology is both faithful to the Catholic tradition and philosophically coherent. Thus, as we shall demonstrate, John Paul II's moral vision can easily withstand the critical scrutiny of his intellectual peers.

Even dissenting theologians have found some things to praise in John Paul II's moral vision. No one, of course, could fault John Paul II's focus on the theme of human dignity, which was the central moral teaching of his long pontificate. His indefatigable work for this cause has been singled out even by his harshest critics. Most moral theologians applaud the attention given to the "culture of life," though they may disagree on how some of the life issues could be morally resolved. They also affirm many of his progressive social teachings and his emphasis on the virtue of solidarity.

But support for the natural law framework and for the idea of intrinsically evil acts in the pluralistic environment of the twenty-first century has been tepid among some moral theologians. And this uneasiness with the natural law paradigm has been the primary source of their problems with John Paul II's moral theology. Here are the major criticisms proposed by Curran but voiced by other dissenters as well:

- John Paul II's moral theology suffers from "physicalism," since the human moral act is identified "with the physical or biological structure of the act" (111). In Curran's view, John Paul II focuses too narrowly on the biological side of the human person when he evaluates moral actions. Moreover, by following a natural law ethic, John Paul II appears to regard the natural (i.e., the natural inclinations) and the bodily as "absolutes that cannot be interfered with for the good of the relationships in which the person is involved" (115). The problem, claims Curran, is that John Paul II adopts a static Thomistic anthropology with its three layers of inclinations: what we share with all living beings (the dynamism of life), what we share with animals (for example, reproductive capability), and what is distinctively human (for example, our rational intellect). But, in Curran's view, this anthropology implies that "human reason . . . can never interfere with the physical act of marital sexual intercourse" (114).

- John Paul II has an "overly simplistic" view of truth. According to Curran, the Holy Father "claim[s] to have the certitude of truth too quickly and too readily" (250). On the contrary, "John Paul II needs to recognize explicitly the limits on truth and certitude especially in the moral area" (34). There is a big difference, Curran argues, between "speculative" truth (for example, the truths of physics and geometry) and moral truth. Moral truth means "true for the most part" and admits of exceptions. Curran cites the work of Aquinas, who also recognized that the precepts of the moral law apply to particular moral cases only "in most cases" (*ut in pluribus*).[13] Curran concludes that the notion of truth employed by John Paul II "suffers from significant deficiencies in light of the Catholic tradition itself" (34). The implication is that the Holy Father is at odds with the Catholic tradition, which has a more nuanced and balanced view of truth.

- A related criticism concerns John Paul II's failure to attribute enough importance to "historical consciousness" and to the historical development of moral doctrine (179–184). The presumption is that moral and social truth is historical and always evolving. John Paul II has adopted a "classicist approach," and he does not seem to appreciate how the Church has changed its teaching on issues such as slavery, usury, and religious freedom over the centuries (184). According to Curran, "John Paul II's encyclicals fail to recognize that the church not only teaches the truth about humankind but must also learn it; the church is both learner and teacher" (42).

- John Paul II puts too much emphasis on absolute moral norms and intrinsically evil acts; according to Curran, *Veritatis Splendor* "distorts the meaning of Christian morality as found in Scripture . . . [by] making primary the insistence on obedience to the commandments" (52). This represents an inadequate "legal model" of morality, and "law should not be the primary model for understanding the moral life" (128). For Curran, "morality, as portrayed throughout scripture, involves much more than just obedience to commandments" (52). He cites Matthew 25 (31–46), where Jesus tells us that those who feed the hungry, clothe the naked, and visit prisoners will be the ones who are saved. Thus, love of one's neighbor and not obedience to the commandments is "proposed here as the criterion for entry into eternal life" (52). Other moral theologians have made similar claims. According to Richard McCormick, things considered intrinsically evil (*intrinsece malum*) "in the Catholic tradition are human interpretations and judgements, and share neither in the absoluteness of divine wisdom nor exclude the possibility of error."[14]

- Curran points to the dichotomy in John Paul II's thought between his teaching on sexual morality and his teachings on social issues such as economic rights (see chapter 6). Whereas John Paul II's social teaching is flexible and generally sensitive to the historical and social context, his sexual morality is characterized by classicalism and an outmoded legalism. For example, John Paul II cites the text of Genesis to support the permanence of the traditional family structure and monogamous nature of marriage. However, he has not advocated that an economic structure such as capitalism is appropriate for all people at all times. But Curran would like to see the same kind of historical consciousness and flexibility applied to sexual morality. According to Curran, "John Paul II makes no claim about a plan of God for political society existing from the beginning of the world, as he does for marriage and sexuality" (250). As a result the Holy Father stays on the level of generality and "his social teaching does not claim to have the certitude on very concrete issues, as is the case in papal sexual teaching" (250). Curran goes on to demonstrate that John Paul II's physicalism, which taints his sexual morality, does not interfere with his social teachings, and hence those teachings are superior to his pronouncements on sexuality.

The first criticism is that John Paul II's moral theology falls into the trap of physicalism. This allegation has been made before and capably addressed by moral theologians faithful to the Magisterium such as William May and Germain Grisez.[15] An objective person will see that it has no merit so long as one reads John Paul II's words with care. John Paul II disagrees with dissenting theologians who argue that the moral act (taking of a human life, the use of contraceptives, etc.) does not possess an independent moral quality since it must always be judged in reference to circumstances and the broader purpose of the moral agent. According to Curran, John Paul II is too preoccupied with the physical act that can be judged right or wrong regardless of these other "human" factors. So while Curran might say that masturbation could be morally acceptable depending on the circumstances, he rebukes John Paul II for arguing that an act like masturbation is always immoral because the physical act itself is wrong and disordered. But John Paul II definitely does not say this. In a key passage of *Veritatis Splendor*, which bears reading and rereading by his critics, he writes the following:

> The morality of the human act depends primarily and fundamentally on the "object" rationally chosen by the deliberate will. . . . In order to be able to grasp the object of an act which specifies that act morally, it is therefore necessary to place oneself in the perspective of the acting person. . . . *By the object of a given moral act, then, one cannot mean a process or an event of the merely physical order, to be assessed on the basis of its ability to bring about a given state of affairs in the outside world. Rather, that object is the proximate end of a deliberate decision which determines the act of willing on the part of the acting person.* (VS, 78; my emphasis)

Notice that John Paul II explicitly disavows merely inspecting the physical act as the basis for a moral judgment about a human action. Instead he maintains that we judge the action by considering what the acting person chooses and deliberately wills, and by what he calls the "proximate end" (see the last sentence of the Holy Father's passage). Consider again the example of masturbation. Sexual self-stimulation for the sake of pleasure is the same *physical* act as self-stimulation to give a semen sample, but the acts are *morally* different. Natural law proponents like Germain Grisez clearly recognize this difference, and so would John Paul II.[16] Obtaining a semen sample in this fashion may still be morally problematic if one were to indulge in sexual fantasy or if one willed sexual satisfaction in the process. This is especially so if there are alternative methods for obtaining the semen sample. But the key point is that the two actions *are not the same*, because the objects or proximate ends differ: in one case the will is seeking sexual pleasure, and in the other case it is carrying out a medical procedure.

The larger point, made evident by this example, is that John Paul II's moral philosophy is most definitely not committed to some sort of crass physicalism. The moral act (or choice) is not evaluated in terms of the outward deed or by the physical effects caused by that deed. Rather, it must be understood in light of the acting person's will, his choice, and his immediate or proximate intention (for example, to assert what is false to deceive one's superiors).

In addition, Curran's analysis of John Paul II's natural law philosophy is weakened by a dualistic fallacy, since it presupposes an opposition between reason and nature (or the lower natural inclinations). Curran polarizes these inclinations and overlooks their integration and unification in the exercise of our human reason.[17] According to theologian Martin Rhonheimer, "through practical reason, the natural tendencies and inclinations become a good for reason, they are rationally ordered, and in the order of reason—but only at this intellectual level—they are confirmed as human goods."[18] In this respect we are much different from animals, with whom we share certain inclinations such as self-preservation.

Although these inclinations can be described as hierarchical, they operate in an "ascending order of excellence and a descending order of fundamentality."[19] In the order of excellence, the lower inclinations (self-preservation) are subordinate to the higher ones (reason). At the same time, "there is an order of fundamentality that prevents the lower inclinations from being destroyed by the higher inclinations; . . . the lower inclinations are the necessary preconditions for the higher levels."[20] There is no dichotomy between reason and the lower inclinations in the thought of Aquinas or John Paul II. On the contrary, as discussed in chapter 3, John

Paul II's anthropology consistently underscores the unity of the acting person as a thinking, feeling, willing, sensing, physical being.

If we apply John Paul II's understanding of Thomistic natural law to Curran's example of contraception, we can see where Curran goes wrong. There is no opposition or disjunction between human reason and the function of sexual intercourse and procreation. Curran has argued elsewhere that our biological fecundity "ought to be assumed into the human sphere and be regulated within it."[21] But this claim reveals Curran's own dualistic leanings, since it assumes that this fecundity is outside the human and the personal.

Aquinas says that we share certain natural inclinations with animals. But when a human being's natural inclination toward sexual intercourse is grasped and properly ordered by reason, it becomes conjugal love between a man and a woman. Human sexual intercourse, therefore, is not the same as the sexual activity of animals, since animals cannot engage in acts of conjugal love. Conjugal love is a gift of the self to another and as such it requires exclusivity, lasting fidelity, and respect for the integral value of procreation. Contraception interferes with the gift of the whole self to one's spouse. As such, the act of contraception is an act contrary to the good of marriage. In the words of John Paul II,

> Consequently, sexuality, by means of which man and woman give themselves to one another through the acts which are proper and exclusive to spouses, *is by no means something purely biological, but concerns the innermost being of the human person as such.* It is realized in a truly human way only if it is an integral part of the love by which a man and a woman commit themselves totally to one another until death. (FC, 3; my emphasis)

John Paul II goes on to say that "this totality required by conjugal love also corresponds to the demands of responsible fertility" (FC, 3). Conjugal love requires self-giving, and in its fullness that love must include an openness to procreation. Beyond any doubt, whatever one thinks of John Paul II's views on marriage and sexual relations, this citation demonstrates that he can hardly be accused of "physicalism," of reducing the sexual or procreative act to the merely physical or biological.

What about the larger objection advanced by proportionalists that a choice to engage in an action such as adultery (or extramarital intercourse) does not have an independent moral quality? Proportionalists contend that the circumstances of the adulterous action along with the motivating purposes must always be factored in when considering this action's rightness or wrongness. According to John Paul II, however, it is possible "to qualify as morally evil according to its species—its 'object'— the deliberate choice of certain kinds of behavior or specific acts, apart from a consideration of the intention for which the choice is made or the totality of foreseeable consequences of that act for all persons concerned" (VS, 79). John Paul II follows Aquinas in arguing that an action can be wrongful by reason of the person's choice (*electio*) and the immediate or proximate purpose (*finis proximus*). Moreover, like Aquinas, he differentiates the object or immediate purpose from the ultimate, motivating purpose (*finis ultimus*), which cannot justify an evil choice.[22]

Thus, as chapter 5 stated, a destitute person may choose to smother his stingy grandfather so that he can inherit the family fortune in order to feed his starving children. In this case, he intends the death of his grandfather (*finis proximus*) by means of suffocation, even though his motivating purpose (*finis ultimus*) is noble. This motivation, however, can never justify his willing to kill his grandfather. On the other hand, if a woman shoots a man who is approaching her with a knife, her proximate end is to avoid being stabbed and mortally wounded, and the means is to impede the man by shooting him. Depending upon how she fires the gun, she may or may not kill this attacker, but she wills only to save herself from his attack. Obviously, the moral nature of the two acts described here is quite different. Thus, the decisive element for moral judgment is the object that specifies the human act. John Paul II turns to St. Thomas Aquinas to support his position: "it often happens that man acts with a good intention, but without spiritual gain, because he lacks a good will; let us say that someone robs in order to feed the poor: in this case, even though the intention is good, the uprightness of the will is lacking; consequently no evil done with a good intention can be excused" (VS, 78).[23]

Proportionalists, however, do not concede that moral actions are specified by their object, that is, by the proximate end or immediate intention, such as the intention to have sexual intercourse outside of marriage. They claim that without knowing the motivating purpose or ultimate end we cannot adequately assess the actions' rightness or wrongness, since there may be mitigating circumstances, particularly if net benefits are the result. This approach precludes the Church's teaching, based on revelation and tradition, that there are intrinsically evil actions, wrong always and under any circumstances, no matter what the motivating purposes happen to be. For proportionalists, we cannot really know whether an act is morally evil without considering the greater net good or lesser evil it brings about. According to this theory, there can even be exceptions to norms that forbid adultery or intentional killing of the innocent because there may be a proportionate reason for validating such acts.

But how do we know when a reason is proportionate? There are no fixed criteria for making such a determination. John Paul II was right to expose the salient problem with this theory: "the impossibility of evaluating all the good and evil consequences and effects . . . of one's own acts" (VS, 77). The theory of proportionalism, which departs from the tradition in a significant fashion, is incompatible with the absoluteness of fundamental human rights and the promotion of equal dignity. John Paul II rightly appreciates that moral absolutes are the only ground on which human rights and universal dignity can be protected: "only a morality which acknowledges certain norms as valid always and for everyone, with no exception, can guarantee the ethical foundations of social co-existence" (VS, 97).

The Holy Father's argument bears repeating: *without certain moral absolutes, "social co-existence" loses its foundation.* The problem in relying on a moral methodology dedicated to finding the overall net good is that one person's "proportionate reason" is another's rationalization. Is telling a few lies to investors in order to preserve jobs and keep a manufacturing plant open morally wrong? Some might plausibly argue that the overall net good provides a justification for the means of lying, while others would disagree. Once we accept the proportionalist's premise that "we must look at all dimensions (morally relevant circumstances) before we know what the action is and whether it [is] contrary to . . . natural law,"[24] the push for expediency begins to dominate moral decision making. The result is inevitable: an expedient solution or a "good" objective can blind us to the injustice of the means such as the killing of an innocent person through abortion or the willful deception of corporate investors. When this happens, human rights, such as the right to life, are sacrificed for the sake of achieving this "worthy" objective. Morality, the surest foundation of "social co-existence," is devoid of any meaningful objectivity. The only antidote to this loss of objectivity is the one John Paul II presents with such vigor in *Veritatis Splendor*—there must be some exceptionless moral norms so that the "good" is not the adversary of what is just and right.

The second criticism pertains to John Paul II's "overly simplistic" view of truth. Curran juxtaposes speculative and scientific truth against moral truth and argues that truth is an analogous concept, and not a univocal one as John Paul II supposes. He also claims that the Holy Father's views on moral truth are not compatible with the Catholic tradition.

However, the Catholic tradition has *always* held that there is moral truth, and that even for some specific issues we can have complete moral certitude. Consider Aquinas's teaching on this matter. Curran cites Aquinas to support his criticism, but his selective use of Aquinas's texts is disputable. According to Aquinas, there are some moral norms, such as "one should keep promises" or "one should return things deposited for safekeeping," that are in force "always but not for every occasion" (*semper sed non pro semper*). If someone gives me a weapon for safekeeping but later seeks that weapon to kill an innocent person, the obligation to return the weapon to the rightful owner is nullified. But there are other negative norms, such as "one should not commit adultery," that hold "always and on every occasion" (*semper et ad semper*). Those norms, revealed in Sacred Scripture and confirmed by the Magisterium, are universally and absolutely true and do not permit exceptions. Thus, moral propositions such as "in no way is it permissible to kill an innocent person" have the same level of objective veracity as the propositions of science.[25]

Vatican II also supports John Paul II's conception of moral truth. In *Dignitatis Humanae*, the Council tells us that "all men . . . are by their own nature impelled, and are morally bound, to seek the truth." Moreover, "they are bound to . . . order their whole life according to the requirements of the truth." The truth the Council has in mind is the "unchanging truth" of the natural law. The document goes on to affirm that moral truth is to be found in "the principles of the moral order that flow from human nature itself."[26] Both *Dignitatis Humanae* and *Gaudium et Spes* make it unmistakably clear that there are true, objective standards of morality that are quite specific. The latter document insists that there are certain specific moral norms that are permanently true and not subject to revision. These norms include prohibitions against abortion and genocide.[27] It is quite difficult to see how John Paul II's pronouncements on moral truth are not fully compatible with the Catholic tradition. On the contrary, Curran's skepticism is consonant with neither Aquinas's moral theology nor the teachings of Vatican II.

The third general criticism made by Curran and other dissenters is that the natural law approach favored by John Paul II fails to pay enough attention to the changing nature and historical development of moral doctrine. The suggestion is that morality evolves, and hence moral theology should not be so insistent on "absolute" standards. What is behind this sentiment is a desire to induce the Catholic Church to be more open to cultural change even if such change is inconsistent with its established traditions.

This persistent criticism invites several remarks. First, the morality of the Catholic Church has actually been remarkably stable over the centuries. For example, even Curran concedes that legal historian John Noonan is accurate when he reports that the Church has been consistent in its opposition to abortion from its earliest days until the present. Morality does evolve at some level, but the intrinsic human goods such as life and knowledge are permanent because they perfect our human nature and we cannot flourish without them. Therefore, the moral precepts predicated on these goods, such as "it is always wrong to intentionally kill the innocent," can never change. Thus while the Church has refined its teachings on things such as usury and religious liberty, its teaching on core moral values has been quite consistent.

Curran contends that the Church must learn before it teaches. This proposition is absolutely true if it means that the Church must refine its teachings to keep up with the research of science and social science. John Paul II repeatedly asserted his willingness to be open to such new sources of knowledge—who could deny that he was an eager "learner" throughout his long pontificate? Also, according to John Paul II, "The Church values sociological and statistical research, when it proves helpful in understanding the historical context in which pastoral action has to be developed and when it leads to a better understanding of the truth" (FC, 74).

But the Church does not learn in a vacuum. Rather, with the help of the Holy Spirit it must evaluate new learning or the results of research in reference to the Word of God, its traditional values, and its accumulated wisdom. How else can the Church judge whether the source of that new learning is a "deceitful spirit" (1 Tim. 4:1–2) rather than the Holy Spirit?

The real issue is which norms or traditions of the Church should be variable and which ones are unchangeable. We get little help from the dissenters on this crucial point. Natural law moralists, on the other hand, have done a reasonably good job of differentiating intrinsic goods from instrumental goods and arguing that certain values (forbidding adultery or intentional killing of the innocent) associated with the former are absolute. Consider marriage, which is regarded by some secularists merely as a social institution that is culturally determined and therefore subject to some degree of change. But to what extent should the secular culture's views on marriage encroach upon the Catholic understanding of this institution? This question often surfaces in the current debate over the possibility of same-sex marriage. But marriage is also a sacrament and an intrinsic human good, and, as such, it cannot change. The Catholic Church has affirmed that exclusivity and indissolubility are essential in order to realize the intrinsic good of marital communion. As chapter 6 disclosed, this normative understanding of marriage is based on Jesus's teachings, which demand marital fidelity and indissolubility.

Some postmodern Catholic philosophers, however, like Gianni Vattimo, now question this teaching: "must we really believe . . . that man is by nature one thing or another or that the family is by nature monogamous and heterosexual, that matrimony is by nature indissoluble?"[28] But what if Vattimo gets his way and the culture redefines marriage by completely removing the exclusivity and indissolubility requirements? This transformation of marriage, which is already under way, would welcome various forms of polygamy or "serial monogamy." If that were to happen, wouldn't the Church be right to resist this development and insist upon exclusivity as a necessary condition for realizing the intrinsic goodness of marriage? Are those within the Church who are so eager to embrace historicism willing to accept such radical change in the institution of marriage and willing to accept the proposition that marriage is "historically relative"? Or do they accept the continuity of the Church's position, based on its own experience, the unambiguous Word of Jesus, the teachings of the great Councils, and the reflections of theologians like Aquinas, that exclusive commitment is a basic requirement of marriage? Just how far are the advocates of cultural accommodation and historicism willing to go in their rejection of the great traditions? Would they really want to see the revival of practices like polygamy sanctioned by the Catholic Church?

The key question is whether the Church's perception of cultural change should lead it into new normative directions. The only valid criterion for making this type of decision is a consideration of whether or not the Holy Spirit is calling the Church to change, and since the Holy Spirit is most unlikely to contradict itself, such change must be carefully evaluated in light of the previous Church teaching. As Catholics, we are called upon to conform to the Word of God no matter what we "learn," and hence there are and there should be significant constraints on the Church's ability to change or jettison centuries-old moral teachings, grounded in Sacred Scripture.

According to Cardinal Newman, any development of Catholic doctrine must be "in accordance with, or in consequence of, the immemorial principles" of the Church's teaching, since those principles have maintained their "continuity down to this day." Otherwise that development is a corruption of doctrine. Heresies, Newman writes, "which have from time to time arisen, have in one respect or other, as might be expected, violated those principles with which [the Church] rose into existence, and which she still retains."[29] Note the critical importance of *continuity* for Cardinal Newman—a radical moral teaching, which is discontinuous with the moral tradition of the Church, must be highly suspect.

But we must concede that the Church's moral teaching has apparently evolved in certain areas. Curran cites the issues of slavery, usury, and religious liberty. Slavery, for example, was part of the cultural landscape for a good portion of the Church's history. It is important, however, to understand the historical context. In earlier eras, it would have been economically impossible to imprison the armies and families of defeated countries. As a result, humane slavery was tolerated by the Church as an alternative to execution. In recent years the Church has denounced slavery as incompatible with human dignity. The Vatican II document *Gaudium et Spes*, for example, classified slavery as a social evil and called it "shameful." Yet this judgment does not contradict anything the Church itself has explicitly taught or handed down as a deposit of the faith. The Church now has a keener sense of the degradation of slavery, which is no longer necessitated by historical circumstances. What we have here is an evolution of moral doctrine, but not the rejection of a moral proposition that was once authoritatively asserted by the Church (for example, "slavery in all its forms is morally acceptable"). Also, as Germain Grisez points out, true moral development "is not toward accepting something previously considered wrong, but toward seeing the unacceptability of something previously considered permissible."[30]

As for usury, it is worth noting that what the Church condemned was the charging of interest to the poor along with the greed of usurers. According to Thomas Divine, "In the writings of the early Fathers, we find only reiterations of the scriptural precepts that it is contrary to charity and mercy to exact usury of the poor, without any intimation that these precepts imply a universal prohibition."[31] Also, the original meaning of usury was the charging of interest for a fungible or perishable good. Money is different, however, and a reasonable interest payment reflecting the time-value of money seems legitimate. Thus, the Church's teaching did not preclude the charging of interest per se, and it did not envision a situation where money would have a time-value and where interest rates would be determined by capital markets. Because of changing historical circumstances, Church teaching on usury has surely evolved. But once again it is difficult to make a convincing case that there has been some dramatic reversal in the Church's position on usury, since it still condemns exorbitant or excessive interest rates.

Finally, there is the matter of religious liberty. We no longer live in a world where church and state are inseparable and where the state enforces religious belief. In such societies, heresy was often tantamount to treason. But given the separation of church and state in contemporary society, Vatican II recognized the state's duty to protect the religious liberty of its citizens. This liberty includes freedom of conscience, but it does not include the right to teach religious error. John Courtney Murray, a theologian with particular expertise in this area of theology, has asserted that while there was "authentic progress," there was not "a change of faith."[32] As with slavery, so with religious liberty there has been an organic development of doctrine but not some sort of radical change that signals discontinuity in Church teaching. According to Avery Cardinal Dulles, "The Church has applied the unchanging principles of the right to religious freedom and the duty to uphold religious truth to the conditions of an individualist age . . . but the principle of noncoercion of consciences in matters of faith remains constant."[33]

The lesson here is simple: conceptual clarification of Church teachings alleged to have changed over time often reveals the remarkable stability of Church doctrine even in the area of morality. Over the centuries certain moral doctrines have evolved in light of new knowledge or changing historical circumstances, but the Church's basic teachings have remained the same. It is ironic that revisionists who are so quick to find fault with the Church for changing its moral teachings simultaneously complain about the Church's "inertia" and unwillingness to revise its "medieval" doctrines.

The next criticism is that John Paul II has distorted the Christian notion of morality by overemphasizing the Decalogue and the intrinsically evil acts (such as adultery) that it identifies. This issue has been a great stumbling block for dissenters. Intrinsically evil acts are those acts that do not conform to the natural moral law as discerned by practical reason. First, despite claims to the contrary, the Catholic tradition has never looked upon the existence of intrinsically evil acts as some type of "human judgment" that is subject to change. Rather, the Church has always regarded the intrinsic wrongness of certain actions as an objective reality. Second, as John Paul II observes, "The existence of particular norms regarding man's way of acting in the world, which are endowed with a binding force that excludes always and in whatever situation the possibility of exceptions, is a constant teaching of Tradition and the Church's Magisterium."[34]

Curran's claim that John Paul II has "distorted" the meaning of the Scriptures by putting too much emphasis on the Decalogue is particularly puzzling. Other theologians infer that the prohibitions found in the Decalogue and the New Testament are less absolute than they seem to be. Recall that some proportionalists regard the commands of the Decalogue in more formal terms. In their view, the imperative not to commit "murder" should be seen as an imperative to avoid "unjust killing."[35] Let us carefully consider both of these criticisms.

First, it is simply beyond dispute that the Decalogue is frequently referred to throughout the New Testament. In the synoptic Gospels we find repeated references to the commandments as the path to salvation and as a *necessary condition* for inheriting eternal life (Mark 7:8–13; Mark 10:17–22; Mark 12:28–34; Matt. 19:16–20; Luke 18:18–21). We have already referred to Jesus's insistence on the need to follow the commandments in his encounter with the rich young man (Matt. 19:16–19). Moreover, in the Sermon on the Mount, after Jesus proclaims the Beatitudes he reminds his followers that he has not come to abolish the commandments but to fulfill them (Matt. 5:17–48). In that same discourse Jesus warns people that "whoever then relaxes one of the least of these commandments and teaches men so, shall be called least in the kingdom of heaven" (Matt. 5:19). Jesus's reaffirmation of specific commandments such as the prohibition against adultery is found in several Gospels (Matt. 19:4–9; Mark 10:4–12; Luke 16:18). Furthermore, the mandate to keep the commandments is not confined to the synoptic Gospels. It is reiterated in John's Gospel as well (cf. John 15:10). Also, St. Paul refers to the law of the Decalogue written on the hearts of men and women (Rom. 2:14–15 and 13:8–10). Finally, in the First Letter of John we read: "by this we may be sure that we know him, if we keep his commandments; he who says 'I know him' but disobeys his commandments is a liar" (1 John 2:3). These and many other examples are proof of the Decalogue's special prominence in the New Testament along with its timeless moral relevance.

John Paul II emphasizes the Decalogue simply because it has been resolutely proclaimed by Jesus Himself, who tells us repeatedly that we must follow the commandments to inherit eternal life. Its importance has been underscored in the epistles of St. John and St. Paul. *Scripture makes it abundantly clear that following Jesus means faithfully keeping His commandments.* Therefore, given the many texts we have cited, it is untenable to assert that John Paul II has exaggerated the importance of these commandments of the Sinai.

Curran and other proportionalists are uncomfortable with these absolute norms, which in their view represent a harsh "legalism" and the imposition of inflexible rules on unwilling moral agents. But as previous chapters have indicated, these norms are necessary for the protection of basic human goods such as life and marriage. When we keep the commandments, we manifest love for our neighbor by respecting his or her goods. A careful reading of chapter 1 of *Veritatis Splendor* clarifies that in John Paul II's mind the importance of the Decalogue is not what it proscribes. Rather, the Decalogue is an opportunity to acknowledge and follow God as His people; it is a great gift, "the offer of a share in the divine Goodness revealed and communicated in Jesus" (VS, 11).

Of course, John Paul II clearly recognized that there is more to morality than the Decalogue, despite its centrality in Sacred Scripture. Recall that he refers to the Sermon on the Mount as the *"magna charta* of Gospel morality" (VS, 15). In that sermon, which includes the Beatitudes, Jesus proclaims: "Do not think that I have come to abolish the Law and the Prophets; I have come not to abolish them but to fulfill them" (Matt.

5:17). Thus, Jesus does not neglect the commandments in this magnificent moral teaching but demonstrates that He is "the living 'fulfillment' of the Law" (VS, 15). John Paul II goes on to explain how the Beatitudes are also an important part of Jesus's moral message:

> The Beatitudes are not specifically concerned with certain particular rules of behavior. Rather, they speak of basic attitudes and dispositions in life and therefore they *do not coincide exactly with the commandments*. On the other hand, there is *no separation or opposition* between the Beatitudes and the commandments: both refer to the good, to eternal life. The Sermon on the Mount begins with the proclamation of the Beatitudes but also refers to the commandments (Matt. 5:20–48). At the same time, the Sermon on the Mount demonstrates the openness of the commandments and their orientation toward the horizon of the perfection proper to the Beatitudes. These latter above all are *promises*, from which there also indirectly flow *normative indications* for the moral life. In their originality and profundity they are a sort of *self-portrait of Christ*, and for this very reason are *invitations to discipleship and communion of life with Christ*. (VS, 16)

While the commandments outline the initial path to moral perfection, the Beatitudes provide a "normative indication" of the heroic heights to which we can aspire as moral beings. The Beatitudes suggest a morality of giving and self-sacrifice that beckons us to keep following the path of moral perfection as we aspire to a higher level of Christian discipleship and fellowship.

Curran cites Matthew 25 as the acid test of moral conformity with the Gospel and as "the criterion for entry into eternal life." There is no doubt that this passage proposes important moral norms that require us to help our fellow humanity in need. But it is invalid to claim that these acts of charity are enough to win eternal life and that this moral teaching is superior to all other moral pronouncements in the New Testament. Can someone who deceives his wife for many years in order to carry on adulterous affairs still find favor with God even if he consistently performs acts of charity? The norms proposed in Matthew 25 about feeding the hungry and clothing the naked are part of the fabric of New Testament morality, but by no means do they supersede or displace the Decalogue, which Cardinal Ratzinger has rightfully called the "moral axis of the Sacred Scripture."[36]

The second objection about the Decalogue brings us back to the issue of intrinsic evil acts. There seems to be very little support in the Catholic tradition for regarding the commands of the Decalogue as "human interpretations" that do not share in "the absoluteness of divine wisdom." The early Church Fathers, for example, accepted the absolute prohibitions on actions such as adultery as a mandate from God. Citing the research of French scholars, John Finnis describes how these apostolic fathers "reformulate the Decalogue's prologue and envisage the Ten Commandments as a manifestation of God's sovereignty in the perspective not simply of exodus but now rather of creation itself."[37] There is also little doubt that the theologians St. Augustine, St. Albert the Great, St. Thomas Aquinas, and Francis Suarez were quite insistent on the existence of intrinsically evil acts specified in the Decalogue.

And, of course, there is no ambiguity about what these commands mean. The Decalogue lays out specific negative precepts such as "do not bear false witness" and "do not commit adultery." This latter injunction is always presented as an absolute or categorical command with no exceptions permitted even for proportionate reasons. Moreover we all know what adultery means—sexual intercourse outside of marriage by or with a married person. It is disingenuous to reinterpret this command euphemistically and claim that Jesus was really referring to "wrongful sex." As Robert George has observed,

> For centuries, no Jew or Christian imagined that precepts such as 'do not murder' or 'do not commit adultery' meant not to kill or commit adultery unless one had a proportionate reason for doing so. . . . If [modern] theologians are correct, then the whole body of believers— Jews and Christians alike—would have been mistaken about crucial matters pertaining to salvation until the final third of the twentieth century.[38]

When certain moral theologians tell us that "we cannot expect the Bible to lay out rights and wrongs in detail,"[39] one wonders just what they make of the Decalogue and the other moral commands that pervade the Gospels. When Jesus confronts those who are about to stone the woman caught in adultery (John 8:1–11), he is upset with their hypocrisy. Jesus is merciful with her, as we would expect, but He also tells her, "Go, and do not sin again" (John 8:11), making abundantly clear His disapproval of her adulterous actions. Notice carefully the tone of Jesus's parting remark. He gives her a command, not an exhortation (such as "go and try not to sin again") or a suggestion to avoid "wrongful sex." Why would it be so unheard of for Jesus to reveal the moral truth in the form of commands or specific moral laws (no adultery, the indissolubility of marriage, and so on) that will assist the People of God to determine how they should live?

Thus, regardless of these assertions by dissenters like Curran and McCormick, there is ample evidence that John Paul II, and not these dissenters, has Albert the Great, Aquinas, Augustine, the Church Fathers, and Scripture on his side.[40] These are formidable allies. Accordingly, John Paul II bids wavering moral theologians to reconsider their disavowal of the "universality and immutability of the moral commandments" (VS, 115) and to return to a belief in this basic moral truth that has been propagated down through the centuries.

Finally, we come to the criticism that there is a dichotomy between John Paul II's social and sexual teachings. There is some validity to this claim, which has been made by other revisionist theologians as well. John Paul II speaks in more general terms when he discusses social issues such as economic justice. While he calls for fair wages and just working conditions, he certainly does not contend that there is some preordained economic structure that should be adopted over all others. At the same time, as Curran points out, he is quite specific in the sphere of sexual or marital ethics.

But there are valid reasons for this divergence. The Holy Father and his predecessors have rightly refrained from offering specific solutions to complex economic and social problems. As Pope Paul VI explained, "In the face of such widely varying situations, it is difficult for us to utter a unified message and to put forward a message which has universal validity."[41] Many of these issues are highly technical, and they are not within the ambit of the Church's teaching authority. Second, while the family structure has remained stable, there has been enormous change in the social sphere as the economy has advanced from the industrial age to the information age and from localization to globalization. According to John Paul II, the family was "from the beginning" and remains today God's divine plan (FC, 19). To cast aside this claim is to open up the possibility of relativizing the family structure by support for polygamy and other variations of the sacred marital covenant.

Third, social and economic issues are far more complicated than issues arising at the level of marital ethics. Consider injustices such as economic inequality in countries like Latin America. The causes of such inequality are varied and disputed: colonial history, poor property rights, lack of education, regressive social spending, and so forth. And there is even more disagreement about the possible solutions. Is land reform the best route to economic justice? Or is more social spending the answer? What about simply relying on the economic growth that will come from embracing globalization and free trade? Curran wants to treat all moral problems in the same way, as complex and open ended so that they preclude being resolved by specific norms. But moral problems are not uniform. Rather, they have varying levels of complexity. Just because some moral problems are quite complex and defy a definite resolution, it does not follow that all moral problems lack a settled solution.

Fourth, we do not find Jesus Himself addressing social or economic issues in specific terms, but, as we have seen, He is quite specific about other moral issues such as adultery and divorce. While there are some moral truths that are clearly specified ("thou shalt not commit adultery") and receive their ultimate justification in Scripture, other moral questions are left unresolved by revelation. Those questions such as economic justice must be addressed at a more general level, as John Paul II and Paul VI have done.

In summary, John Paul II's critics come up short. The Holy Father's potent reaffirmation of exceptionless moral norms and inviolable human rights is both philosophically tenable and consistent with Scripture and the long tradition of Catholic theology. Without specific moral absolutes, few in number but powerful in their normative force, each person's supreme dignity cannot be protected. Without those absolutes the darkness of moral contingency cannot be overcome. The faithful should not be obliged to ponder whether actions such as adultery *might* be right under some circumstances if there is a proportionate reason. Discerning that reason depends on assessing the consequences of one's adulterous behavior, which are impossible to predict. Adultery is always wrong and always to be avoided—there is no ambiguity and no need for endless moral deliberation, which is often rationalization in disguise. John Paul II also has articulated a nuanced natural law philosophy that is certainly not susceptible to the problem of "physicalism." Finally, his moral theology allows for some evolution of moral doctrine, such as condemnations of practices once ignored or tolerated by the Church, while emphasizing that certain principles are unchanged since they are necessary to protect basic human goods, which are invariant.

In contrast to proportionalism, John Paul II presents a moral vision with the clarity and simplicity necessary to make righteous living accessible for everyone. As we have demonstrated, his moral theology has a spiritual richness and sophistication that is often unappreciated by some critics who are eager to dismiss the principles underlying his moral teaching. But as we have shown, that teaching is based solidly upon "Sacred Scripture and the living Apostolic Tradition" (VS, 5).

The Future of Moral Theology

The purpose of John Paul II's moral writings is to inaugurate a renewal of moral theology that reaffirms the moral substance of the Catholic faith. At the same time, he develops a new methodology that puts more emphasis on Scripture. In his writings he labored to show the problematic positions of revisionist theologians. In an effort to accommodate the culture, these theologians have offered new theories on anthropology, conscience, autonomy, the fundamental option, and proportionalism. At the same time, they have discarded traditional Church teaching on intrinsically evil acts and ignored the lasting effects of individual moral choices.

In the concluding sections of *Veritatis Splendor* John Paul II calls upon moral theologians to "exercise careful discernment in the context of today's prevalently scientific and technical culture, exposed as it is to the dangers of relativism, pragmatism, and positivism" (VS, 112). Only Christian faith, not the behavioral sciences, can reveal moral truth. Thus, he encourages them to consult the Scripture for indications of valid moral norms:

> It is the Gospel which reveals the full truth about man and his moral journey, and thus enlightens and admonishes sinners; it proclaims to them God's mercy, which is constantly at work to preserve them from despair at their inability fully to know and keep God's law and from the presumption that they can be saved without merit. God also reminds sinners of the joy of forgiveness, which alone

grants the strength to see in the moral law a liberating truth, a grace-filled source of hope, a path of life.

Teaching moral doctrine involves the conscious acceptance of these intellectual, spiritual and pastoral responsibilities. Moral theologians who have accepted the charge of teaching the Church's doctrine, thus have a grave duty to train the faithful to make this moral discernment, to be committed to the true good and to have confident recourse to God's grace. (VS, 112–113)

The implication of this passage is clear enough: the proper renewal of moral theology will begin when moral theologians return to the authentic teaching of the Gospel, which articulates the moral requirements of the faith. In Scripture they will find specific prohibitions against certain activities such as adultery, lying, and the taking of innocent life. According to the Holy Father, "Jesus Himself reaffirms that these prohibitions allow no exceptions" (VS, 52). Dissenting theologians may still deny that these prohibitions are not really absolute despite the language to the contrary, but they cannot deny that up until the past several decades people believed that the command "You shall not commit adultery" meant just what it said. Were the faithful, the Magisterium, and previous generations of Church Fathers and moral theologians all wrong until these revisionists finally came along to enlighten us?

The Holy Father does not seek a return to classical moral theology, which was overly concerned with arcane laws and negative restrictions. Prior to Vatican II, moral theology was taught from manuals. It was excessively legalistic and sometimes veered toward voluntarism. It was also disconnected from other areas of theology and not focused on Christ as the ultimate norm of morality. But the biggest problem was the failure to ground moral norms in the basic human goods required for personal human flourishing. Thus, Vatican II's call for a renewal of moral theology was surely justified.

That renewal, however, went in the wrong direction thanks to the work of several dissenting theologians. Those theologians stressed the complexities of the moral life and the need for new methods of moral analysis such as proportionalism. The result of this, according to George Weigel, was to make it increasingly difficult "to condemn radical evil in a century pockmarked by its lethal and brutalizing consequences."[42] At the same time, the rejection of metaphysics has made it virtually impossible to construct a unifying moral vision anchored in the goodness of God's creation.

John Paul II's moral theology, however, has overcome the deficiencies of preconciliar Catholic moral theology. This has been accomplished in part by the integration of personalism into John Paul II's own distinctive theological vision. John Paul II has also changed the wayward course set by the dissenters with a return to "the very foundations of moral theology, foundations which are being undermined by certain present-day tendencies" (VS, 5). As a result, John Paul II has accomplished a more authentic renewal that is creative but consistent with the Catholic tradition and teachings of the Magisterium. There is much work to be done, but the Holy Father's writings provide many insights for the continuation of this authentic renewal, firmly grounded in Scripture and tradition. We humbly suggest a few possibilities for how theologians can profitably advance John Paul II's pioneering work for the continuing renewal of moral theology.

First, moral theologians should follow John Paul II's example and develop a theology that is authentically Christocentric, one that always regards Jesus Christ the Logos as the ultimate norm of morality and the "center of history" (RH, 1). His eternal Word transcends time and history. Moral theology should also be carefully nurtured by Scripture, as Vatican II has suggested. This aspect of a renewal is essential since "much recent work in moral theology is neither centered on Christ . . . nor oriented toward the heavenly calling of the Christians."[43] As Cardinal Ratzinger has pointed out, recent work in moral theology has "marginaliz[ed] Sacred Scripture even more completely than the pre-conciliar manualist tradition."[44] Yet as John Paul II reminds us, "from the beginning Christ has been at the center of the faith and life of the Church, and also at the center of her teaching and theology" (CTH, 44).

Second, moral theologians should follow John Paul II's advice to initiate a revival of Thomistic realism that takes seriously "God as the necessary ground . . . of all created beings" and as the source of all goodness (MI, 8). As John Paul II constantly reminded us, "the good has its foundation in God alone" and a proper theory of the good is indispensable for a viable moral theology (MI, 15). The retreat from Thomistic metaphysics has led to specious philosophies arguing that goodness is not naturally given but is creatively determined by the human subject. As chapter 1 stated, moral theology depends on the right philosophical partners, and Aquinas has been an exemplary aide to theologians in the past. This does not imply that openness to insights of contemporary philosophy should be discouraged if that philosophy has discerned the truth. The Holy Father himself found some accommodation between the Thomist tradition and personalism. Similar creative retrievals of Aquinas's philosophy, especially his natural law ethic and his philosophy of the person, would be immensely helpful for the future trajectory of moral theology.

Third, those theologians who espouse a dualistic anthropology, or who are dubious about a valid nondualistic anthropology, should reassess their philosophies especially in light of John Paul II's profound work on the theology of the body. The issue of anthropology is of crucial importance for bioethics, so theologians can ill afford to ignore or discount the Holy Father's holistic view of the human person. Dualism and materialism have led to obstinate errors in moral reasoning. As we have seen, for John Paul II the human body forms an integral part of the human person. This insight is expressed with great eloquence throughout *The Theology of the Body* in passages such as this one:

> When the first man exclaimed at the sight of the woman: "This is bone of my bones and flesh of my flesh" (Gen 2:23), he merely affirmed the human identity of both. Exclaiming in this way, he seems to say that here is a body that expresses the person. . . . It can also be said that this "body" reveals the "living soul" such as man became when God-Yahweh breathed life into him. (TB, 61)

Moral theologians must expose the fallacious reasoning underlying anthropologies that promote materialism or a dualism of material body and spiritual soul. They should also explore more thoroughly the implications of a nondualistic anthropology for bioethics. Without a properly conceived anthropology, moral theology will fail to do justice to our personhood and to the tangible reality of human life.

Fourth, moral theologians must reevaluate the validity of the fundamental option theory and ponder the significance of human choices as free and self-determining. The arguments advanced by John Paul II against this theory seem quite compelling. In describing and assessing cases in moral theology they should adopt the perspective of the acting person: "In order to be able to grasp the object of an act which specifies that act morally, it is therefore necessary to place oneself *in the perspective of the acting person*" (VS, 78). Proportionalism considers morality from the perspective of the neutral observer. It focuses on expected outcomes when it assesses moral rightness, and it largely neglects the acting person's practical deliberation and choice. The Holy Father has reaffirmed the primacy of the "inwardness" of the moral subject for understanding and evaluating moral actions. This perspective recognizes the forgotten truth that morality is about the will and the heart, the deliberate, interior choice of a specific action.

Moral theologians should also elaborate upon John Paul II's unique contribution to this discourse about human action, and explore the theological implications of *The Acting Person*. The notion that moral actions have existential or soul-making significance for the acting person needs more attention in a pragmatic world obsessed with results. The Socratic question posed in Plato's *Gorgias* is still an apt one for meditation: "is it not better to suffer injustice rather than do it?"[45] Given the lasting effect on one's character, isn't it better to be the victim of evil rather than its perpetrator?

Finally, moral theology must be prepared to accept that leading a moral life is difficult. It must not succumb to the temptation to soften the message of Jesus in the Gospel. As John Paul II writes, if morality "strives toward values, if it brings a universal affirmation of good, it can be nothing but extraordinarily demanding. Good, in fact, is not easy, it is always the 'hard road' of which Christ speaks in the Gospel (Matt. 7:14)" (CTH, 22). Like the early Christians, we are called to "live according to the new way" (Acts 9:1). A theology that models itself on the facile standards of conventional morality is propagating an illusion that will dilute the moral substance of the faith. Such a theology will lead to a soft humanism that cannot distinguish good from evil or vice from virtue. No one disputes the presence of moral ambiguity in this world. But when the lines between good and evil become so blurred that we cannot tell one from the other, we edge closer to the precipice of moral nihilism. Such nihilism, Nietzsche warns us, gives rise to the "omni-satisfied" (*Allgenügsamen*), those "whitewashed souls . . . who consider everything good."[46] They affirm all values, lifestyles, or commitments as equally valid and refuse to be selective. True moral judgment, however, implies that a certain moral choice should be validated and affirmed because the alternatives are morally unacceptable. Nietzsche saw with great clarity a simple truth that has eluded his postmodern followers: we cannot affirm what is right and just unless we negate and renounce what is wrong and unjust.

Moral theology, therefore, must acknowledge that there are durable, sacred values worth our sacrifice and effort. In John Paul II's view, moral courage and even martyrdom reveal what it means to be human because they show us that sometimes it is better to suffer evil than to give evil its due (VS, 90). According to Cardinal Ratzinger, "In martyrdom, it becomes clear that a good exists that is worth dying for."[47]

Last Words

Of course, there is much more to be said about all these issues, but I am confident and hopeful that this book will not be the last word about John Paul II's prophetic moral vision. Others will continue to carefully mine his prolific output and offer a more substantial defense of the late Holy Father's teachings and his sustained effort to preserve the fundamental moral principles of the Catholic faith.

What is particularly impressive about those teachings, even for his critics, is his unwavering belief in the transcendent dignity of each human person. This viewpoint will continue to come under assault in the twenty-first century by those who are determined to redefine human nature or those who wish to attribute dignity only to individuals who have "achieved" the status of personhood. And it will be casually cast aside by others who advocate an ephemeral morality instead of one that offers the confident assurance of fixed moral norms grounded in the absolute dignity of personhood.

But John Paul II has prayerfully spoken the truth about these matters, and when the truth is communicated, it is always accompanied by God's grace. John Paul II's heroic efforts, which are slowly beginning to reap results, are to be commended. If Catholic laypeople, clergy, and theologians prayerfully meditate on the Holy Father's writings, they will be impressed by their wisdom and insight, their continuity with the tradition, and their sensitivity to the inviolable rights of *all* persons. Once we begin to reformulate the precepts of the Decalogue or to make exceptions about fundamental rights and duties, morality begins to lose its objectivity and stability. As Shakespeare puts it: "Take but degree away, untune that string, / And, hark, what discord follows."[48]

There are some hopeful signs, of course, that the Catholic Church itself has begun to feel the stirrings in her own faithful members for moral teachings "in tune" with Sacred Scripture and the natural law. So we must not be timid about proclaiming and teaching the moral principles that John Paul II has so carefully articulated and defended. This pope's inspiring words on moral truth represent a challenge for all of us, a challenge to face an uncertain future as decisively and full of hope as he did.

Notes

1. *Gaudium et Spes*, in *Vatican Council II: The Conciliar and Post Conciliar Documents*, ed. Austin Flannery, O.P. (Northport, N.Y.: Costello, 1975), 74. John Finnis points out that this phrase is poorly translated in some editions as "natural law and the Gospel." See "The Natural Law, Objective Morality, and Vatican II," in *Principles of Catholic Moral Life*, ed. William May (Chicago: Franciscan Herald Press, 1980), 113–149.

2. Karol Wojtyla, "Human Nature as the Basis of Ethical Formation," in *Person and Community: Selected Essays*, trans. Theresa Sandok (New York: Peter Lang, 1993), 96.

3. St. Thomas Aquinas, *Summa Theologiae* I-II, q. 100, a. 3.

4. Immanuel Kant, *Foundations of the Metaphysics of Morals*, trans. Lewis Beck (Indianapolis: Bobbs-Merrill, 1959), 16.

5. Kant, *Foundations*, 64.

6. Karol Wojtyla, "Subjectivity and the Irreducible in the Human Being," in *Person and Community: Selected Essays*, 213.

7. Karol Wojtyla, "The Person: Subject and Community," in *Person and Community: Selected Essays*, 229.

8. St. Thomas Aquinas, *Sent.* III, d. 35, a. 4, sol. 1c.

9. Kevin Schmiesing, "A History of Personalism," Acton Institute for the Study of Religion and Liberty, www.acton.org/schmiesing. (December 19, 2005).

10. Wojtyla, "Subjectivity and the Irreducible," 213.

11. Rocco Buttiglione, "Introduction to the Third Polish Edition of the Acting Person," in *Karol Wojtyla: The Thought of the Man Who Became Pope John Paul II* (Grand Rapids, Mich.: Eerdmans, 1997), 359.

12. Charles Curran, *The Moral Theology of John Paul II* (Washington, D.C.: Georgetown University Press, 2005). The citations to this book refer to page numbers.

13. St. Thomas Aquinas, *Summa Theologiae* I-II, q. 94, a. 4.

14. Richard McCormick, S.J., "Some Early Reactions to *Veritatis Splendor*," *Theological Studies* 55 (1994): 500.

15. For example, see William May, "Moral Theologians and Veritatis Splendor," www.cfpeople.org/Apologetics/page51a079.html.

16. Germain Grisez, *Living a Christian Life* (Quincy, Ill.: Franciscan Herald Press, 1983), 648.

17. See St. Thomas Aquinas, *Summa Theologiae* I-II, q. 17, a. 1.

18. Martin Rhonheimer, "Natural Moral Law: Moral Knowledge and Conscience: The Cognitive Structure of the Natural Law and the Truth of Subjectivity," *Pontifical Academy for Life*, February 2002, www.academiavita.org/nat_dig/rhonheimer (January 22, 2006).

19. John Grabowski and Michael Naughton, "Catholic Social and Sexual Ethics: Inconsistent or Organic," *The Thomist* (October 2000): 555–578.

20. Grabowski and Naughton, "Catholic Social and Sexual Ethics," 565.

21. Charles Curran et al., *Dissent In and For the Church: Theologians and "Humanae Vitae"* (New York: Sheed and Ward, 1969), 25.

22. St. Thomas Aquinas, *Sent.* II, d. 40, a. 2.

23. This text is from *In Duo Praecepta Caritatis et in Decem Legis Praecepta*, 250. For full reference see *Veritatis Splendor*, 78.

24. Curran et al., *Dissent In and For the Church*, 25.

25. For the relevant texts of Aquinas, see *Summa Theologiae* II-II, q. 33, a. 2c, and q. 79, a. 3, ad. 3, along with *De Malo*, q. 7, a. 1, ad. 8. For Aquinas's position on the absolute prohibition on the taking of innocent life, see *Summa Theologiae* II-II, q. 64, a. 6. See also John Finnis, *Aquinas* (Oxford: Oxford University Press, 1998), 164–167.

26. *Dignitatis Humanae* in *Vatican Council II: The Conciliar and Post Conciliar Documents*, ed. Austin Flannery, O.P. (Northport, N.Y.: Costello Publishing, 1975), 2.

27. *Gaudium et Spes*, 79.

28. Gianni Vattimo, "The Age of Interpretation," in *The Future of Religion*, ed. S. Zabala (New York: Columbia University Press, 2005), 53.

29. John Henry Cardinal Newman, *An Essay on the Development of Christian Doctrine* (New York: Longmans, Green, 1949), 329–330.

30. Germain Grisez, *Christian Moral Principles* (Quincy, Ill.: Franciscan Press, 1983), 220.

31. Quoted in David Palm, "The Red Herring of Usury," www.catholic.com/thisrock/1997/970fea3.asp (January 3, 2006).

32. Quoted in Avery Cardinal Dulles, S.J., "Development or Reversal," *First Things* (October 2005): 60.

33. Dulles, "Development or Reversal," 60.

34. John Paul II, "Address to Moral Theologians," November 12, 1988, in *Acta Apostolicae Sedis* 81 (1989): 1209.

35. See John Dedek, "Intrinsically Evil Acts: An Historical Study of the Mind of St. Thomas," *The Thomist* (July 1979): 385–413.

36. Joseph Cardinal Ratzinger, "The Renewal of Moral Theology: Perspectives of Vatican II and *Veritatis Splendor*," *Communio* (Summer 2005): 119.

37. John Finnis, *Moral Absolutes: Tradition, Revision and Truth* (Washington, D.C.: Catholic University of America Press, 1991), 7.

38. Robert George, contribution to "The Splendor of Truth: A Symposium," *First Things* (January 1994): 14–29.

39. McCormick, "Some Early Reactions to *Veritatis Splendor*," 500.

40. See William May, *Moral Absolutes* (Milwaukee: Marquette University Press, 1989).

41. Pope Paul VI, *Octogesima Adventens*, Acta Apostolicae Sedis 59 (1967): 26.

42. George Weigel, *Witness to Hope* (New York: HarperCollins, 1999), 690.

43. Grisez, *Christian Moral Principles*, 15.

44. Ratzinger, "Renewal of Moral Theology," 120.

45. Plato, *Gorgias*, trans. W. C. Helmbold (Indianapolis: Bobbs-Merrill, 1952), 469c.

46. Nietzsche, "Vom Geist der Schwere," in *Also Sprach Zarathustra* (Stuttgart: Philipp Reclam, 1962), 183. For English translation see Walter Kaufmann, ed., *The Portable Nietzsche* (New York: Viking, 1954), 306.

47. Ratzinger, "Renewal of Moral Theology," 120.

48. William Shakespeare, *Trolius and Cressida*, in *The Complete Works of Shakespeare*, ed. Hardin Craig (Glenview, Ill.: Scott Foresman, 1961), 109.

Appendix: The Life and Writings of Pope John Paul II

KAROL JÓZEF WOJTYLA was born on May 18, 1920, in Wadowice, a small town near the city of Kraków in southern Poland. He was the second of two sons born to Karol Wojtyla and Emilia Kaczorowska. His mother died in 1929. Shortly thereafter his older brother, Edmund, passed away, and his father, a noncommissioned army officer, perished in 1941.

Upon his graduation from Marcin Wadowita, the high school in Wadowice, Karol enrolled in Kraków's Jagiellonian University in 1938. However, the Nazi occupation in Poland forced the closure of the university in 1939. As a result, the young Karol had to work in a quarry (1940–1944) and then in the Solvay chemical factory to earn his living and to avoid deportation to Germany. Fortunately, he found some solace in acting and writing. He composed several dramatic and poetic pieces, including "The Jeweler's Shop." An artistic career seemed to be on the horizon, but God had other plans.

During those difficult years Karol felt the stirrings of a call to the Catholic priesthood, and, in 1942, he began studies in a clandestine seminary operated in Kraków by Adam Stefan Cardinal Sapieha, the city's archbishop. The defiant Cardinal Sapieha represented "the moral resistance of the nation against the Nazis."[1] When World War II finally came to an end in 1945, he continued his studies in the major seminary of Kraków after it reopened; he later studied at the Faculty of Theology of the Jagiellonian University. He was ordained to the priesthood in Kraków on November 1, 1946.

Shortly after his ordination, Cardinal Sapieha sent Father Wojtyla to Rome, where he worked under the guidance of the French Dominican Thomist Garrigou-Lagrange. He finished his doctorate in theology in 1948. His thesis focused on the issue of faith in the works of St. John of the Cross. The focus of this work, *Faith According to St. John of the Cross*, was on the experiential reality of faith, which is always inextricably bound up with love.

After he finished graduate studies, he returned to Poland and was promptly assigned to a parish in Niegowic. But his stay in this small village lasted only six months. In March 1949, he was transferred to St. Florian's parish in Kraków, a place where he made many good friends who stayed close to him for many years.

In 1951, he returned to his studies at the Jagiellonian University, pursuing his second doctorate degree. His habilitation thesis was written on the ethical system of the phenomenologist Max Scheler. Scheler's main philosophical work was *Formalism in Ethics*, and in this book Scheler sought to develop an ethical system predicated on the emotional experience of value. Since Scheler was a phenomenologist, he sought to understand ethical values through an analysis of common experience. Scheler's philosophy also belonged in the personalist tradition so attractive to Karol Wojtyla because of its attention to the significance of moral choices. Scheler's work was a reaction to the Kantian ethical system, which was characterized by its sterile focus on duty and the disjunction between happiness (or fulfillment) and morality. In his own work on ethics, Wojtyla looked for some common ground between these two philosophers, emphasizing both the objective (duty) and subjective (personalism) dimensions of morality.

With two doctorates in hand, he was now eligible to become a university professor, and in 1954, he was assigned to the philosophy department at the Catholic University of Lublin. Several years later, he was appointed to the Chair of Ethics at that university. During this period, Lublin was an exciting place to be teaching philosophy. In the spirit of St. Thomas Aquinas, the faculty sought to integrate the disciplines of metaphysics, ethics, and anthropology. As Christopher West points out, the Lublin School "believed their work—if given the proper exposure—could redirect the entire course of modern philosophy."[2]

On July 4, 1958, Father Wojtyla was appointed auxiliary bishop of Kraków by Pope Pius XII, and he was consecrated September 28,

1958, in Wawel Cathedral, Kraków, by Archbishop Baziak. He became the archbishop of Kraków in December 1963. Bishop Wojtyla was a major contributor to the Vatican II proceedings, writing major portions of the document *Gaudium et spes*. He also addressed Vatican II on the topic of religious freedom. He was made a cardinal by Pope Paul VI on June 26, 1967.

As a professor at Lublin, Karol Wojtyla was quite prolific. His books included *Love and Responsibility* (1960) and his major philosophical opus, *The Acting Person* (1969). He also composed numerous articles that appeared in various scholarly journals and in a work of collected essays called *Person and Community*. *Love and Responsibility*, "born out of pastoral necessity," was one of his most popular works. It delineated a Catholic sexual ethic that taught that conjugal love had both procreative and unitive dimensions.[3]

After the untimely death of Pope John Paul I, Cardinal Wojtyla was elected to the papacy on October 16, 1978. During the first few years, there were clear signs that this pontificate would be one of historic accomplishment. Within several months, he wrote his first encyclical, *Redemptor Hominis*, focusing on the mystery of Christ's redemption. In June 1979 he made his first pilgrimage to Poland, a visit that gave great comfort to the workers' Solidarity movement. Thanks to his support of Solidarity and his courageous opposition to communism, he is credited with helping to bring about the final collapse of Soviet communism in 1991.

In May 1981, he was the victim of an assassination attempt by Mehmet Ali Agca, but he recovered and returned to the Vatican from the Gemelli hospital in early June. The pope saw the hand of divine providence in all this: "One hand fired, and another guided the bullet" (MI, 159).

The assassination attempt never impeded John Paul II's determined efforts at global evangelization. The Holy Father completed 104 pastoral visits outside of Italy and 146 within Italy. There were several pilgrimages to places such as the United States, Poland, France, Germany, and Latin America. The Holy Father drew some of the largest crowds in history, including six million people at an outdoor mass in Manila. In 1998, he embarked on the first papal pilgrimage to Cuba. The Holy Father worked tirelessly to improve Jewish-Christian relations. To this end, he made an historic visit to the Holy Land in March 2000. The pope visited Yad Vashem, Israel's Holocaust memorial, and the Western Wall. According to one reporter, "the sight of the aging, stooped pope praying as he pressed a trembling hand against the ancient stones of the Western Wall struck a chord with Jews around the world."[4]

During his papacy, John Paul II wrote fourteen encyclicals, fifteen apostolic exhortations, eleven apostolic constitutions, and forty-five apostolic letters. The most well known of those encyclicals included *Veritatis Splendor* (1993), *Fides et Ratio* (1998), and *Evangelium Vitae* (1995). He wrote several encyclicals on social issues, such as *Centesimus Annus* (1991), which marked the centenary anniversary of Pope Leo XIII's *Rerum Novarum*. His last encyclical, *Ecclesia de Eucharista*, written in 2003, was devoted to the topic of the Eucharist, which "is at the center of the process of the Church's growth" (EE, 21). While the encyclicals have several unifying themes, George Weigel contends that it is instructive to "imagine [them] as a set of keys for understanding and unlocking the teaching of Vatican II." For example, the encyclical *Redemptoris Missio* provides the "key" for interpreting the Council's document on missions (*Ad Gentes Divinitus*).[5]

John Paul II also oversaw the production of the *Catechism of the Catholic Church*, "one of the most important cultural accomplishments of the pontificate."[6] While he was not directly involved in writing this document, it relied heavily on his teachings, which, according to Father Schönborn, were "often the basis of a *Catechism* text."[7] Despite the admonitions of some skeptics, the *Catechism* was well received within the Catholic Church—within a few years of its publication, eight million copies were in print.

The pope also published five popular books: *Crossing the Threshold of Hope* (1994), *Gift and Mystery: On the 50th Anniversary of My Priestly Ordination* (1996), *Roman Triptych—Meditations* (2003), *Rise, Let Us Be on Our Way* (2004), and *Memory and Identity* (2005).

Pope John Paul II presided at 147 beatification ceremonies, during which 1,338 men and women became *beati* (or blesseds) of the Church. He also canonized 482 saints at fifty-one ceremonies. Those saints included Maximillian Kolbe, a martyr of charity who gave his life to save an inmate at Auschwitz; the German philosopher and Jewish convert Edith Stein (who became Sister Teresa Benedicta of the Cross); Sister Faustina Kowalska, the inspiration for the Divine Mercy movement; Padre Pio; Gianna Beretta Molla, an Italian physician who sacrificed her life for the life of her unborn baby; and Katherine Drexel. The new *beati* included Mother Theresa of Calcutta and Pope John XXIII.

During his pontificate, he presided over the installation of 232 cardinals and appointed 3,995 bishops. With many of these inspired appointments he transformed the face of the Catholic hierarchy. He also convened six plenary meetings of the College of Cardinals and presided at fifteen synods of bishops.

World Youth Days were another distinctive feature of John Paul II's pontificate. They attracted millions of young people in cities like Rome, Denver, Toronto, Manila, and Paris. The Holy Father seemed to have a special bond with young people as evidenced by the great success of these unprecedented events.

John Paul II suffered from Parkinson's disease and other ailments. He was frail and always in physical pain. By 2003 his progressive immobility forced him to begin using a hydraulic wheelchair so that he could say Mass while seated. He no longer walked in public and often allowed other Vatican officials to take his place at major ceremonies. In the final years of his life he was described by the Vatican press secretary, Joaquin Navarro-Valls, as a "a body pulled by a soul." But even during this time, he never faltered. His unflagging spirit and complete dedication to God are best expressed in his Last Will and Testament: "I feel that much more profoundly that I am totally in God's Hands—and I remain continually at the disposition of my Lord, entrusting myself to Him in His Immaculate Mother ('Totus Tuus')."[8]

Pope John Paul II was the longest-serving pope of the twentieth century, but on April 2, 2005, his long reign as pope came to an end. Millions came to Rome for the Holy Father's funeral, loudly proclaiming *Magnus* and *Santo subito!*

Notes

1. Rocco Buttiglione, *Karol Wojtyla: The Thought of the Man Who Became Pope John Paul II* (Grand Rapids, Mich.: Eerdmans, 1997), 30.

2. Christopher West, *Theology of the Body Explained* (Boston: Pauline Books, 2003), 36.

3. See George Weigel, *Witness to Hope* (New York: HarperCollins, 1999), 140, 142.

4. Jerry Filteau, "Reconciliation with Jews a Hallmark of John Paul II's Papacy," *The Pilot*, April 8, 2005, 21.

5. George Weigel, *God's Choice* (New York: HarperCollins, 2005), 33.

6. Weigel, *God's Choice*, 44.

7. Quoted in Weigel, *Witness to Hope*, 661.

8. John Paul II, "Last Will and Testament," April 7, 2005, www.zenit.org/.041105.html (November 30, 2005).

Bibliography

Works by Karol Wojtyla

Person and Community: Selected Essays. Trans. Theresa Sandok. New York: Peter Lang, 1993.

Collected Plays and Writings on Theater. Trans. Boleslaw Taborski. Berkeley: University of California Press, 1987.

Faith According to St. John of the Cross. San Francisco: St. Ignatius Press, 1981.

Love and Responsibility. Trans. J. J. Willetts. San Francisco: HarperCollins, 1981.

Sources of Renewal: The Implementation of the Vatican Council. Trans. P. S. Falla. New York: Collins, 1980.

The Acting Person. Trans. A. Potocki. Analecta Husserliana, vol. 10. Dordrecht, Holland: D. Reidel, 1979.

"The Person, Subject, and Community." *Review of Metaphysics* 33, no. 2 (December 1979): 277.

"The Structure of Self-Determination as the Core of the Theory of the Person." In *Tommaso d'Aquino nel suo VII Centennario.* Roma: Edizioni Domenicane Italiene, 1974.

For the works of John Paul II and St. Thomas Aquinas used in writing this book, see the Abbreviations section in the front.

General Bibliography

Aristotle. *Metaphysics.* Trans. R. Hope. Ann Arbor: University of Michigan Press, 1968.

———. *Nicomachean Ethics.* Trans. J. A. K. Thomson. New York: Penguin, 1976.

Bauman, Zygmunt. *Life in Fragments: Essays in Postmodern Morality.* Cambridge: Blackwell, 1995.

Boyle, Joseph. "Freedom, the Human Person, and Human Action." In *Principles of Catholic Moral Life*, ed. William May. Chicago: Franciscan Herald Press, 1980.

Buttiglione, Rocco. *Karol Wojtyla: The Thought of the Man Who Became Pope John Paul II.* Grand Rapids, Mich.: Eerdmans, 1997.

Caputo, John. *Radical Hermeneutics: Repetition, Deconstruction and the Hermeneutic Project.* Bloomington: Indiana University Press, 1987.

Catechism of the Catholic Church. New York: Doubleday, 1995.

Clarke, Norris, S.J. *The One and the Many.* Notre Dame, Ind.: Notre Dame University Press, 2001.

———. *Person and Being.* Milwaukee: Marquette University Press, 1993.

Colson, Charles, and N. de S. Cameron. *Human Dignity in the Biotech Century.* Downers Grove, Ill.: InterVarsity Press, 2004.

Curran, Charles. *The Moral Theology of John Paul II.* Washington, D.C.: Georgetown University Press, 2005.

———. *New Perspectives in Moral Theology.* Notre Dame, Ind.: Fides, 1974.

Curran, Charles, and Richard McCormick, S.J., eds. *Readings in Moral Theology No. 1: Moral Norms and Catholic Tradition.* New York: Paulist Press, 1979.

Curran, Charles, et al. *Dissent In and For the Church: Theologians and "Humanae Vitae."* New York: Sheed and Ward, 1969.

Dawson, Christopher. *The Dynamics of World History.* La Salle, Ill.: Sherwood Sugden, 1978.

Dedek, John. "Intrinsically Evil Acts: An Historical Study of the Mind of St. Thomas." *The Thomist* (July 1979): 385–413.

De Lubac, Henri. *At the Service of the Church.* San Francisco: Ignatius Press, 1993.

Derrida, Jacques. *Positions.* Trans. A. Bass. Chicago: University of Chicago Press, 1981.

Dworkin, Ronald. *Life's Dominion: An Argument about Abortion, Euthanasia and Individual Freedom.* New York: Knopf, 1993.

Dworkin, Ronald, et al. "Assisted Suicide: The Philosopher's Brief." *New York Review of Books*, March 27, 1997, 41–49.

Dulles, Avery, S.J. "Can Philosophy Be Christian?" *First Things* (April 2000): 24–29.

———. "Development or Reversal." *First Things* (October 2005): 57–61.

———. *The Splendor of Faith.* New York: Herder and Herder, 2003.

Farley, Margaret. "How Shall We Love in a Postmodern World?" In *The Historical Development of Fundamental Moral Theology in the United States*, ed. Charles Curran and Richard McCormick, S.J. New York: Paulist Press, 1999.

Finnis, John. "Euthanasia, Morality and Law." *Loyola of Los Angeles Law Review* 31 (June 1998): 1123–1145.

———. *Fundamentals of Ethics*. Washington, D.C.: Georgetown University Press, 1983.

———. *Moral Absolutes: Tradition, Revision and Truth*. Washington, D.C.: Catholic University of America Press, 1991.

———. "On the Practical Meaning of Secularism." *Notre Dame Law Review* 73 (March 1998): 491–516.

Flannery, Austin, O.P., ed. *Vatican Council II: The Conciliar and Post Conciliar Documents*. Northport, N.Y.: Costello, 1975.

Fletcher, Joseph. *Moral Responsibility: Situation Ethics at Work*. Philadelphia: Lippincott, 1967.

Foot, Philippa. "Moral Relativism." In *Moral Relativism: A Reader*, ed. Thomas Carson and P. Moser. New York: Oxford University Press, 2001.

Fuchs, Josef. *Human Values and Christian Morality*. Dublin: Gill, 1970.

———. *Personal Responsibility and Christian Morality*. Washington, D.C.: Georgetown University Press, 1984.

George, Robert, et al. "The Spendor of Truth: A Symposium." *First Things* (January 1994): 14–29.

Gilson, Etienne. *The Spirit of Medieval Philosophy*. New York: Charles Scribner & Sons, 1932.

Grabowski, John, and Michael Naughton. "Catholic Social and Sexual Ethics: Inconsistent or Organic." *The Thomist* (October 2000): 555–578.

Green, Ronald. "Business Ethics as a Postmodern Phenomenon." *Business Ethics Quarterly* 3, no. 3 (1993): 219–225.

Grisez, Germain. *Abortion: The Myths, the Realities, and the Arguments*. New York: Corpus, 1970.

———. *Living a Christian Life*. Quincy, Ill.: Franciscan Herald Press, 1983.

Hegel, G. W. F. *Vorlesungen über die Geschichte der Philosophie III*. In *Sämtliche Werke XV*, ed. G. Lasson and J. Hoffmeister. Leipzig: Meineer Verlag, 1905.

Heidegger, Martin. *Einführung in die Metaphysik*. Tübingen: Niemeyer, 1953.

———. *Holzwege*. Frankfurt: Klostermann, 1950.

———. *Vorträge und Aufsätze*. Pfullingen: Neske, 1954.

———. *Was Heißt Denken*. Tübingen: Niemeyer, 1954.

Hittinger, Russell. *First Grace*. Wilmington, Del.: ISI Books, 2003.

Hudson, Deal. "Does Life Begin at Implantation?" *The Window*, May 15, 2005, 1–3.

Hütter, Reinhard, and Alan Mitchell, eds. *Ecumenical Ventures in Ethics: Protestants Engage Pope John Paul II's Moral Encyclicals*. Grand Rapids, Mich.: Wm. B. Eerdmans, 1998.

Introna, Lucas. "The 'Measure of Man' and the Ethics of Machines." In Proceedings of Computer Ethics Philosophical Enquiry (CEPE) Conference, ed. Richard Spinello and Herman Tavani. Boston College, June 2003.

Kant, Immanuel. *Foundations of the Metaphysics of Morals*. Trans. Lewis Beck. Indianapolis: Bobbs-Merrill, 1959.

Kiely, Bartholomew, S.J. "The Impracticality of Proportionalism." *Gregorianum* 66 (1985): 676–683.

Küng, Hans. *On Being a Christian*. Trans. E. Quinn. New York: Doubleday, 1976.

Kupczak, Jaroslaw. *Destined for Liberty*. Washington, D.C.: Catholic University of America Press, 2000.

Lacan, Jacques. "Of Structure as an Inmixing of an Otherness." In *The Structuralist Controversy: The Languages of Criticism and the Sciences of Man*, ed. R. Mackey and E. Donato. Baltimore: Johns Hopkins University Press, 1972.

———. "The Seminar of Jacques Lacan." Book VII. In *The Ethics of Psychoanalysis*, ed. J. A. Miller. Trans. D. Porter. New York: W. W. Norton, 1983.

Lear, Jonathan. *Happiness, Death and the Remainder of Life*. Cambridge, Mass.: Harvard University Press, 2000.

Lee, Patrick. *Abortion and the Unborn Child*. Washington, D.C.: Catholic University of America Press, 1997.

———. "Personhood, Dignity, Suicide, and Euthanasia." *The National Catholic Bioethics Quarterly* (Autumn 2001): 37–48.

———. "Soul, Body and Personhood." *American Journal of Jurisprudence* 49 (2004): 87–125.

Pope Leo XIII. "Aeterni Patris: Encyclical Letter on the Restoration of Christian Philosophy." In *One Hundred Years of Thomism: Aeterni Patris and Afterwards—A Symposium*, ed. U. C. Brezik. Houston: University of St. Thomas, 1981.

Lewis, C. S. "The Abolition of Man." In *Philosophy and Technology*, ed. C. Mitcham and R. Mackey. New York: Free Press, 1972.

Lyotard, Jean-Francois. *The Post-Modern Condition: A Report on Knowledge*. Minneapolis: University of Minnesota Press, 1984.

MacIntyre, Alasdair. "How Can We Learn What *Veritatis Splendor* Has to Teach?" *The Thomist* 58 (1994): 171–195.

May, William. *Moral Absolutes*. Milwaukee: Marquette University Press, 1989.

———. "Moral Theologians and Veritatis Splendor." www.cfpeople.org/Apologetics/page51a079.html.

———. "Philosophical Anthropology and *Evangelium Vitae*." 2002. www.christendom-awake.org/pages/may.

McCormick, Richard, S.J, ed. *Notes on Moral Theology, 1965–1980*. Washington, D.C.: University Press of America, 1981.

McCormick, Richard, S.J. "Some Early Reactions to *Veritatis Splendor*." *Theological Studies* 55 (1994): 181–200.

McDermott, John, S.J., ed. *The Thought of Pope John Paul II*. Roma: Editrice Pontificia Università Gregoriana, 1993.

Molla, Pietro, and Elio Guerriero. *Saint Gianna Molla*. San Francisco: Ignatius Press, 2004.

Murray, John Courtney, S.J. "The Problem of Religious Freedom." *Theological Studies* 25 (1964): 503–575.

Newman, John Henry Cardinal. *Certain Difficulties Felt by Their Anglicans Considered: A Letter Addressed to the Duke of Norfolk*. London: Longmans, Green, 1897.

———. *An Essay on the Development of Christian Doctrine*. New York: Longmans, Green, 1949.

Nietzsche, Friedrich. *Also Sprach Zarathustra*. Stuttgart: Philipp Reclam, 1962.

Noonan, John. *The Scholastic Analysis of Usury*. Cambridge, Mass.: Harvard University Press, 1957.

O'Connell, Robert, S.J. *St. Augustine's Early Theory of Man*. Cambridge, Mass.: Harvard University Press, 1968.

O'Connell, Timothy. *Principles for a Catholic Morality*. New York: Seabury, 1978.

Paine, Lynn S. "Ideals of Competition and Today's Marketplace." In *Enriching Business Ethics*, ed. C. Walton. New York: Plenum, 1990.

Pegis, Anton. *At the Origins of the Thomistic Notion of Man*. New York: MacMillan, 1962.

Plato, *Gorgias*. Trans. W. C. Helmbold. Indianapolis: Bobbs-Merrill, 1952.

Plotinus. *Enneads*. 6 vols. Trans. A. H. Armstrong, Cambridge, Mass.: Harvard University Press, 1946.

Rahner, Karl, S.J. *Theological Investigations*, vol. 6. New York: Seabury, 1964.

Ratzinger, Joseph Cardinal. "Morality Should Be Inspired by Encounter with Jesus." Congress on the Encyclical *"Veritatis Splendor,"* November 26, 2003.

———. "The Renewal of Moral Theology: Perspectives of Vatican II and *Veritatis Splendor*." *Communio* (Summer 2005): 112–120.

Rawls, John. "The Idea of an Overlapping Consensus." *Oxford Journal of Legal Studies* 7, no. 1 (1987): 4–16.

Rhonheimer, Martin. *Natural Law and Practical Reason*. New York: Fordham University Press, 2000.

Richardson, William J., S.J. *Heidegger: Through Phenomenology to Thought*. The Hague: Martinus Nijoff, 1963.

———. "Heidegger's Truth and Politics." In *Ethics and Danger*, ed. A. Dallery and C. Scott. Albany, N.Y.: SUNY Press, 1992.

Rowland, Tracey. *Culture and the Thomist Tradition*. London: Routledge, 2003.

Sartre, Jean-Paul. *Being and Nothingness*. Trans. Hazel Barnes. New York: Philosophical Library, 1956.

———. *Dirty Hands*. In *No Exit and Three Other Plays*. Trans. L. Abel. New York: Vintage International, 1989.

———. *Existentialism and Human Emotions*. Trans. Hazel Barnes. New York: Citadel Press, 1957.

Schmiesing, Kevin. "A History of Personalism." Acton Institute for the Study of Religion and Liberty. www.acton.org/schmiesing.

Schmitz, Kenneth. *At the Center of the Human Drama: The Philosophical Anthropology of Karol Wojtyla/Pope John Paul II*. Washington, D.C.: Catholic University of America Press, 1993.

Schnackenburg, Rudolf. *The Moral Teaching of the New Testament*. New York: Herder and Herder, 1965.

Singer, Peter. *Practical Ethics*. 2nd ed. New York: Cambridge University Press, 1993.

Smith, Adam. *The Wealth of Nations*. London: Cannan, 1876.

Smith, Janet. "The Preeminence of Autonomy in Bioethics." In *Human Lives: Critical Essays on Consequentialist Bioethics*, ed. D. Oderberg and J. Laing. London: McMillan, 1997.

Spinello, Richard A. "Competing Fairly in the New Economy: Lessons from the Browser Wars." *Journal of Business Ethics* 57 (2005): 343–361.

Taylor, Charles. *The Ethics of Authenticity*. Cambridge, Mass.: Harvard University Press, 1991.

———. "Die Immanente Gegenaufklärung." In *Aufklärung Heute*. Stuttgart: Kett-Cotta, 1991.

Vacek, Edward. "Contraception Again—A Conclusion in Search of Convincing Arguments: One Proportionalist's [Mis?]Understanding of a Text." In *Natural Law and Moral Inquiry*, ed. Robert George. Washington, D.C.: Georgetown University Press, 1998.

Vattimo, Gianni. *Belief*. Trans. Lucas DeSanto and David Webb. Stanford, Calif.: Stanford University Press, 1999.

Weigel, George. *God's Choice*. New York: HarperCollins, 2005.

———. *Witness to Hope*. New York: HarperCollins, 1999.

West, Christopher. *Theology of the Body Explained*. Boston: Pauline Books, 2003.

Zabala, Santiago. "A Religion without Theists or Atheists." In *The Future of Religion*, ed. S. Zabala. New York: Columbia University Press, 2005.

Index

About the Author

RICHARD A. SPINELLO is an associate research professor in the Carroll School of Management at Boston College, where he also directs the school's ethics program. He has written and edited several books on business ethics and related topics.